Dollars, Debts, and Deficits

Dollars, Debts, and Deficits

Rudiger Dornbusch

Published jointly by
Leuven University Press
Leuven, Belgium
and
The MIT Press
Cambridge, Massachusetts
London, England

Second printing, 1987

First MIT Press edition, 1986
First published by Leuven University Press, 1986
© 1986 by Rudiger Dornbusch

Printed and bound in the United States of America by Edwards Brothers, Inc.

Library of Congres Cataloging-in-Publication Data

Dornbusch, Rudiger.
  Dollars, debts, and deficits.

  Includes bibliographies and index.
  1. Foreign exchange problem—United States. 2. Dollar, American. 3. Debts, External—Developing countries. 4. Economic stabilization—Developing countries. 5. Budget deficits—Europe. I. Title.
HG3903.D67 1986   339.5   85-24100
ISBN 0-262-04085-9

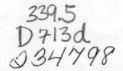

Contents

Foreword

The "Professor Dr. Gaston Eyskens Lectures" are published under the auspices of the chair established on the occasion of the promotion of Professor Doctor Gaston Eyskens to Professor Emeritus on 4 October 1975 and named after him. This chair is intended to promote the teaching of theoretical and applied economics by organizing biannually a series of lectures to be given by outstanding scholars.

The pursuance of this goal is made possible through an endowment fund established by numerous Belgian institutions and associations as an expression of their great appreciation for the long and fruitful teaching career of Professor Gaston Eyskens.

Born on 1 April 1905, Gaston Eyskens has taught at the Catholic University of Leuven since 1931. For an unusually large number of student generations Professor Eyskens has been the inspiring teacher of general economics, public finance, and macroeconomic theory. He is recognized as the founder of Dutch language economic education in Leuven. It should also be mentioned that he was a founder of the Center for Economic Studies of the Department of Economics. As a member of the Governing Board of the university from 1954 to 1968, he succeeded in adding an important dimension to the social service task of the university.

As member of parliament, minister, and head of government, he dominated the Belgian political scene for many years. His influence on the cultural and economic emancipation of the Flemish community has been enormous.

Professor Dr. M. Loeys
Chairman of the Administrative Committee of the
Gaston Eyskens Chair

Preface

This book brings together a collection of essays on economic policy problems of the world economy. The occasion for developing the material into its present form was provided by an invitation to deliver the Gaston Eyskens Lectures at the Katholieke Univebsiteit Leuven, Belgium, in the fall of 1984.

The subject of the lectures, "Dollars, Debts, and Deficits," covers my policy research of the past few years: exchange rate questions, issues of LDC debt and adjustment, and the problems raised by budget deficits and European stagnation. Even though the three topic areas cover widely different policy problems, it makes sense to bring them together. This is the case because international economic interdependence links exchange rates, budgets, adjustment opportunities, and debt service across countries. But there is also a common political economy perspective with which I have approached these issues which gives the collection a coherent perspective. The message is that modern macroeconomics is useful, more than ever, as a framework for active policy.

In developing my ideas on these policy problems, I have benefited greatly from discussions with Stanley Fischer. He has been generous with friendship and advice. As a member of the CEPS Macro Group I had the advantage of working with a very stimulating team and I wish to acknowledge especially my collaboration with Olivier Blanchard and Richard Layard. On Latin American issues Eliana Cardoso and Mario Simonsen have freely given their advice. It is a pleasure to acknowledge these debts and hope for more. I would also like to thank Carol McIntire for her editorial assistance.

I wish to express my gratitude to the faculty and administration of the Katholieke Universiteit Leuven for their challenging invitation. Their generous hospitality is only rivaled by the enjoyment they take in offering a tough debate.

I

Exchange Rate Theory and the Overvalued Dollar

Introduction to Part I

The experience with flexible exchange rates in the past fifteen years raises challenging questions of theory and policy. Among the most significant are the following three:

1. What factors can explain the persistent, large deviations from purchasing power parity (PPP)?

2. What are the effects of real exchange rate changes, and should exchange rates be used as a means of inflation stabilization?

3. Is exchange rate-oriented monetary policy or sterilized intervention effective in containing exchange rate movements and should either be employed for that purpose?

Explaining Deviations from PPP

Figure I.1 shows the U.S. real exchange rate measured by the relative deflators in manufacturing of the U.S. and its trading partners. The long

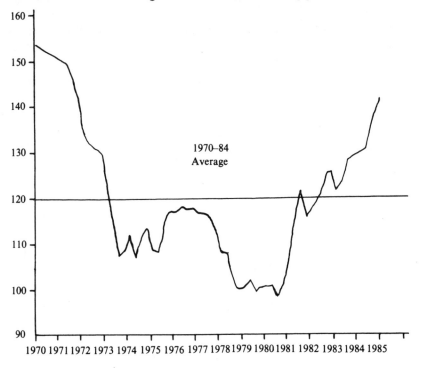

Figure I.1
The U.S. real exchange rate (index 1980 = 100)

period highlights the swings in the real exchange rate coinciding with the shift to flexible exchange rates. From an initial overvaluation of the 1960s, much advertised by Houthakker and Samuelson, the dollar depreciates in real terms, and the depreciated level, with large fluctuations, is sustained throughout the 1970s. The Carter period brought with it the collapse of the dollar in 1978–80. Then, in 1980–84, the dollar appreciated in real terms by 40 percent from the trough.

By the strict standards of PPP one would not expect large persistent movements in real exchange rates.[1] PPP theory makes a sharp distinction between the real influences on relative price levels and monetary-macroeconomic factors. According to the theory exchange rate movements reflect primarily divergent monetary trends, and these monetary trends are almost exclusively reflected in divergent price level trends. Hence there is little or no room for macroeconomic factors to effect relative price level changes. (It is understood that money is the only macroeconomic source of disturbance.) Only transport costs, tariff disruptions, or long-term shifts in international comparative advantage would be admitted as sources of relative price change.

At the outset of the flexible rate period PPP theory was clearly on the minds of many economists. Monetarism was then in its heyday and rapidly spilling over to international issues. From the monetary approach to the balance of payments it was a short step to a monetary approach to exchange rates. Of course the facts did not allow us to sustain for long a PPP interpretation of exchange rate movements and the Mundell-Fleming model made a rapid recovery as the main frame of reference for exchange rate questions.

Among the interpretations encountered today are chiefly three. The first emphasizes safe haven aspects. Observers in financial markets are impressed with the magnitude of capital flows into the U.S. These flows, which more than finance (ex ante) the current account deficit, are thought to be in search of political security and economic prosperity. The Reagan image is the magnet for all the world's money; investors are deserting a sclerotic Europe and escaping from Latin America which is seen ravaged by the debt crisis, the IMF, and essays at democracy.

The argument is unimpressive. Money had gone with equal enthusiasm only a few years before to Europe and Latin America. Indeed, it is already preparing to leave the "overvalued dollar" at exactly the place that only a moment ago seemed unthinkable. There is no question that investors are looking for profit opportunities—interest and especially capital gains. The stories about safe haven must be seen primarily as rationalizations of why the overvalued dollar should not collapse, bringing with it capital losses that would tilt the balance of benefits toward holding nondollar assets.

The second line of argument emphasizes that the U.S. economy is a service economy, bringing with it a new international competitive advantage. In this view long-term real exchange rate comparisons are a poor instrument to judge equilibrium relative prices. If the underlying equilibrium creates a new competitiveness in services, then a deterioration in manufacturing competitiveness is simply a reflection of the resource pull of the new industries. Trade imbalance in manufacturing is sustainable because services provide the leeway and financing. This argument is respectable but does not carry sufficient quantitative weight. The U.S. service balance surely does not show a large improvement, nor are there indications of a major shift to come. Indeed, the prospective shift would need to be large enough to offset the losses in manufacturing plus the burden of a reduction in net external assets that is now underway.

The third line of argument emphasizes monetary disturbances. One direction has been forcefully developed by Ron McKinnon. In a series of articles he has developed the view that international currency substitution—shifts from one country's $M1$ to another's—and the failure to accommodate these shifts lie behind the dollar's strength. The argument lacks both plausibility and evidence. International investors hold CDs, not $M1$, and hence this view cannot even start to explain what has happened to the dollar. More on the policy implications shortly.

The Mundell-Fleming model does help explain what has happened. Relatively tight U.S. policies in the monetary area and relatively easy fiscal policy would lead to the prediction of a real appreciation of the dollar on each count. But the dollar appreciation on account of monetary tightness would be transitory, evaporating as the tightening of money translates itself into adjustment in inflation and nominal interest rates. The initial appreciation would therefore be soon followed by a path of depreciation toward the initial real exchange rate.

To see this point consider the linkage between nominal interest rates and the rate of depreciation

$$i_t = i_t^* + e_t',$$
(1)

where a prime denotes a percentage rate of change. This equation arises from the assumption that perfect capital mobility can be rewritten in terms of real interest rates (r, r^*) and the rate of change of the real exchange rate, q':

$$r_t = r_t^* + q_t', \tag{1a}$$

where the real exchange rate is defined as $q = \log (eP^*/P)$. Note next that in Mundell-Fleming models the real exchange rate adjusts to its long-run level q asymptotically (see Dornbusch and Fischer 1986), so we can write

$$q_{t+1} = q + v(q_t - q), \quad 0 < v < 1, \tag{2}$$

where q_t denotes the current real rate and q (without time subscript) the given long-run equilibrium real rate. The key parameter is the speed of adjustment v. The speed of adjustment can be thought of in terms of the mean lag $v/(1-v)$, say 4 years. Combining (1a) and (2) yields an equation for the real exchange rate in terms of the current real interest rate differential:

$$q_t = q - x(r_t - r_t^*), \quad x = \frac{1}{1-v}. \tag{3}$$

The model shows that a rise in the real interest rate, as a result of a tightening of money, will lead to an immediate nominal and real appreciation which then is followed by a gradual depreciation to the initial long-run equilibrium. The smaller the speed of adjustment of the real exchange rate, v, the larger the impact of real interest rate changes on the current real exchange rate. Specifically suppose the mean lag is four years ($v = 0.8$), then a 1 percent rise in the real interest differential would lead to an immediate real appreciation of 5 percent. The model thus does explain large real exchange rate movements as the counterpart of monetary policy changes. Although the model explains the movement in the real exchange rate, it is open to the criticism that it does not explore the current account and cumulative debt implications of the sustained overvaluation. Krugman (1985) has made this point particularly strongly in calling the high dollar "unsustainable."

Four years of continuing appreciation, however, can only be explained, in this perspective, by an unending string of monetary surprises. The monetary explanation alone would therefore strain belief. But fiscal policy helps. Fiscal expansion in the U.S., and contraction in other major OECD countries, shifts demand toward U.S. goods and hence calls for a rise in the equilibrium relative price of U.S. goods and increased real interest rates. The larger and the more persistent the policy shift, the larger is the real appreciation.

The monetary-fiscal explanation needs some qualifications. One is that the dollar appreciation is large relative to Europe and small relative to Japan. It would therefore be important to understand the differential. The other question concerns the persistence of appreciation. In the long run budget constraints must be met, and hence a period of fiscal expansion requires that ultimately trade surplusses be generated to finance the increased interest bill. Those surplusses require a real depreciation, and the prospect of future real depreciation should limit the extent and persistence of the initial real appreciation. The resulting time path of real exchange rates depends on both the elasticity of trade flows to real exchange rates and on the substitutability of assets in portfolios. The more substitutable are domestic and foreign assets, the more the course of exchange rates is governed by the near-term monetary and fiscal policies.

The preceding discussion emphasizes fundamentals as determinants of the large dollar appreciation. But there is also room for bubbles.[2] There is no reason to rule out that a path of growing appreciation be entirely driven off equilibrium by expectations of capital gains. From a policy point of view, of course, it makes all the difference whether it is fundamentals or bubbles that are behind the overvalued dollar.

The Effects of Real Exchange Rate Changes

Real exchange rate changes have major impact on the inflation process and on output, profitability, and employment in trade-sensitive sectors. In both respects the dollar appreciation has split the U.S. economy, with the domestic sector running ahead in terms of output and prices and the international sector showing a decline in both respects.

The inflation impact of appreciation is perhaps best highlighted by figure I.2 which shows the U.S. levels of prices. The figure shows the GDP deflator trending steadily upward. Import prices are seen to rise more steeply in the depreciation phase up to 1980 and then to peak at the trough of the dollar before they start to fall in absolute terms.

The dollar appreciation affects U.S. inflation through at least four channels. First, there is a significant decline in the dollar prices of materials. To some extent this applies also to administered prices, in particular, petroleum prices. Second, import prices of commodities, other than materials, tend to fall and inflation of export prices slows down. This effect is stronger on the import side the more foreign suppliers' prices are based on their own costs, rather than on prices of

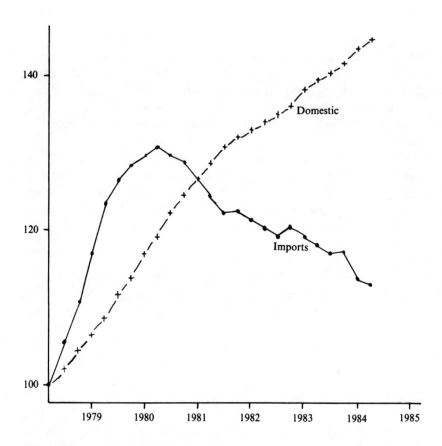

Figure I.2
The U.S. price level (index 1979 = 100)

competing products in the U.S. market. Conversely, on the export side appreciation slows prices more, the more suppliers base their pricing on foreign markets rather than home costs. Third, import competing domestic firms and firms that export will tend to restrain their price increases in the face of falling import prices. Fourth, the loss in competitiveness involved in real appreciation leads to reduced rates of wage inflation in the sectors most exposed to foreign competition and reduced cost of living inflation everywhere.

The combined impact of these channels is to reduce U.S. inflation significantly below what it otherwise would be. There is considerable disagreement, however, on the quantitative magnitude of these effects. Older estimates suggest that a 10 percent dollar appreciation reduces inflation by about 1 percent. More recent estimates, however, are of 2 to

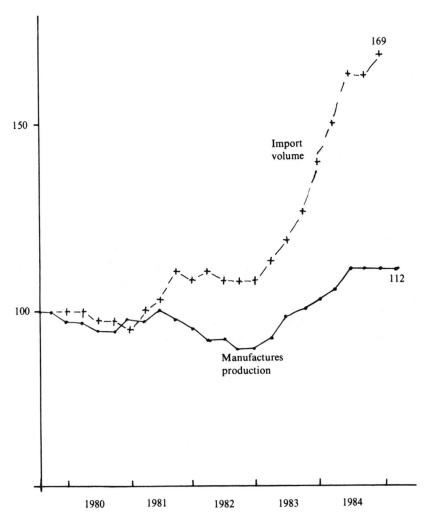

Figure I.3
Manufactures: import volume and domestic production (moving average, 1979:2 = 100)

3 percent. These effects are particularly large if the slowdown in inflation in turn exerts a favorable impact on wage settlements.[3]

The overvalued dollar has had a major impact on trade and domestic production. Figure I.3 gives an idea of the impact in manufacturing. While import volume grew nearly 70 percent over the period 1979 to 1984, the level of domestic manufactures production rose only 12 percent. Adjusting for high-tech industries and for space- and defense-related production, the domestic expansion becomes even smaller and in some sectors negative. Manufacturing, agriculture, and other trade-sensitive sectors thus feel left out of the recovery.

At an aggregate level there is clear evidence that the real exchange rate has a definite and sizable effect on the trade balance. A 10 percent real appreciation deteriorates the trade balance, measured as a fraction of GDP, by about 0.8 percent. The large dollar appreciation, in conjunction with the relatively more rapid U.S. expansion since 1982, thus readily explain the trade and current account deterioration.

In the early phase of the overvaluation, well into 1984, the strong dollar was not much of a political issue because rapid domestic recovery overshadowed the growing lack of competitiveness.[4] A year later, with a full response of trade flows to the overvaluation and a slowing down of the economy, there is wild furor. Congress is up in arms against the "deindustrialization" and is looking for remedies. Senator Bill Bradley sponsored a Sense-of-the-Senate resolution calling for easier monetary policy, to take down the "yo-yo dollar." His argument was:

The level of the dollar is killing jobs, business plans, and future economic opportunity. Unless we immediately address the problem posed by the value of the dollar, we will be putting U.S. industry into an economic hole out of which it will be incredibly hard to grow.[5]

Under the incredible heading of "Trade Emergency and Export Promotion Act" the Rostenkowski-Gebhardt-Bentsen bill singles out countries with large bilateral trade imbalances for special protection measures:

... to assure that international trade occurs in a balanced open and fair manner, and to assure the people of the United States that their Government will take trade actions to protect the vital interest of the United States.[6]

The prime target is of course Japan, but also some developing countries. In the eagerness for protection, the bill encourages the administration to negotiate away free trade by yet further administrative action. It also proposes import barriers on trade surplus/debt servicing countries like Brazil. Surely that affords Brazil with a singular opportunity to stop debt service altogether.

Congress always enjoys talking protection. The threat is that this time the economy may run out of steam and the dollar may be slow coming down, with yet slower adjustment to the real depreciation, so that increased protection becomes almost inevitable. Not surprisingly, many people see protection as an attractive way to move toward budget balance by collecting import duties.

Exchange Rate Policy

In the area of exchange rate policy there are two chief questions: one is whether the large appreciation of the dollar reflects a policy failure of monetary policy; the other is whether target zones, or even fixed rates, are a preferable, practicable option.

The most influential idea in exchange rate policy is McKinnon's call for an exchange-rate-oriented monetary policy. Stabilizing the exchange rate, it is argued, makes money supplies endogenous and thus minimizes the impact of asset market disturbances. A first variant of this theory is the currency substitution version which holds that $M1$ shifts from foreign monies toward the U.S. dollar are behind the dollar appreciation. Because monetary policy is constrained by national aggregate targeting, the authorities fail to accommodate the shift in the composition of $M1$ demanded and hence give rise to exchange rate fluctuations that revalue the relative supplies to restore portfolio balance.[7]

That view of international asset markets found little reception. The criticism of the position is this: the basic premise of the McKinnon prescription, and its flaw, is that it assumes that exchange rate instability is induced by shifts in the currency denomination of the public's money holdings, that is, by currency substitution. But surely international currency speculation is not carried out by shifts between different countries' $M1$'s (currency plus demand deposits) but by shifts between interest-bearing assets. McKinnon now recognizes the problem and has shifted his continued support of exchange-rate-oriented monetary policy to a new ground: indirect currency substitution, otherwise known as capital mobility.[8]

In the case of direct currency substitution McKinnon had the right cure for a nonexistent problem—international money demand shifts. Now recognizing that in fact currency speculation means shifts in international bond portfolios, McKinnon develops the notion of *indirect* currency substitution and gets the wrong cure for the right problem. He argues that even in the case of portfolio shifts not involving monetary assets, the proper response is a change in the *money* supply to sustain the exchange rate:

Why should changes in international portfolio preferences between *nonmonetary assets* affect the demand for domestic *money*? The short answer is that the domestic transactions balances demand increases *indirectly* when international investors desire more bonds denominated in the domestic currency.[9]

The point is this: A portfolio shift without any accomodation leads to an adjustment in equilibrium interest rates and exchange rates for asset markets to continue clearing in the face of unchanged supplies. The fact that interest rates change leads McKinnon to believe that accommodating monetary policy would be a good idea. But surely this is *exactly* the case that Poole (1970) developed when he showed that portfolio shifts should be accommodated *in the same market*. By responding to a portfolio shift through *sterilized intervention*, the central bank offsets *all* impact of the disturbance, on interest rates and on the exchange rate. This happens because sterilized intervention allows the public to determine the currency composition of the international bond portfolio. By contrast, fixing the exchange rate by nonsterilized intervention as McKinnon would have us do means that interest rates will change and hence that the pure portfolio disturbance is shifted into the goods markets without any reason.

Using monetary policy to fight international bond disturbances simply represents an inappropriate (perhaps third-best) assignment.[10] There are no theoretical or even operational reasons for such a choice. It would be as poor an idea as offsetting the impact of a money demand increase by a fiscal expansion simply to keep interest rates constant. Surely everybody recognizes that in such a case an increase in money would be appropriate. There should be no serious issue about the proper assignment: portfolio shifts between bonds of different denomination call for sterilized intervention, currency substitution (if it ever happened) for nonsterilized intervention.

In the past two years the call for exchange market intervention and exchange rate targeting is becoming louder. Intervention would make sense, as noted earlier, in the case of portfolio shifts. It also makes a lot of sense if there are bubbles that need crushing. But if exchange overvaluation reflects fundamentals (monetary and fiscal policy) it becomes very doubtful.

There is a proclivity of the habitués of international financial markets to see exchange-rate-oriented monetary policy as the panacea for exchange rate problems. This is particularly clear in the growing cry for exchange rate target zones, whether rigid or of the Williamson kind, that is, with soft bumpers and bleepers.[11] The problem with this recommendation is twofold. First, it is quite clear that with exchange-rate-oriented monetary policy the U.S. would not have been able to have the disinflation that in fact took place. Certainly for stabilization periods it is an inappropriate recommendation. But worse yet, for the U.S. the exchange-rate-oriented monetary policy would have meant the reckless monetization of gigantic budget deficits. Surely somewhere in the discussion it must be remembered that both monetary and fiscal policy matter. Fixing the exchange rates without any kind of agreement on target zones for budgets and for real interest rates is unjustifiable.

Any observer of fiscal policies in the main industrial countries will have noted that they are not conducted primarily with international considerations in mind. It is simply unrealistic to expect that the U.S. Congress will set budget targets with a view toward defending the exchange rate. Neither the exchange rate nor the equally important real interest rate has been effective in containing Congress. Agreeing on exchange rate targets might merely mean giving Congress a freer hand in pursuing unbalanced fiscal policies.

In an international perspective it is true that the dollar is overvalued. But it is also true that Europe has record unemployment. One cannot simply look at the exchange rate alone, disregarding real interest rates and the fiscal stance. A policy of bringing the dollar down by U.S. monetary expansion would (rightly) be met by a European cut in interest rates to enjoy disinflation, the perpetuation of export-led growth, and the extra stimulans of lower real rates of interest. The first issue then is coordination of monetary policies to reduce real interest rates, but not the dollar. The second, discussed in part III of this book, is to force European fiscal expansion while consolidating the U.S. budget. For neither of these objectives does exchange rate targeting seem very suitable. It would be even less suitable to cope with the problem of Japan unless targeting means setting the yen at 150 and forcing Japan to try to live with the rate.

Notes

1. See Dornbusch (1986a, b) for a discussion of PPP and an analysis of the impact of exchange rates on relative prices.

2. See Frankel (1985a) for a recent evaluation of the bubble argument in the context of the U.S. dollar.

3. For recent discussions, see Woo (1984) and Sachs (1985).

4. See J. Frankel (1985b) on concepts of overvaluation.

5. *Congressional Record*, May 15 1985, S6151.

6. Quoted from Section 3 of the proposed "Trade Emergency and Export Promotion Act" dated July 15, 1985.

7. See McKinnon (1982).

8. See McKinnon (1984a) and (1984b).

9. See McKinnon (1984, p. 30).

10. For further discussion, see also Cuddington (1982) and Spinelli (1983).

11. See J. Williamson (1985).

References

Cuddington, J. 1985. "Currency Substitution: A Critical Survey from a Portfolio Balance Perspective." Federal Reserve Bank of San Francisco *Conference Supplement, Economic Review*, Fall.

Dornbusch, R. 1986a. "Purchasing Power Parity." *New Palgrave Dictionary of Economics*, forthcoming.

Dornbusch, R. 1986b. "Exchange Rates and Prices." *American Economic Review*, forthcoming.

Dornbusch, R. and S. Fischer, 1986. "The Open Economy: Implications for Monetary and Fiscal Policy." In R. Gordon (ed.), *The American Business Cycle: Continuity and Change*, NBER and University of Chicago Press.

Frankel, J. 1985a. "The Dazzling Dollar." *Brookings Papers on Economic Activity*, 1.

Frankel, J. 1985b. "Six Meanings of Overvaluation: the 1981–85 Dollar." *Princeton Essays in International Finance*.

Krugman, P. 1985 "Is the Strong Dollar Unsustainable?" *The U.S. Dollar*, Federal Reserve Bank of Kansas City.

McKinnon, R. 1982. "Currency Substitution and Instability in the World Dollar Standard." *American Economic Review* 72 (30).

McKinnon, R. 1984a. "*An International Standard for Monetary Stabilization*. Institute for International Economics. Policy Analyses in International Economics, No. 8.

McKinnon, R. 1984b. "Why Floating Rates Fail." Discussion paper No. 42. Banca d'Italia, November.

Poole, W. 1970. "Optimal Choice of Monetary Policy Instruments in a Simple Stochastic Macro Model." *Quarterly Journal of Economics*, May.

Sachs, J. 1985. "The Dollar and the Policy Mix 1985." *Brookings Papers on Economic Activity* 1.

Spinelli, F. 1985. "Currency Substitution, Flexible Exchange Rates, and the Case for International Monetary Cooperation: Discussion of a Recent Proposal." *IMF Staff Papers*, December.

Williamson, J. 1985. *The Exchange Rate System.* Institute for International Economics, Policy Analyses in International Economics, No. 5 (revised).

Woo, W. T. 1984, "Exchange Rates and the Prices of Nonfood, Nonfuel Products." *Brookings Papers on Economic Activity,* 2.

1   The Overvalued Dollar

The number one policy problem for the world economy is to achieve a soft landing, locking in the gains of the past two years. The overly strong dollar has been immensely successful in generating a noninflationary recovery in the U.S. but has done so at the cost of a very large loss in international price competitiveness. High real interest rates have not stood in the way of a brisk recovery while fiscal expansion pushed the economy, but now impose a heavy levy on profits in an economy where growth is becoming moderate. The solution to the twin problems of high real rates and the overvalued dollar is decidedly *not* a reform of the international monetary system, monetization of budget deficits, or a collapse of the dollar.

The intelligent solution is to correct our budget deficit and to persuade our trading partners, especially Germany, the U.K., and Japan that the time has come for them to take the initiative for sustaining growth by long overdue fiscal expansion. In addition, given these fiscal policy adjustments, monetary authorities here and abroad should accommodate a continuing recovery by allowing a decline in real interst rates. Such a policy package would limit the decline of the dollar (and the attendant risk of a steep increase in U.S. inflation) and ensure a continuation of world recovery under sounder financial conditions.

International agreements about intervention, target zones, or even fixed exchange rates are implausible as long as Congress and the administration cannot agree on a restoration of fiscal balance. Equally important, exchange rate commitments are premature as long as

Adapted from testimony before the Committee on Finance of the U.S. Senate, April 24, 1985.

governments in the countries with excessive fiscal tightness do not cease taking a free ride on the world economy.

Once the fiscal alignments are underway and real interest rates are allowed to ease, the dollar will move down, restoring a sustainable current account. Without those fiscal realignments we should certainly not commit the U.S. to target exchange rate zones. We certainly should not be prepared to monetize deficits in an effort to take the dollar down, and we should resist freezing the dollar at the present level, except as the counterpart of a strong and sustained foreign expansion. Until basic macroeconomic policies are locked in by actions on the budget here and abroad, we should certainly not undertake any exchange rate commitments.

The Strong Dollar

Since 1979–80 the dollar has undergone a massive appreciation in world currency markets. The extent of the appreciation, reaching a peak earlier this year, is shown in table I.1. Even though the decline since the peak in February 1985 is already large, the remaining cumulative appreciation from 1980 to April 1985 is huge. This is particularly clear from the movement in the Morgan Guaranty index for the trade-weighted dollar exchange rate.

Table 1.1
Dollar appreciation since 1980

	1980	1982	May 1985	Percent change 1980–85
Yen/$ rate	227	249	252	11.0
DM/$ rate	1.83	2.43	3.11	69.9
Morgan $ index [a]				
Nominal	90.7	109.8	132.0	45.5
Real	89.5	109.8	125.0	39.7

a. An increase in the trade weighted index represents an appreciation of the dollar.

Given the attention that Japan is attracting, it is important to recognize that Germany (and Europe) had in fact a vastly larger depreciation. The movements in nominal currency values are already sizable, but their impact has been reinforced by the fact that U.S. inflation was higher and productivity growth lower than that abroad. As a result our international competitiveness has been impared by the combined effect of these three factors. The point is perhaps most effectively made by noting the data on hourly compensation in manufacturing in the U.S. and abroad, shown in table I.2.

Table 1.2
Changes in wages measured in U.S. dollars (cumulative percentage change)

	1975–1979	1980–1984
U.S.	42.8	29.6
Germany	82.3	− 22.4
Japan	80.0	14.4

Source: Bureau of Labor Statistics.

Of course U.S. competitiveness suffered even further than the wage data in table 1.2 indicate, because productivity growth abroad was significantly higher than in the U.S. economy. The deterioration of external competitiveness is quite apparent in comparative industry price data. For example, in the period 1980 to 1984 the price of U.S. exports of electrical and electronic measuring devices increased by 54 percent over the price of comparable imports; for telecommunications parts the deterioration in price competitiveness is 32 percent, 57 percent for thermal household appliances and 48 percent for textile finishing machinery. These are not special cases; the same pattern prevails throughout manufacturing.

The loss in external competitiveness is patently obvious from a number of trade indicators. Table 1.3 shows data on growth of export and import volumes for several countries in the period 1981 to 1984. Cumulative U.S. export growth has been negative while import volume has increased sharply. These data are affected by differences in economic growth at home and abroad, but they also reflect our loss in international cost competitiveness.

Table 1.3
Growth in trade volume (cumulative percentage change: 1981–84)

	U.S.	Europe	Japan	Latin America
Exports	− 12.7	15.8	32.1	17.7
Imports	27.8	7.0	9.0	− 36.9

Source: IMF *World Economic Outlook*, April 1985.

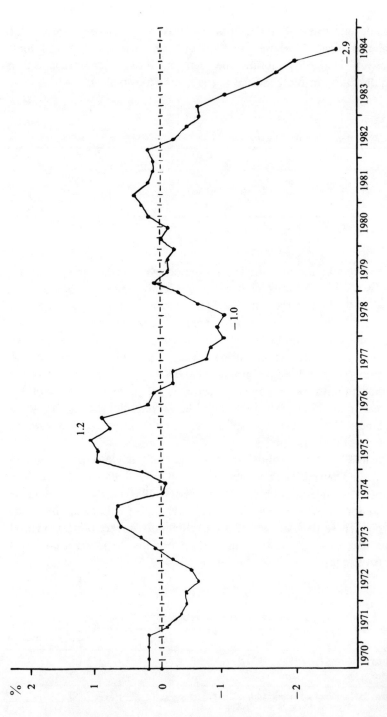

Figure 1.1
The U.S. current account (percent of GDP)

The deterioration in external performance is summarized in figure 1.1, which shows the U.S. current account deficit as a fraction of GDP. The deficit is at an all time high. Econometric estimates suggest that as much as 60 percent of the deterioration is due to the loss in international competitiveness. The remainder is accounted for by the relative cyclical position of the U.S. and the rest of the world and by the sharp trade adjustment of Latin America. Our spending growth has run strongly ahead of spending increases abroad. This is particularly true of course for debtor LDCs where the adjustment programs have led to increases in their exports and deep cuts in our exports to them. Although some of these trade losses may be transitory, Latin America is bound to have significantly less access to external capital in the coming years and hence will have to run persistent trade surplusses to earn the dollars with which to pay interest to our banks.

The large divergence between U.S. import and export performance is of course the channel through which the U.S. has spread growth abroad. Our spending has increased significantly more rapidly than our income, and the divergence has sustained, or made possible income growth, budget improvements and debt service abroad.

Dollar Appreciation and the U.S. Economy

The rise in the dollar has been a major factor in the slowing down of inflation in the U.S. economy. The normal pattern is for inflation to fall in a recession but to show a sharp increase in the recovery. From one business cycle to the next (measured from peak to peak) inflation used to increase, thus ratcheting upward over the past 30 years. That pattern, for the moment, is broken. Inflation and wage settlements are low and for the time being do not show signs of the normal cyclical recovery. Several complementary factors that help explain this development follow.

Deregulation and the weakening of unions are clearly important factors. The dominant element is likely to be the record high, and still high, level of unemployment. But the strong dollar must also be counted. The appreciation of the dollar has lowered import prices absolutely and thus has directly contributed to disinflation. But the increased import competition has also exerted a dampening effect on the price increases domestic firms could afford and on the wage increases they could concede. Dollar overvaluation thus has exerted a chilling influence on the entire wage-price setting mechanism. This is particularly the case for raw materials, where the normal cyclical recovery has simply not taken place.

The fall in dollar prices of agricultural commodities has helped keep food price inflation and hence wage demands low.

The rule of thumb is that a 10 percent dollar appreciation reduces inflation by about 1 percentage point. But that number may be a considerable underestimate of the pervasive effects of a sustained, large appreciation. Taking into account direct effects as well as wage channels, a 10 percent dollar appreciation may reduce inflation by 2 percentage points or even more. Given the size of the dollar appreciation since 1980, this suggests that in addition to unemployment the strong dollar may be the main reason we have been able to enjoy a noninflationary recovery so far.

The dollar overvaluation has also involved costs, most obviously in the deterioration of manufacturing competitiveness, profitability, and employment. Manufacturing has been bypassed in the recovery, and this is particularly true for the capital goods industry, excepting space- and

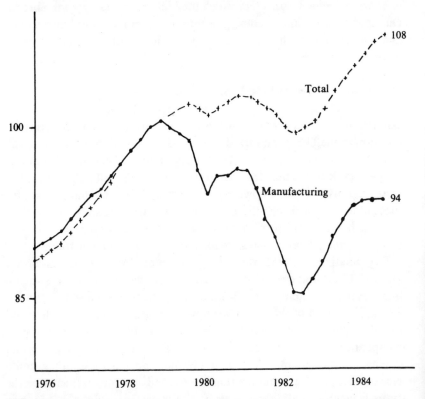

Figure 1.2
U.S. employment trends (index 1979:1 = 100)

defense-related firms. While total industrial output grew 8 percent since 1979, defense and space related production grew by 58 percent. This suggests a decline of civilian production in the midst of a strong recovery.

The poor performance of manufacturing is reflected in the decline of manufacturing employment since 1979. Figure 1.2 shows total employment (nonagricultural establishments) as well as employment in manufacturing. While total employment has grown by 8 percent since 1979, manufacturing employment today is more than 6 percent lower than six years ago. Part of the reduction in manufacturing employment reflects productivity growth and thus must be welcomed. But that will not go far enough to explain the significant fall. The recovery of the past two years was simply insufficient to make up for the inroads of import competition and loss of exports on manufacturing employment.

The common argument against excessive fiscal expansion is that it leads to crowding out, as high interest rates displace private sector investment spending and thus growth of potential output and employment. But there is a more immediate crowding out as firms that lose competitiveness cease operations in the high wage country and shift operations abroad. There is accordingly a direct loss of useful capital and of employment opportunities. This process will be more intense the larger and the more persistent the overvaluation. In the U.S. the recovery has for a while overshadowed these effects of the strong dollar, but they are now becoming quite apparent.

Why Is the Dollar High?

The strength of the dollar has been explained by three basic arguments: safe haven factors, bubbles, and the divergent policy mix here and abroad. They are not necessarily alternative explanations, and each may well have played a role.

The safe haven argument asserts that the U.S. has become a relatively safer place for investment, given increased uncertainty and instability in the rest of the world. It is difficult to put the finger on the increased uncertainty, especially in 1984 and early 1985, when some of the sharpest appreciation occurred. The argument is also surprising in view of the fact that as recently as 1980, the U.S. was definitely not the place sought out by foreign capital. Of course the Reagan presidency must have made some difference.

The bubble argument emphasizes that asset markets can set prices of currencies, long-term bonds, stocks, or real estate that are unrelated to fundamentals. For example, stock prices might be set in excess of the value of prospective earnings of capital or land prices in excess of the prospective value of rentals. Similarly currency values might be set outside a range that is sustainable considering the impact of the exchange rate on economic activity or the external balance. Expectations of high capital gains carry these markets and compensate for the fully perceived risk of a collapse to fundamentals. Such bubbles have occurred in the past, and they may well be at work in foreign exchange markets. Bubbles are a serious problem whenever capital gains dominate by a large margin interest differentials. In these conditions the speculation centers on whether further capital gains can be sustained or whether changes in fundamentals could force a shift in the market. In the exchange market this speculation has focused on the trend of U.S. interest rates and on the strength of the economy. A weakening of rates is seen as the signal that the stampede from the dollar will get underway.

The safe haven and bubble argument have in common that they recognize an overvaluation of the dollar. Nominal exchange rate movements, in this view, have taken the rate away from a sustainable level, and thus ultimately a collapse is inevitable. The persistence of the exchange rate at this disequilibrium level in turn is seen as distorting resource allocation. An alternative approach argues that the fundamentals have changed and thus warrant a high value of the dollar, even if it is troublesome for some sectors and unwise as a policy. The argument focuses on fundamentals in that the U.S., and other industrialized countries have followed a sharply diverging trend of policies that is responsible for the dollar appreciation.

Table 1.4 shows data on fiscal policy that support this view. While the U.S. has shifted dramatically toward a deficit, Germany, other European

Table 1.4
Government budget trends (percent of GDP)

	Actual budget deficit		Change in adjusted budget deficit, 1980–1985
	1984	1985	
U.S.	3.2	3.6	−4.5
Germany	1.7	0.9	+4.2
Japan	2.2	0.8	+3.2

Note: The adjusted deficit data are corrected for the effect of unemployment and inflation.

countries, and Japan have moved in the opposite direction with as much vehemence.

The divergent shift in fiscal policy was reinforced by a much stronger increase in interest rates in the U.S. compared to the rest of the world. Even today U.S. interest rates exceed those in Germany or Japan by more than 250 basis points, and by even more when adjustments for inflation are made. The long-term interest differential, between the U.S. and Germany or Japan, exceeds 400 basis points. If the probability of a dollar collapse were negligible, these differentials would imply a really huge incentive to hold U.S. securities. As it is, that possibility cannot be ruled out, but in the early stages of the recovery, it may well have been the case that depreciation was as likely as appreciation, thus leaving a net incentive to shift toward U.S. securities.

The strong dollar can thus be seen primarily as a reflection of monetary and fiscal policies here and abroad. The dollar is clearly overvalued from the point of view of manufacturing, but even so our aggregate growth performance has been above average by the standards of postwar recoveries. Without a deterioration in our trade balance, the growth in 1983–84 would have been entirely unreasonable, and the interest rates, in the absence of accommodation, would have shifted difficulties to housing and interest-sensitive manufacturing sectors. Given the enormous fiscal stimulus, crowding out was simply unavoidable, except if the Fed had chosen to accommodate even higher growth by an exchange-rate-oriented monetary policy which might have meant a very strong monetary growth so as to monetize the deficits. The only choice would have been to take the crowding out in interest-rate-sensitive sectors rather than in the external balance. As it is, our growth during the recovery has been above average for the postwar period; asking for more is unreasonable.

The Exchange Rate System

For at least 100 years the international monetary system has been considered inadequate, whatever the arrangements: the gold standard, bimetallism, the gold exchange standard, dollar standard, fixed rates, managed rates, and floating rates. Throughout the interwar period international monetary conferences sought to cope with the conflicts posed by divergent national policies and interests. The problems were not solved then, nor at Bretton Woods, the Smithsonian, or Ram-

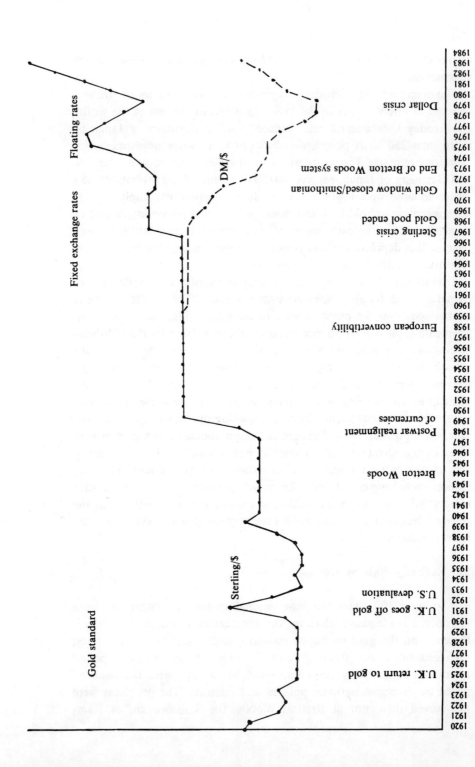

bouillet. They will also befuddle any new initiative the U.S. Treasury might promote.

Figure 1.3 shows the international monetary system in the past 60 years in the light of two key exchange rates: the sterling/$ rate was the center piece until the 1960s; and the deutsch mark/$ rate has been the focal point since. Our problems today are not unlike those of 1931–32 when every country sought to gain employment by competitive devaluation or undervalued currencies. Again in 1971 the U.S. was faced with overvaluation. At that time President Nixon devalued the dollar and imposed an import surcharge. Here is a statement that sounds uncomfortably familiar today:

As a temporary measure, I am imposing an additional tax of 10 percent on goods imported into the United States... It is an action to make certain that American products will not be at a disadvantage because of unfair exchange rates. When the unfair treatment is ended, the import tax will end as well... The time has come for exchange rates to be set straight and for the major nations to compete as equals. There is no longer any need for the United States to compete with one hand tied behind her back. (quoted in J. Odell, *U.S. International Monetary Policy*)

Those who call for a step in the direction of international monetary reform start from the premise that flexible rates have failed. A strong advocate of that position is C. F. Bergsten, who has argued recently (*New York Times*, April 21, 1985):

It is clear that the monetary system is failing in its basic purpose of accurately equating the competitive positions of national economies. Its reform is essential to achieve and maintain a healthy world economy.

These complaints about the behavior of the flexible rate system are misplaced; they command as much persuasion as a drunk driver complaining, after the crash, that cars are simply not safe. The fact is that the extreme divergence of the policy mix in the U.S. and abroad is to be blamed, not the exchange rate system. U.S. growth has been high, above average for a recovery, *despite* record high real interest rates and high dollar, and that suggests that some very peculiar policies were in place. Moreover there is no reason to single out exchange rate difficulties, neglecting the high real interest rates as a very damaging feature of the recovery. A balanced, open-minded approach will focus on both distortions to balanced growth.

It used to be said that exchange rates fail to function properly when they do not lead to balanced trade or balanced current accounts. That view is no longer fashionable because it is recognized that international borrowing or lending need not be all bad. The new version shifts to "equating underlying competitive positions of national economies," which one assumes means exchange rate movements that to not deviate too much from purchasing power parity levels, whatever the consequences for national unemployment rates. But suppose that the dollar had indeed been maintained in line with inflation differentials. Our much stronger external balance would have added yet further to growth and also to inflation. Growth abroad would have been much smaller and unemployment correspondingly higher. But abroad, the unemployment problem is already very serious indeed. In Europe unemployment is now 11.3 percent and rising, *even* with the strong dollar.

Even with the overvalued dollar Europe feels that real wages are too high to have full employment. With a weaker dollar their unemployment problem would be much worse. The point of all this is that the dollar cannot improve both Europe's unemployment and our manufacturing problems at the same time. Without a deliberate shift in underlying monetary and fiscal policies, exchange rate fix-ups are simply beggar-thy-neighbor policies that are unlikely to succeed because the rest of the world badly needs remedies for unemployment, even as we hope to improve our manufacturing profitability. If that point is conceded, we might as well speak directly of the required policy changes that will simultaneously cope with dollar overvaluation and overly high real interest rates, rather than pretend that exchange rate fix-ups miraculously solve all inconsistencies of national macroeconomic policies. That would lend a welcome realism to the discussion because it would make clear that we are talking about European and Japanese fiscal expansion and U.S. budget cuts, and about sharply lower real interest rates.

No international monetary system can cope effectively with sharply divergent macroeconomic policies, especially under conditions of international capital mobility. The Bretton Woods system came under pressure in the late 1950s and thoughout the 1960s, because the U.S. policy mix was not acceptable to our major trading partners. To escape from dollar overvaluation under fixed rates, the world went to flexible rates, which now are said to have failed. Moving to more rigid rates will not cope with the problem of integrated capital markets and divergent fundamentals. Limiting exchange rate movements, without internationally agreed target zones for budgets and for real interest rates, is simply absurd.

The reason is that there is no instrument available to implement the exchange rate commitment. The policy instruments available to affect exchange rates are primarily monetary and fiscal policy. With the right fiscal policy still out of reach, monetary policy would have to do whatever is necessary to make the exchange rate stay within bounds. But of course few people would be foolish enough to argue that the monetary policy should be geared to defending the exchange rate, *at any price*. In the U.S. conditions of 1983–84, that would have meant monetizing budget deficits and preventing disinflation altogether. It is therefore surprising that as impracticable an alternative as target zones should continue to attract public interest and the support of some policy advisors.

We have already discussed the merits of changes in monetary and fiscal policies. If such policy changes were made, it is not obvious why there would be any further need for exchange rate targets. But if these more basic changes in macro policies were not to occur in the near future, are there alternatives? Target zone supporters might hope to implement their exchange rate objectives either via changes in underlying macro-economic policies or via foreign exchange market intervention. With unchanged monetary policy, intervention will have to be sterilized. That means the world supply of public debt would be reshuffled between dollar and DM denominations.

The effectiveness of sterilized intervention has not been established, and therefore we should not oversell the scope for intervention to achieve orderly exchange rate movements. A significant body of research produced by the Federal Reserve leads to the conclusion that inter-vention with unchanged monetary and fiscal policies does nothing to exchange rates. Indeed, the effectiveness of intervention would at best be limited to creating outright "disorderly markets" in a effort to depress the exchange rate. That is an effective way to burst a bubble, though not in the case of an equilibrium exchange rate that is high because underlying policies call for a high rate. As to the bubble case, the logic that calls for bursting bubbles carries over to bond markets where disorderly markets should be created to bring down overly high long-term rates by pushing up bond prices.

Economics has as yet no definite criteria for establishing whether a particular economywide asset price represents a price that optimally allocates resources between alternative uses. We use the presumption that the free market knows best, but have to confess to some uncertainty on this question. But it is equally important not to throw all organized thinking overboard and react to manufacturing problems by a piecemeal fix-up of the exchange rate, as if there were no concern for economywide interactions. Anyone who is willing to act on the exchange rate must also be willing to announce views and actions on interest rates and the stock market. They are part of the same economywide price system and determine, in conjunction with fiscal policy the level of output, employment and the allocation of resources in the world economy. It is not appropriate to think that one single price—the exchange rate—can be identified as "wrong" and moved around at will without worldwide effects on every other price. If the dollar could be talked or intervened down without changes in monetary and fiscal policy, then we would probably have higher interest rates. It is difficult to believe that a lower dollar and a higher interest rate are any better than what we have now.

The best of all worlds would be one where policymakers can draw on international exchange for the gains from trade but isolate economies from the spillover effects of macroeconomic policies and disturbances. We would like strong exchange rates for disinflation, but without the import consequences. We would like to draw on capital inflows to hold down interest rates but would like to avoid running trade deficits or incurring foreign debts. For better or worse, there is no way we can run smaller trade deficits and have higher growth and lower interest rates except by a reversal of the past few year's policy mix here and abroad.

Neither an import surcharge nor capital control is a substitute for a change in fundamentals.[1] An interest equalization tax to reduce the attractiveness of U.S. assets to foreign holders is the proper response to a bubble or to safe haven capital flight into the dollar, which as a result becomes overvalued. A restoration and increase of the withholding tax on foreign holders of U.S. assets would be altogether appropriate, if only as a way of charging rent on the safe haven. The policy would yield some revenue in the process of taxing foreign asset holders who may otherwise escape taxes altogether. There would be little doubt that the dollar would decline as a result, perhaps precipitously. But the weakening of the dollar would leave us still with the problem of the right policy mix. The weaker dollar would increase (or sustain) growth, but it also would raise interest rates and thus merely shift the crowding out to other sectors of the economy. The basic problem that needs attention therefore is to correct the policy mix here and abroad.

Note

1. I have critized the import surcharge idea in an editorial entitled, "The Illusions of Protectionism," in the *Los Angeles Times*, April 4, 1985.

2   Equilibrium and Disequilibrium Exchange Rates

Milton Friedman's 1950 essay "The Case for Flexible Exchange Rates" brought persuasive arguments against exchange control and fixed exchange rates and established firmly the profession's preference for flexible rates. The case rested on a triple advantage: no need for direct controls and inefficiency, the advantage of monetary sovereignity and the convenience of adjusting the exchange rate rather than the entire domestic price structure. The analogy with daylight savings time plainly made the case that "it is far simpler to allow one price to change, namely, the price of foreign exchange, than to rely upon changes in the multitude of prices that together constitute the internal price structure."[1] When the collapse of the Bretton Woods system led to flexible rates, the profession accepted this as progress; that belief continues and predisposes us to see the experiment with flexible exchange rates as successful.

It is not always easy, however, to believe that the experiment has been an outright success. We do observe large, apparently self-reversing movements in exchange rates, both nominal and real. More importantly, we often have no good idea, either in theory or more informally, in what manner the current level of the exchange rate represents an equilibrium. It is at such times, of course, that we are reminded of the history of flexible exchange rates in the 1920s, especially the French episode, and the argument of the time that exchange rates were moved, under the influence of speculation, in ways incompatible with fundamentals and aggravating the problems of domestic stabilization. That view had been advanced by Nurkse:

>...anticipations are apt to bring about their own realization. Anticipatory purchases of foreign exchange tend to produce or at any rate to hasten the anticipated fall in the exchange value of the national currency, and the actual fall may set up or strengthen expectations of a further fall.... Exchange rates in such circumstances are bound to become highly unstable, and the influence of psychological factors may at times be overwhelming. French economists were so much impressed by this experience that they developed a special 'psychological theory' of exchange fluctuations, stressing the indeterminant character of exchange rates when left to find their own level in a market swayed by speculative anticipations.[2]

Nurkse's view was challenged by Friedman[3] who argued that no professional case had been made to the effect that speculation was destabilizing. On the contrary, speculation against the currency only anticipated a depreciation bound to come of its own. That criticism has been largely endorsed by the profession and ratified in exchange rate models where the current equilibrium exchange rate correctly reflects the anticipated path of future (exogeneous) money. The exchange rate then is merely a barometer of a government's inflationary intentions.

But such an interpretation misses an important point in Nurkse's view, namely, that there is an exchange rate indeterminancy because financial policies, which supposedly anchor the system, are in fact endogeneous and may be substantially caused by movements in the exchange rate. It is true that the exchange rate only reflects the possible paths the economy might take. But the likelihood of a particularly adverse path becomes higher once speculators' recognition of that possibility is reflected in the exchange rate and, from there, in prices and the requirements of monetary accommodation. This, of course, was very much the scenario that Nurkse was commenting on in pre-Poincare France.

The possibility that flexible rates may adversely affect the macro-economy is certainly coming to be recognized. The idea of "virtuous and vicious circles" makes that point, as does the notion that flexible rates make the Phillips curve steeper.[4] But while it is certainly recognized that flexible exchange rates may not do their work, this is not yet a commonly shared belief. Indeed, it is only controversy over sterling in 1979–80, the yen in 1978–79, and the current controversy over the dollar that loudly suggests a fundamental problem with our exchange rate system.[5]

In fact there appear to be several separate problems. One emerges from international real interest differentials that arise in the course of monetary stabilization which lead to real appreciation and disruptive macroeconomic effects abroad. A second is associated with speculative bubbles that remove the exchange rate from a path dictated by fundamentals. In either event the exchange rate assumes a life of its own that may be seriously at odds with macroeconomic stability and that calls for remedies. This is also the case when extraneous beliefs join fundamentals in influencing the market rate.

There is certainly one thing the experience with flexible rates has done, and that is to disillusion even the true believer on the subject of monetary sovereignty under flexible rates. That there is no sovereignity, but rather sharp conflict of interest is brought out by the present dollar problem.

The *Financial Times* of January 26, 1982, in a commentary entitled "$ Rise Undermines European Bid to Cut Interest Rates" notes:

The fresh wave of higher U.S. interest rates threatens to wreck the independent initiative launched last week by the Bank of England, the West German Bundesbank and other EEC central banks to lower the cost of credit in Europe and speed up economic recovery.

The sharp fall in sterling and other leading European currencies against the dollar yesterday may prolong the European recession just as an upturn had seemed likely.

This is because EEC central banks may be forced to take action to prevent currency depreciation triggering off fresh inflation.

That these concerns go beyond technicalities of day-to-day money markets is represented in a follow-up article on January 28: "Germans Worried by U.S. Deficit" which notes:

However, despite the efforts of European central banks to coordinate a modest fall in interest rates last week, it is stressed here that Europe's scope to "uncouple" itself from U.S. developments remains very small. This is said to apply to West Germany despite its improved current account performance and relatively low inflation rate.

Bonn feels that the upshot may well be a further fall in investment, a rise in unemployment and more social unrest. "All elements of a depression are there", one official stressed.

This chapter will take the perspective that exchange rates in the 1970s have not worked well. From that point of view we attempt to establish in what ways the exchange rate system may have fallen short of what theory and policy beliefs suggest and what possible remedies there are. In the first section exchange rate theories and some empirical evidence are reviewed. The section concludes that theories have across the board failed to account for exchange rate behavior. The next section identifies four specific policy problems: bubbles, the peso problem, extraneous beliefs and the dollar problem. Each deals with the possibility of disequilibrium exchange rates, although in different, possibly over-lapping ways. The last section discusses (and dismisses) intervention as a policy tool and makes a case for real interest equalization taxes.

Exchange Rate Theories

This section develops the main theoretical approaches to exchange rate determination and comments cursorily on their empirical success. The relevant theories are the monetary approach and the current account approach in two variants emphasizing imperfect substitutability of assets and goods, respectively.

The Monetary Approach

The monetary approach, no doubt, is the most popular model of exchange rate determination, anchored as it is in two outrageous simplifications of the economic scene: purchasing power parity and the quantity theory. The model assumes that national price levels are instantaneously flexible and determined by money supplies and real money demands. Moreover, with the "law of one price," prices are equalized internationally with exchange rate movements offsetting divergent national price trends.

The monetary approach gives rise to an exchange rate equation that includes relative nominal money supplies, relative velocities and relative levels of real income. In log form the exchange rate equation then becomes:

$$e = (m - m^*) + (v - v^*) - (y - y^*),$$

where e is the dollar price of foreign exchange and m, v, and y are nominal money, velocity, and real income, with an asterix denoting the foreign country. Early endeavors with this equation were not unsuccessful, but by now there are, I believe, no more serious claims for the empirical relevance of this model.[6]

The monetary model is highly restrictive in its assumption of the law of one price. This is apparent when we move to a transactions version of this model. Let q denote the log of the expenditure deflator, let a denote real spending, and let v denote expenditure velocity. Home money market equilibrium can be stated in terms of the determinants of the expenditure deflator:

$$q = m + v - a, \tag{2}$$

where q is a weighted average of home and import prices,

$$q \equiv xp + (1 - x)(e + p^*). \tag{3}$$

With a similar specification for the foreign country, and assuming foreign expenditure on domestic goods to have a share $x^* \leqslant x$, we derive an exchange rate equation of the form:

$$e = [(m - m^*) + (v - v^*) - (a - a^*)] + (x - x^*)\,\Theta, \tag{4}$$

where $\Theta \equiv e + p^* - p$ denotes the terms of trade.

The extended model maintains the prediction of the monetary approach to the extent that changes in money or velocity are translated into equiproportionate depreciation, *given* the terms of trade. But now there is another source of exchange rate movement, namely, terms of trade changes. Changes in the equilibrium terms of trade affect the equilibrium exchange rate to an extent that depends, among other factors, on the differential in expenditure shares, $x - x^*$.

The extended model is readily applied, in the manner of Fleming and Mundell, to the effects of a shift in demand toward domestic goods. Suppose capital is perfectly mobile and that the home country faces a given, unchanging foreign level of spending and interest rates. Assume also that product prices are given. Figure 2.1 shows the determination of the exchange rate at point A. The IS schedule is positively sloped because a real depreciation creates demand and raises output. The LM schedule is negatively sloped since an appreciation lowers the price level and raises the real money stock thus making room for a real expansion. Figure 2.1 shows that a shift in demand toward domestic goods will raise income and lead to an appreciation. The expansion will be larger the larger the share of importables in the deflator. By contrast, a large import share in the expenditure deflator will tend to dampen the expansionary impact of a money expansion.

Even before we move to issues of imperfect asset substitution or expectations, exchange rate determination is already a macroeconomic problem involving the interaction of goods and asset markets. Consider now the extension to the case where output adjusts gradually to long-run excess demand and exchange rate expectations conform to perfect foresight. Under the assumption that capital mobility is perfect, home

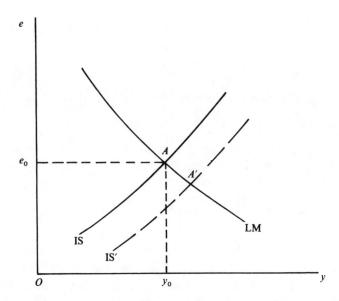

Figure 2.1

nominal interest rates equal those abroad plus the anticipated rate of depreciation:

$$i = i^* + \dot{e}. \tag{5}$$

In figure 2.2 we show the phase diagram, noting that now the rate of depreciation $\dot{e}$, is a determinant of home velocity. From an initial equilibrium at A a monetary expansion leads to an immediate depreciation at point A' on the saddlepath. The exchange rate in the short run must overshoot as output expansion is sluggish. At A' the exchange rate has overdepreciated, and thus anticipated appreciation lowers velocity relative to a static expectations world. Over time the economy converges to point A'' as output expands to meet the increase in demand. The economy proceeds from A' to A'' along the perfect foresight path PP.

The analysis of expectations is readily extended in three directions. One is to add sluggish price adjustment and thus allow long-run neutrality. The second extension is to consider the impact of anticipated future shocks. Third, and perhaps most important, we can introduce an explicit consideration of the current account as a source of dynamics. Current account imbalances, by redistributing net assets internationally, may affect demand to the extent that marginal spending patterns differ. If this is the case, current account imbalances lead to changes in equilibrium relative prices and thus to changes in the exchange rate.

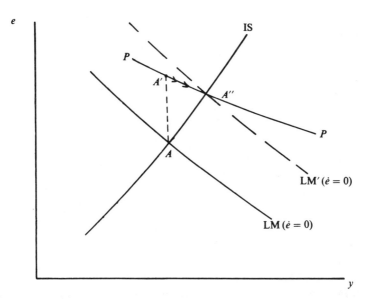

Figure 2.2

We have reached the point where the *current* exchange rate is determined not only by current monetary factors—the relative supply and demand of money—but also by prospective monetary factors as well as the present and future demand for goods. An anticipated fiscal expansion, for example, will lead to immediate currency appreciation even though the demand expansion has, as yet, not materialized. But there is one important complication still left out, namely, the possibility of imperfect substitution among assets.

Imperfect Asset Substitutability

If asset holders are risk averse, and returns on securities denominated in different currencies are not perfectly correlated, risk premia may emerge that depend on relative asset supplies.

A risk premium modifies the relation between interest rates and expected depreciation in (5). The equation now becomes

$$i = i^* + \dot{e} + \phi\left(\frac{B}{W}, \frac{W}{\bar{W}}\right); \quad \phi_1 > 0, \phi_2 \leqslant 0, \tag{6}$$

where B denotes the supply of domestic outside nominal assets, while W

and $\bar{W}$ are home wealth and world wealth all measured in home currency. The extent to which the risk premium increases with a rise in the relative supply of domestic currency assets depends on the degree of risk aversion and the variance of relative asset returns. The exchange rate affects the variables $B/\bar{W}$ and $W/\bar{W}$ since it influences the domestic currency value of world wealth. A depreciation lowers the relative supply of domestic assets and domestic relative wealth.

The risk premium model of asset markets, in conjunction with money and goods markets, extends the range of exchange rate determinants which now include the current and prospective relative supplies of nominal outside assets and, possibly, the distribution of world wealth. It is interesting to note, in this context, that imperfect asset substitutability need, by no means, establish a link between current accounts and the exchange rate. Frankel[7] among others, has noted that what is at issue in the risk premium is the relative supply of nominal outside assets. Privately financed current account imbalances will not affect the world supplies of outside assets. Furthermore, even if the deficits were publicly financed there is no necessity that they be financed in terms of home currency denomination. More important, as has been noted, the relative supply of outside nominal assets is also affected by intervention and budget financing, thus obliterating any special role for the current account.

There remains the question whether current accounts, by redistributing world wealth, interact with a preferred domestic habitat in portfolios to change the risk premium and therefore, affect exchange rates. As Krugman[8] has shown this possibility requires a coefficient of risk aversion larger than unity. Again it must be borne in mind that the relevant measure of wealth in the risk premium will also include real assets so that there is typically no direct relation between the current account alone and the distribution of world wealth. A stock market boom will have much larger effects on relative wealth than likely current account imbalances.

Empirical Evidence

Claims for empirically successful exchange rate equations are disappearing rapidly. Recent papers by Frankel (1982), Isard (1981), Meese and Rogoff (1983) and Hacche and Townsend (1981) conclude that *simple* structural models of exchange rate determination all fail to account well for actual exchange rate behavior. This is the case whether a monetary approach is adopted, a Mundell-Fleming-Frankel model, or models that include, in addition, current account or relative wealth variables.

Hacche and Townsend summarize their findings as follows:

> The predominant impresion left by our results is one of failure: we have not succeeded in finding empirical regularities in the data to help explain in any satisfactory way the fundamental determinants of sterling's effective exchange rate during the floating rate period. Our research has failed, often dramatically to yield support for any of the theories tested....[9]

The same conclusion is reached by Meese and Rogoff who conclude:

> major bilateral exchange rates and the trade weighted dollar are all well approximated by a random walk. The representative structural models do not perform well out-of-sample; they predict poorly even when uncertainty about future values of the explanatory variables is removed.[10]

Isard (1980) and Artus (1984) similarly find that their tests are unsatisfactory except with the inclusion of a Reagan dummy.

There are some reasons why tests may be fairing poorly. First the models tend to give too much emphasis to money supply disturbances neglecting shifts in money demand, fiscal and demand disturbances which, of course, are as important as money supply changes. The neglect of demand and fiscal variables in empirical work is, in fact, quite complete.

The more important point is that exchange rate testing has given no room to the role of anticipated future events. But it should be clear that when major changes in the determinants of exchange rates are anticipated, they must affect the level of the exchange rate, given current values of the exchange rate determinants. This point is readily made with the help of figure 2.3. The economy sits initially at point A, and there develops the expectation of a *future* increase in money and government spending, respectively. The exchange rate will immediately jump in response to the news. In response to an anticipated future money increase, it will depreciate to A', in response to anticipated higher spending or tax cuts, it will appreciate to A''.[11] Thus, given current money and fiscal policy, today's exchange rate may be any of three, A, A', or A'' depending on whether we anticipate easier money or easier fiscal policy or neither. Neglecting these "news" effects on exchange rates may thus eliminate most of the explanatory variables for the observed noise. This is more likely to be the case the more proximate and larger the anticipated changes.

The same point can be made, using the equation for the relationship

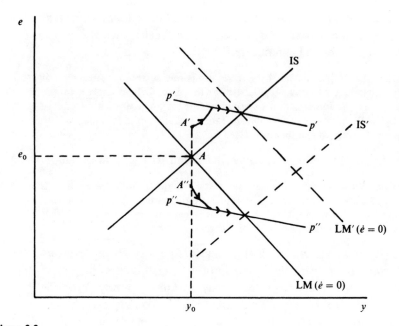

Figure 2.3

between interest differentials, depreciation, and the risk premium. Noting that in (6) $\dot{e}$ denotes the expected rate, we can write:[12]

$$\dot{e}_{actual} = i - i^* + \phi\left(\frac{B}{\bar{W}}, \frac{W}{\bar{W}}\right) + \text{"news,"} \tag{7}$$

where we have used the fact that with rational expectations the actual depreciation rate is equal to the expected rate plus a white noise error or "news." Equation (7) singles out news as one of the determinants of movements in the exchange rate. Given current income, money, and prices as well as the relative supplies of assets, the exchange rate may appreciate or depreciate because the expectation of a change in exchange rate determinants emerges. While that idea has been immediately accepted in the literature and, indeed, reminds us of the 1920s discussion, it has received practically no empirical testing.[13]

The literature differs sharply from the extensive and careful testing which expectations-based macroeconomics has received in closed economy applications. Research here has particularly focused on questions that run quite parallel: the effect of money, unanticipated versus anticipated, on unemployment and the real rate of interest.[14] It remains a question whether the very poor empirical performance of exchange rate

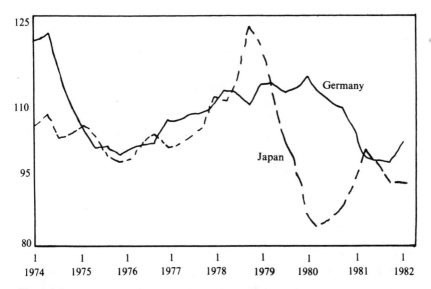

Figure 2.4
Real effective exchange rates (1975 = 100). Source: IMF.

models is due to a failure to distinguish news and anticipated realizations of the determinants of exchange rates. The work on anticipated future disturbances on the time path of exchange rates, for example, has amply shown that exchange rates may well lead anticipated money.

Four Problems

In this section we sketch four problems that may have arisen under the flexible exchange rate regime of the 1970s. The first is the adverse side effect of inappropriate monetary-fiscal policy mixes. The second concerns the role of expectations about future policy changes that render current policy more difficult, a variant of the peso problem. The third concerns the possibility of speculative bubbles. The fourth involves extraneous beliefs.

Bubbles

Important research on the volatility of asset prices has forced the question whether asset prices move "too much" given the path of fundamentals such as interest rates or dividends.[15]

The same question arises in the context of exchange rates. Observing real exchange rates in figure 2.4, where we show the yen and DM rates, we might ask whether this large movement in real exchange rates is warranted by beliefs about the fundamental determinants of exchange rates.

Work by Blanchard (1979), Blanchard and Watson (1982), and Tirole (1980), among others, discusses the conditions under which speculative bubbles or cumulative divergences from the path warranted by fundamentals may arise. An interesting model is that of Blanchard (1979) where risk neutral speculators are aware that a particular asset price is off the path of fundamentals. Indeed, they expect with probability a a crash and probability $1 - a$ the continuation of the bubble.

Suppose domestic and foreign assets are perfect substitutes. The interest rate differential must equal the expected rate of depreciation:

$$i - i^* = \tilde{e}_{t+1} - e_t, \tag{8}$$

where $\tilde{e}_{t+1}$ is the expected future exchange rate. But given the probabilities a associated with a crash to the fundamental rate, $\bar{e}_t$ and $1 - a$ of a continuing bubble, we have

$$e_{t+1} - e_t = \frac{i - i^*}{1 - a} + \frac{a}{1 - a}(e_t - \bar{e}). \tag{8a}$$

Equation (8a) describes a "rational" bubble. The exchange rate in the absence of a crash depreciates at a rate determined by three factors: the interest differential, the probability of a crash, and the undervaluation, $e_t - \bar{e}$. The more undervalued the exchange rate and the higher the probability of a crash, the more rapid is the rate of depreciation. A positive interest differential implies depreciation, more so the higher the probability of a crash.

Leaving aside interest differentials, the equation shows the fundamental problem of bubbles: the more *over*valued the exchange rate, the more rapidly it is *ap*preciating; the more *under*valued, the more rapidly the rate is *de*preciating. Bubbles are not self-correcting except by a crash. Bubbles, while they last, involve the possibility of temporary, cumulative deviations from fundamentals.

The presence of interest differentials introduces the possibility that the exchange rate can remain unchanged even though there is over or undervaluation. From (8a) we have the special case where the exchange rate remains constant:

$$\bar{e} - e_t = \frac{(i - i^*)}{a} \tag{9}$$

Thus a positive interest differential in favor of the home country can sustain an overvaluation, while a negative interest differential can sustain an undervaluation.[16] The bubble will be larger the larger the interest differential and the probability of a crash. For example, a 20 percent probability of a crash and a five percentage point interest differential sustain a 25 percent overvaluation!

The analysis has shown the possibility of temporary deviations of the exchange rate from the fundamental rate warranted by "the" model or fundamentals. Why should we be concerned about such deviations? The obvious reason is that given the path of policy variables, an exchange rate bubble will have real effects on competitiveness, inflation, and employment. It represents a macro-shock that, if possible, we would want to offset. The possibility of rational bubbles is important to recognize because is represents a fundamental departure from the view that markets do things right, all the time.

The Peso Problem

In the case of a bubble all market participants are aware that the current exchange rate deviates from the fundamental rate, but the bubble may be sustained by new entrants and the belief that it may grow fast enough, thus providing existing asset holders with a commensurate return. A different kind of exchange rate problem emerges when expectations about the path of fundamentals affect the current level of the exchange rate. Such a possibility, particularly when it involves the consideration of a large change in policy regime, has an effect on the current exchange rate and therefore on the difficulty of macroeconomic management. Specifically, the expectation of expansionary monetary policy (whether justified or not) will lead to current actual depreciation and thus to current inflationary pressures ahead of any expansion. Conversely, the belief in tightening will lead to appreciation and deflationary pressure.

This is the so-called "peso problem."[17] Salant and Henderson (1976) have shown that it is a generic problem of asset markets where speculators have to recognize the possibility of a future change in regime that affects future asset prices. The point is illustrated with a simple log-linear monetary model of the exchange rate in the tradition of Mussa (1975). Suppose there is full purchasing power parity and price flexibility and that real money demand depends on expected inflation or depreciation:

$$m_t - e_t = -b(\tilde{e}_{t+1} - e_t). \tag{10}$$

Suppose also that in the next period and ever thereafter the money stock is with probability $(1-a)$ current m_t and with probability a equal to $m_t + x$. The forward solution to (10) yields a level of the current exchange rate:

$$e_t = m_t + \frac{b}{1+b} ax \tag{11}$$

Thus the higher the probability of an increase in future money the higher is the current equilibrium exchange rate.

The problem raised here is very much like that of a bubble if the contingencies contemplated by the public are not in fact the intention of policymakers. The rate today is off the equilibrium path that policymakers have in mind for the economy. But there is of course the possibility that the fact of a depreciation, due to the beliefs about the possibility of an expansion, will force the actual expansion. Policies are rarely exogenous, and they may be largely or entirely endogenous. If such were the case, then random variations in beliefs about future policies could shape actual policies, and the economy would be without anchor.

There is a sense in which the exchange rate, in this setting, behaves exactly right. Asset holders are concerned about the possibility of capital losses and in response to reassessments about the path of policies, so they shift their portfolios and thus move the exchange rate. But there is also a sense in which this forward-looking, asset-market-oriented adjustment of exchange rates works with an overkill. By adjusting to the whims and fears of the moment, the exchange rate moves, and possibly a lot, and it moves relative to other more stable or sticky prices. Thus the *real* exchange rate, which guides the international division of labor, is being moved in response to conjectures about the future course of monetary and fiscal policies.

The importance of the peso problem is well-illustrated by the French experience in 1925–26. While the actual budget was in surplus and inflation was under control, the expectation that debt service should possibly be financed by money creation or capital taxation led to a flight out of the franc. Figure 2.5 shows the franc exchange rate collapsing in early 1926 and then, upon Poincare's assuming office with fiscal dictatorial powers, rapidly appreciating again.

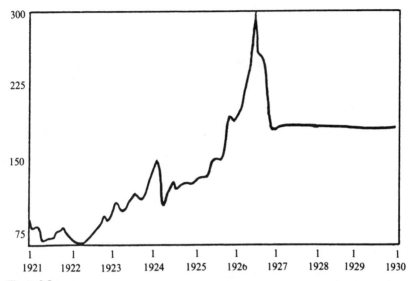

Figure 2.5
The French franc, effective exchange rate (Jan. 1921 = 100)

The exchange rate links asset and goods market in a sticky price world. The double allegiance creates trouble because the exchange rate moves like an asset price and not as a real exchange rate should. But movements in the nominal exchange rate also effect the price level, through import prices, wages, and competitive effects. Therefore movements in exchange rates, provoked by changing expectations about policy, have immediate effects on inflation. The moment the public comes to believe that a particular anti-inflation program is less likely to succeed, the ensuing exchange rate depreciation will make that a fact. Clearly here we face the unusual problem of a price that may be too flexible.

Extraneous Beliefs

There is another manner in which the public's perception of the world can lead the exchange rate to deviate from fundamentals. This arises when extraneous beliefs about the determinants of asset prices, via expectations, actually come to influence asset prices. This point has been made by Blanchard (1976) with respect to the Phillips curve and by Shiller (1981) in the context of the stock market. If fads, fashions, or misperceptions are highly autocorrelated, asset prices can persistently and (in finite samples) undiscoverably deviate from fundamentals. The same point can be easily demonstrated in the context of exchange rates.

Suppose the model of the exchange rate is in fact (10) but that market participants believe the exchange rate is influenced by both the money supply and the current arrount, C_t:

$$\tilde{e}_{t+1} = Em_{t+1} + \phi E(C_{t+1}),\tag{12}$$

where the actual current account follows a first-order autoregressive process and the money stock is a constant, m, plus white noise:

$$C_t = \Theta C_{t-1} + u_t, \quad m_{t+1} = m + v_{t+1}, \quad 0 < \Theta < 1,\tag{13}$$

with u_t and v_t white noise. Using (12) and (13), we arrive at the equilibrium exchange rate:

$$e_t = m + kC_t + v_t', \quad k \equiv \frac{b\phi\Theta}{(1+b)}, \quad v_{t=1}' = \frac{v_t}{(1+b)}.\tag{14}$$

Accordingly, the current account does affect the equilibrium exchange rate, even though it is not part of the structural model. Note next that the forecast errors, $e_{t+1} - \tilde{e}_{t+1}$ are given by

$$e_{t+1} - \tilde{e}_{t+1} = ku_{t+1} + v_{t-1}' - \Theta(\phi - k)C_t.\tag{15}$$

If the autocorrelation of the current account is high so that Θ is close to unity and if the response of money demand to the alternative cost of holding money b, is high, $\Theta b/(1+b)$ is close to unity, and the coefficient of C_t is close to zero. Regressions will not uncover that forecast errors are predictable on the basis of the current account. They cannot reject, except in extremely large samples, the hypothesis that the forecast errors are white noise.

The example is of interest because it suggests that extraneous beliefs about exchange rate determinants may introduce persistent and large deviations of the exchange rate from fundamentals and that these deviations are undetectable. The full rational expectations exchange rate (setting $\Theta = 0$) would be $\bar{e}_t = v_t' + m$, and therefore the deviation from this "fundamentals rate," $\bar{e}_t$, is equal to kC_t. The variance of the fundamentals rate is $s_e^2 = s_v^2$, whereas the asymptotic variance of the rate including current account beliefs is

$$s^2 = s_v^2 + \frac{k^2 s_u^2}{1 - \Theta^2}.\tag{16}$$

Real interest rate (percent)   Real exchange rate (1975 = 100)

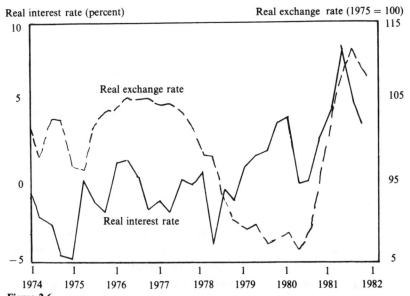

Figure 2.6
The U.S. real exchange rate and the real interest rate. Source: IMF and Morgan guaranty.

It is immediately apparent that with Θ close to unity extraneous current account beliefs introduce a potentially vast variability in the exchange rate.

The Dollar Problem

Since mid-1980, the U.S. dollar has appreciated relative to other currencies and the real exchange rate today is substantially above the levels of 1973 or 1975. Figure 2.6 shows the movement of the real exchange rate (relative value added deflators) and also shows the level of U.S. real interest rates. It is apparent that the real appreciation coincided with a move toward positive and higher average real rates.[18]

Theoretical models built around the idea of sticky prices or inflation rates suggest that a tightening in monetary growth, other things equal, will lead to an immediate appreciation of the real exchange rate in response to higher domestic interest rates and resulting portfolio shifts in favor of domestic assets. But unless there is an ongoing tightening, the move toward tighter money should rapidly translate into falling nominal interest rates and a reduction in inflation. In that adjustment process, the exchange rate would be *de*preciating (following the initial jump appreciation) at a rate that matches interest differentials adjusted for risk premia.

Over the medium term there would be no appreciable change in the real interest rate.

Events, in a number of ways, do not fit the theoretical model. On one side there is an accompanying fiscal expansion which in both the short run and the long run will tend to raise real interest rates. That increase in real interest rates in turn may have a long-run effect on the equilibrium exchange rate while reinforcing the short-run portfolio shifts. On the other hand, the experiment of monetary tightening is very much in the nature of the "peso problem" that was discussed earlier. Continuing nominal and real appreciation occurs as the public reevaluates its belief in tight money in the light of continuing Fed performance while the Fed itself assesses its course in the light of performance and approval. Thus monetary tightening is itself a medium-term exercise in which progressive tightening interacts with resolve to keep up the belief that this will be the case. The mix allows the possibility of continuing real appreciation over a two- or three-year period, the more so if inflation is sticky.

Monetary stabilization, certainly in combination with fiscal expansion, cannot fail to raise the real interest rate in the short run and therefore to lead to international portfolio reshuffling in favor of the dollar. The portfolio shifts, in turn, induce currency appreciation both in real and nominal terms. That appreciation, which is an international side effect of our domestic stabilization policies, is a serious macroeconomic problem as the following evidence shows.

Table 2.1 shows estimates by the Federal Reserve, using their multi-country trade and payments model, of the 20 percent dollar appreciation on a trade weighted basis, on growth and inflation.

Table 2.1
Estimate of the effects of a 20 percent dollar appreciation in 1980:3 to 1980:4

	Incremental inflation			Incremental growth		
	1981	1982	1983	1981	1982	1983
Germany	1.6	1.4	0.7	0.3	2.4	2.1
US	−0.4	−0.5	−0.1	−0.5	−0.4	1.1

Source: Hooper (1982).

The OECD has also reported estimates of the effects of exchange rate changes in their multilateral model. Here the effects of a 10 percent dollar *de*preciation are studied, with the depreciation occurring at the outset.

Table 2.2
OECD estimate of the effects of a 10 percent dollar depreciation (at annual percentage rates)

Half-year	Incremental inflation				Incremental growth			
	1st	2nd	3rd	4th	1st	2nd	3rd	4th
North America	0.4	0.7	0.3	0.1	−0.2	0.1	0.4	0.3
Europe	−0.5	−0.1	−0.6	−0.3	0.0	−0.2	−0.4	−0.3

Source: OECD Economic Outlook, December 1981, pp. 124–125.

The simulations of either model bring out clearly that exchange rates have a very strong impact on inflation and that they also affect real activity. A dollar appreciation will reduce U.S. inflation and raise inflation in Europe. Either model suggests that within a year, a 20 percent dollar appreciation would raise the European price level about 3 percent relative to what it would otherwise be. That *is* a very large inflation shock; it certainly is of the same order as the oil price shock. The inflationary shock is particularly large when there is comprehensive indexation that translates higher import prices into increased unit labor costs and thus speeds comprehensively through the economy.

The inflation shock is accompanied by a change in real GNP growth made up of two opposing tendencies. The terms of trade deterioration in Europe lowers real GNP directly. But there is an offset due to increased competitiveness that increases trade volume. Both sets of estimates show that ultimately the gain in competitiveness increases growth of real GNP, and quite strongly so in the Federal Reserve model. The OECD model, by contrast, shows both slower and smaller responses of growth.

Now it must be recognized that Europe can expand aggregate demand and raise growth, should she wish to do so. We can therefore *not* count the growth benefits of the dollar appreciation as an important offset against the imported inflation. In fact, what we must assume is that Europe in an attempt to contain inflation—after all, that is what every country is trying hard to do—must spend the gain in growth and quite a bit more to confine or offset the inflationary impact. This implies not only a reduction in growth but quite possibly too an environment less hospitable to investment. On balance then the dollar appreciation represents an *adverse supply shock* for Europe. There remains some scope for Europe to affect the composition of the shock between inflation and recession or reduced growth.

In the U.S. the exchange rate appreciation exerts a favorable effect on inflation, although the effect is small compared to those in Europe. The impact on growth is negative but small. It is apparent therefore that the U.S. interests and those of other counties are sharply opposed. What to the U.S. is a favorable side effect to tight money represents an adverse effect abroad. The question then must be whether these spillover effects are part and parcel of a well functioning exchange rate system or whether they represent an important shortcoming that needs serious consideration and remedy.

There is another respect in which U.S. policies, and the changed policy environment, contribute to instability. Engle and Frankel (1982) report that money surprises—deviations of the Friday release of money data from forecasts—exert a significant effect on short-term interest rates and on exchange rates. Cornell (1982) reports the astounding fact that these money news move not only the very short-term rate, as might be expected when Fed correction of money is anticipated, but also the whole maturity structure up to 30 year bonds. The fact that the entire interest rate structure moves up in response to *weekly* money forecast errors reflects the fact that expectations about long term rates have become very diffuse and that now the short-term rate is more nearly thought of as a random walk. In such a world volatility of interest rates may well bring about larger volatility of exchange rates.

What Is to Be Done?

We have identified several problems that place in question the effective operation of the flexible exchange rate system. All issues arise because exchange rates are and behave like asset prices but do play an important role in goods markets as well. We now have to ask whether there are policy remedies to these problems and whether the possible remedies are cost effective. It is important to say at the outset that these issues are unresolved.

There are two possible avenues for influencing and controlling the behavior of exchange rates: one is (sterilized) intervention, the other is a real interest equalization tax (RIET). The case for intervention has been and is an uncomfortable one. The case for a RIET is, at first sight, more controversial but is an avenue that in view of North Atlantic discord and disruption becomes increasingly realistic as an option.

Intervention

The case for intervention rests on the premise that domestic and foreign currency securities are imperfect substitutes and that, accordingly, changes in their relative supplies will induce portfolio disequilibria. At going interest rates there is pressure for exchange rate adjustments, and these adjustment in turn spread to other financial markets as well as to the goods markets. It is thus possible, on the premise of imperfect asset substitutability, to influence exchange rates by affecting the relative supplies of home and foreign currency outside securities or by management of the currency composition of world debt.

Henderson (1982) offers a definitive analysis of the case for intervention. He concludes that intervention is optimal (if feasible) in the case of portfolio shifts, which of course is the traditional case for accommodating financial policies. For disturbances to aggregate demand, by contrast, a policy of maintaining nonintervention in money and exchange markets offers greater employment stability. The latter point is readily made with standard aggregate demand and supply schedules as shown in fig. 2.7. The money wage is assumed fixed, but prices are flexible. Thus there is an upward sloping aggregate supply A_s. The aggregate demand schedule A_d, embodies bond and money market equilibrium, given the alternative policy assumptions. Along the steeper schedule exchange and interest rates are held constant. Therefore a decline in prices stimulates aggregate demand *only* through the effect on competitiveness. Along the dashed and flatter aggregate demand

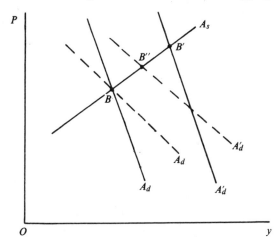

Figure 2.7

schedule, money and debt are held constant. Therefore a fall in prices lowers interest rates and expands demand while at the same time, for bond markets to clear, it induces a depreciation and thus reinforces the gain in competitiveness. Accordingly, a larger rise in output is required to restore balance.

A given autonomous increase in demand shifts the aggregate demand schedules out and to the right, the more so the more accommodating are policies. If interest rates and exchange rates are held constant, the demand expansion is not dampened by higher interest rates and appreciation. Accordingly, under such a "rates constant" policy as Henderson concludes, demand disturbances have a larger impact on employment and domestic prices (point B'') than is the case for an aggregate policy (point b'). There are significant complications to the model once we allow, as we should, supply side effects of exchange rate movements. Once these complications are introduced, it becomes much less clearcut whether rates constant policies are preferred to policies that maintain aggregates. It also becomes more difficult to identify what is the disturbance that is affecting the economy. On both counts the case for an active intervention stance becomes less clearcut, except for obvious portfolio shifts.

The ambiguity in the assessment of intervention is increased once we consider the imperfect substitution issue. There is of course no question that dollar and foreign currency assets are imperfect substitutes. This is the case because their returns are not perfectly correlated, and in some cases are in fact negatively correlated. But there remains the question whether the variance of relative returns and the degree of risk aversion are sufficiently large to make imperfect substitutes an easy policy channel. Long and short bonds are imperfect substitutes, but even so twisting the term structure of interest never was a success. The same question arises in the exchange rate context: how large an intervention is required to move the $/DM rate 1 percent? To that question we have no serious answer.

If intervention does not look like a very reliable tool, are there any options? One option is a (moving) wide exchange rate band within which rates are flexible but at the margins of which rates would be defended. Such a band might be reasonable as a proposition to eliminate extreme risk. But in doing so, we may also increase the mobility of capital and actually aggravate exchange rate instability within the band. The only sense of a band would be as a cooperative venture in forestalling disruptive policies to spill over into excessive appreciation or depreciation. But it is also conceivable that such band setting may well assume protectionist overtones. On balance, there are serious doubts about such a policy.

The case for intervention is usually made as one of countering disorderly market conditions.[19] But there is no very good case why small noise in the market should be smoothed, and there is good reason that large noise cannot effectively be dealt with. A massive disturbance such as the dollar appreciation of 1980–82 probably cannot be dealt with by intervention, unless we allow the exchange authorities to have swings in the size and denomination of their assets. For such massive disturbances we need a more adequate tool.

Real Interest Equalization Taxes

History is aplenty with collapses and surges in exchange rates, whether we look at France in the 1920s, the U.S. in the last years, or the laboratory experiments in Latin America. Invariably, the really vast changes in *real* exchange rates are associated not with changes in comparative advantage but rather with the medium-term adjustment to abandon of fiscal control or, on the other side, monetary stabilization. Taking the case of monetary tightening, real exchange rates easily move by 20 or 40 percentage points and therefore have of course vast effects on the economy over and above what tight money implies. In a small country these effects are largely domestic, but when the policy is pursued in the U.S., unsynchronized with the rest of the world, then the policy spills over as an adverse disruptive supply shock abroad. In the trade field, market disruption is dealt with by quotas or *ad hoc* compensating duties. This is felt to be an effective policy dealing with a *transitory* disturbance. Much the same view should be adopted on capital account. Whenever unsynchronized policies open up disruptively large real interest differentials, we need ad hoc real interest equalization taxes that close the gaps and avoid a major impact on the real exchange rate.[20] There is no sensible argument that tightening of money should involve as a desirable side effect a loss of exports, an increase in imports, and international redistribution of real income and borrowing abroad. Because these side effects are undesirable, both here and abroad, we should attempt to the maximum possible extent to immunize the world economy against these spillovers.

Ad hoc duties to offset trade disruption are neither totally efficient nor totally effective. But nobody questions that they substantially accomplish their purpose of insulating an industry from some transitory foreign disturbance. The same applies to a RIET. There is little doubt that some inefficiency is involved and that certainly more than in the case of trade disruption duties, there is room for circumvention. But it is also true that a RIET is a highly desirable, second-best, instrument.

A real interest equalization tax is a second-best instrument in that at some efficiency costs, it avoids the even larger costs of adverse spillover of U.S. policies abroad. The first-best world is one where transition to lower inflation has no real effects whatsoever, but proceeds with full employment and constant real interest harmony. The moment that scenario is disturbed because prices or inflation rates are sticky, there is a presumption that supplementary policies, both domestic and international, should accompany tight money. The relevant criterion by which to judge supplementary policies (TIPs, wage controls, investment tax credits, RIETs) is whether on balance they make the economy operate more efficiently without prejudicing the disinflation target. Surely that must be the case for RIETs since they avoid, if effective, the adverse and totally unwarranted effects of U.S. policies abroad. The argument against RIETs is that they are costly because they interfere with the free flow of capital. But that argument is empty since it fails to demonstrate that the costs of a RIET are larger than the benefits gained thereby in avoiding the spillover of U.S. policy abroad. At present, we are spending a percentage point or more of GNP every year to try to reduce inflation. We cannot seriously argue that the allocational costs of RIETs are in any sense commensurate with the costs that are avoided by their preventing imported inflation in Europe.

On a cost benefit basis RIETs are assuredly a preferred policy option. The only serious question is how to design the system in a manner that makes coverage complete and administration automatic. One avenue that commends itself is a transitory withholding tax on interest bearing, dollar denominated assets. Because the tax is transitory, the offshore problems, though present, may not be overriding.

Summary

It is shown that modern exchange rate theories have failed across the board to account for exchange rate behavior. Speculative bubbles, expectations about future policy changes, and international side effects of inappropriate monetary-fiscal policy mixes are reasons for deviations of the exchange rate from the rate warranted by the fundamentals. As instruments to influence and control the behavior of the exchange rate, official exchange market intervention as well as a real interest equilization tax (RIET) are discussed. Exchange market intervention is rejected because large noise can not effectively be dealt with this tool. The RIET is a preferred policy option on a cost-benefit basis.

Notes

1. Friedman (1956), p. 173.

2. Nurkse (1944), p. 118.

3. Friedman (1956), pp. 176–177.

4. See Gray and Wallich (1979) and Dornbusch and Krugman (1976).

5. See Appendix 6 to the Treasury and Civil Service Report on Monetary Policy, U.K. House of Commons, London, 1981.

6. For reference see, for example, Dornbusch (1980). See, however, the discussion in the *Economic Report of the President, 1982*.

7. Frankel (1979).

8. Krugman (1980).

9. Hacche and Townsend (1981), p. 253.

10. Meese and Rogoff (1983), p. 23.

11. Wilson (1977) and Rogoff (1979) have studied the role of anticipated future disturbances in exchange rate dynamics.

12. On this point, see Mussa (1976), Dornbusch (1978, 1980), and Isard (1980).

13. See, however, Black (1972), Frenkel (1981), Dornbusch (1980), Engle and Frankel (1982), and Cornell (1983).

14. For references see Mishkin (1982).

15. See, for example, Grossman and Schiller (1980).

16. In (8a) and (9) the fundamental rate $\bar{e}$ is constant. In a more complete model the question must be raised whether this is consistant with nominal interest differentials.

17. See Lizondo (1983) and Krasker (1980).

18. This is the "Reagan dummy" referred to earlier.

19. See *Economic Report of the President, 1982*, pp. 189–191.

20. Tobin (1978) has argued for a permanent tax on foreign currency transactions. Liviatan (1979) argues for transitory taxes associated with monetary stabilization.

References

Artus, J. 1984. Effects of U.S. Monetary Restraint on the DM/$ Exchange Rate and the German Economy. *IMF Staff Papers*, June.

Black, S. W. 1972. The Use of Rational Expectations in Models of Speculation, *Review of Economics and Statistics*, 161–165.

Blanchard, O. J. 1979. Speculative Bubbles, Crashes and Rational Expectations, Economic Letters. North-Holland, pp. 387–389.

Blanchard, O. J. 1976. Three Essays on Macroeconomics. Unpublished Ph. D. dissertation. MIT.

Blanchard, O. J., and M. W. Watson. 1982. Bubbles, Rational Expectations, and Financial Markets. Unpublished manuscript (January).

Buiter, W. H., and M. Miller. 1981. Monetary Policy and International Competitiveness: The Problems of Adjustment. *Oxford Economic Press* 33, Oxford (supplement, July).

Cornell, B. 1983. Money Supply Announcements and Interest Rates: Another View. *American Economics Review*, September.

Dornbusch, R. 1980. *Open Economy Macroeconomics*. Basic Books.

Dornbusch, R. 1980. Exchange Rate Economics: Where Do We Stand? *Brookings Papers on Economic Activity* 1, 143–185.

Dornbusch, R. 1983. Exchange Risk and the Macroeconomics of Exchange Rate Determination. In R. Hawkins et al. (eds.), *The Internationalisation of Financial Markets and National Press*.

Dornbusch, R. 1978. Monetary Policy under Exchange Rate Flexibility. Federal Reserve Bank of Boston, Conference Series, Managed Exchange Rate Flexibility.

Dornbusch, R., and S. Fischer. 1980. Exchange Rates and the Current Account. *The American Economic Review* 70, 960–971.

Dornbusch, R., and P. Krugman. 1976. Flexible Exchange Rates in the Short Term. *Brookings Papers on Economic Activity* 3.

Engle, C., and J. Frankel. 1982. Why Money Announcements Move Interest Rates: An Answer from the Foreign Exchange Risk. Unpublished manuscript. University of California, Berkeley.

Flood, Robert. 1982. Stochastic Process Switching and Inflation. Unpublished manuscript. Board of Governors of the Federal Reserve.

Flood, Robert, and P. M. Garber. 1981. Bubbles, Runs and Gold Monetization. Unpublished manuscript. University of Virginia (October).

Flood, Robert, and N. P. Marion. 1983. Exchange Rates Regimes in Transition: Italy 1974. *Journal of International Money and Finance* 2.

Frankel, J. 1979. On the Mark: A Theory of Floating Exchange Rates Based on Real Interest Differentials. *The American Economic Review* 69.

Frankel, J. 1979. The Diversifiability of Exchange Risk. *Journal of International Economics*.

Frankel, J. 1982. *Tests of Monetary and Balance of Payments Models of Exchange Rates*. University of California, Berkeley.

Frenkel, Jacob. 1981. Flexible Exchange Rates in the 1970s. *Journal of Political Economy* 89.

Friedman, M. 1956. *The Case for Flexible Exchange Rates: Essays in Positive Economics.* University of Chicago Press.

Genberg, H. 1981. Effects of Central Bank Intervention in the Foreign Exchange Market. *IMF Staff Papers.*

Grossman, S., and R. Schiller. 1981. The Determinants of the Variability of Stock Prices. *The American Economic Review* 71.

Hacche, G., and J. Townsend. 1981. Exchange Rates and Monetary Policy: Modelling Sterling's Effective Exchange Rate, 1972–80. *Oxford Economic Papers* 33.

Henderson, D. 1982. Exchange Market Intervention Operations: Their Effect and Their Role in Financial Policy. Unpublished manuscript. Board of Governors of the Federal Reserve System.

Hooper, P. 1982. Impact of the Recent Dollar Appreciation on GNP and Prices in Major Industrialized Countries: Simulations with the MCM. Unpublished memorandum. Board of Governors of the Federal Reserve.

Isard, P. 1980. Expected and Unexpected Exchange Rate Changes. Unpublished manuscript. Federal Reserve Board.

Krugman, P. 1980. Consumption Preferences, Asset Demands and Distribution Effects in International Financial Markets. Unpublished manuscript. MIT.

Liviatan, N. 1979. Neutral Monetary Policy and the Capital Import Tax. Unpublished manuscript. Hebrew University (October).

Lizondo, J. S. 1983. Foreign Exchange Futures Prices under Fixed Exchange Rates. *Journal of International Economics* (February).

Marris, S. 1981. Exchange Rates: Too Fixed or Too Flexible? Unpublished manuscript. Organization for Economic Cooperation and Development.

Meese, R., and K. Rogoff. 1983. Empirical Exchange Rate Models of the Seventies: Are They Fit to Survive? *Journal of International Economics* (February).

Mishkin, F. 1982. Does Anticipated Monetary Policy Matter? An Econometric Investigation. *Journal of Political Economy* 90.

Mussa, M. 1979. *The Empirical Regularities in the Behavior of Exchange Rates and Theories of the Foreign Exchange Market.* Carnegie Rochester Conference Series 11.

Mussa, M. 1976. The Exchange Rate and the Balance of Payments. *Scandinavian Journal of Economics* 2.

Mussa, M. 1969. Three Times the Transfer Problem Plus David Hume. Unpublished manuscript. University of Chicago.

Nurkse, R. 1944. *International Currency Experience: Lessons of the Inter-War Period.* League of Nations. Princeton, New Jersey.

Obstfeld, M. 1982. Can We Sterilize? *The American Economic Review* (May).

Rogoff, K. 1979. Essays on Expectations and Exchange Rate Volatility. Unpublished manuscript. Ph. D. dissertation. MIT.

Salant, S., and D. Henderson. 1978. Market Anticipations of Government Policies and the Price of Gold. *Journal of Political Economy* 86.

Shiller, R. 1981. The Use of Volatility Measures in Assessing Market Efficiency. *Journal of Finance* 36.

Tirole, J. 1982. On the Possibility of Speculation under Rational Expectations. *Econometrica* (September).

Tobin, J. 1978. A Proposal for International Monetary Reform. Cowles Foundation Discussion Paper 506, Yale University.

Wallich, H., and J. A. Gray. 1980. Stabilization Policy and Vicious and Virtuous Circles. In J. Chipman and Charles P. Kindleberger (eds.), *Flexible Exchange Rates and the Balance of Payments*. North-Holland.

Williamson, J. 1982. *The Open Economy and the World Economy*. Basic Books.

Wilson, C. 1979. Anticipated Disturbances and Exchange Rate Dynamics. *Journal of Political Economy* 87.

3   Flexible Exchange Rates and Interdependence

The fundamental argument for flexible exchange rates is that they would allow countries autonomy with respect to their use of monetary, fiscal and other policy instruments.... The argument for flexible exchange rates can be put more strongly still: flexible exchange rates are essential to the preservation of national autonomy and independence consistent with efficient organization and development of the world economy.

Harry G. Johnson (written in late 1960s)[1]

In moving from the exchange control and trade discrimination of the 1950s to the open economic system of the 1960s, the world economy briefly returned to the liberal order that has been credited with fostering economic progress during the 40 years before World War I. There can be little doubt that the 1960s were the best decade the world economy has experienced in this century. But the very source of the success—active management of the macroeconomy that included designing the monetary and fiscal mix to achieve satisfactory, sustained growth—eventually created economic problems that fostered disintegration in the world economy. Differences in inflation preferences between the United States and Europe were irreconcilable, and productivity growth differentials were too large to accommodate a world economy using fixed exchange rates.

Harry Johnson's perceptive assessment, quoted above, was widely shared during the late 1960s. Flexible exchange rates were then seen as an

Reprinted with permission from *International Monetary Fund Staff Papers*, Vol. 30, No. 1 (March 1983), pp. 3–38.

essential further step toward a liberal world system that would allow countries to enjoy the advantages of free markets in goods and assets and yet enjoy domestic macroeconomic independence. Now, after ten years of experience with flexible exchange rates, there is much less confidence that flexible rates and domestic policy autonomy are reconcilable. On the contrary, the exercise of policy autonomy becomes nearly impossible under flexible rates, because many economies are too small and open to accept the exchange rate variations induced by policy. Alternatively, the effects of policies of countries with large economies are exported and interfere with foreign internal stability. What flexible exchange rates are still credited with is an ability to isolate a country from the world inflation *trend*, while it is recognized that they cannot isolate a country from either the effects of policies that initiate a *change in trend* or from any other disturbances.

The traditional argument against flexible exchange rates, derived from the experience of the interwar period, is that flexible rates are unstable, move about erratically, and often aggravate the macroeconomic stability problem. The experience of the last ten years would certainly lead an observer to endorse that view. Anytime there is monetary and fiscal dislocation in a major country, as there was in the United States in the 1970s, flexible rates perform poorly, because they lead to excessive real exchange rate changes and to the export of inflation or deflation. Flexible rates leave us with as much interdependence, or even more, as there is under a fixed rate regime. This chapter reviews the channels of interdependence and asks in what directions one should look for a system that maintains an open world economy but more effectively comes to terms with the high priority given to national policy autonomy.

There are, broadly speaking, three avenues: (1) making exchange rates more fixed, (2) making them less flexible, or (3) as suggested by Modigliani and Tobin, limiting the incentives for short-run capital mobility, either permanently or on an ad hoc basis. It seems certain that free market economics bars consideration of a capital account tax, which might be seen as embodying a wicked infringement on individual freedom. It is also likely that U.S. macroeconomic policies and policies abroad remain unpredictable and uncoordinated to an extent sufficient to preclude establishment of fixed rates or even an exchange rate band. What is left, then, is the spirit of Versailles—that is to say, the recognition that there may be circumstances where it is not impossible that there might be intervention, which could turn out not to be small.

Consequently, a strong case can be made for a different domestic policy mix to go with flexible rates.

Channels of Interdependence

This section sketches a model of interdependence on the aggregate demand and supply sides. The purpose of the model is to draw attention to distinct channels and to identify the relevant parameters in assessing the importance of these sources of interdependence. The section begins by considering a standard macroeconomic model, focusing on prices, aggregate demand, perfect asset substitutability, and rational expectations. Extensions follow in subsequent sections.

Exchange Rates, Employment, and Wages[2]

To study cyclical interdependence, this chapter considers a country that faces a given world interest rate, given import prices, and a given world demand (except for real exchange rate effects) for its exports. The log-linear model is presented in equations (1) and (6):

$$y \quad = a\theta - br + f, \quad \theta \equiv e + p^* - w; \tag{1}$$

$$m - q = hy - ci; \tag{2}$$

$$q \quad \equiv \beta w + (1 - \beta)\,(e + p^*); \tag{3}$$

$$r \quad \equiv i - \dot{q}; \tag{4}$$

$$i \quad = i^* + \dot{e}; \tag{5}$$

$$\dot{w} \quad = \gamma y + a(q - w). \tag{6}$$

Equation (1) represents the IS (investment-savings) schedule with θ denoting the real exchange rate and f denoting a domestic or foreign shift variable. The real interest rate is denoted by r. The LM (demand for money = supply of money) schedule is represented by equation (2), where the price level is denoted by q. The price level is a weighted average of domestic prices, which are set equal to wages, and of import prices. Equation (4) defines the domestic real interest rate, and equation (5) expresses the assumption of perfect asset substitutability, with an adjustment made for anticipated depreciation. Wage dynamics are specified in equation (6) and are linked to the gross national product

(GNP) gap, y, and to the real wage level. The term $q-w$ represents a rigid real wage effect.[3]

This model is appropriate to short-run cyclical issues. It neglects trend inflation, foreign inflation, productivity growth, and the impact of capital formation. It concentrates on aggregate demand and the cyclical interaction between wages, interest rates, and exchange rates. At any point in time—given home wages, money, and fiscal policy—an exchange rate and a depreciation rate can be found that satisfy the international interest rate relation. The wage level and the exchange rate determine external competitiveness and hence aggregate demand and employment. The system can be simplified by noting the relation between home and foreign interest rates:

$$r \equiv r^* + \beta\theta; \ i = r^* + \theta + \dot{w}. \tag{7}$$

The model is slightly more complex than the extended Mundell-Fleming model because of two modifications. On the one hand, care is taken to allow for an impact of import prices on the price level used to deflate real balances and real wages and to define the real interest rate. On the other hand, the domestic producer price index (here, the wage) responds not only cyclically but also to the real wage level.

The role of wage behavior can be appreciated by looking at the long-run behavior of the system as shown in figure 3.1. For a given world interest rate, the IS schedule shows equilibrium in the domestic goods market. A real depreciation creates excess demand, which is met by an increase in output. Along $\dot{w} = 0$, money wages are constant. A real depreciation, because it reduces real wages, leads to wage increases. To keep wages constant, the reduction in the standard of living owing to depreciation must be offset by unemployment that dampens wage demands. Hence $\dot{w} = 0$ is downward sloping. The slope of the constant wage schedule is determined by the relative response of wages to the cyclical position and to the standard of living via the real exchange rate

$$\left.\frac{d\theta}{dy}\right|_{\dot{w}=0} = \frac{\gamma}{a(1-\beta)} \equiv \lambda \dots \tag{8}$$

The pattern of wage response will determine the long-run effects of disturbances on output and the real exchange rate. A reduction in foreign demand or a rise in world interest rates, for example, will shift the IS schedule upward and to the left. The decline in employment is larger, the flatter the $\dot{w} = 0$ schedule or the smaller the cyclical responsiveness of

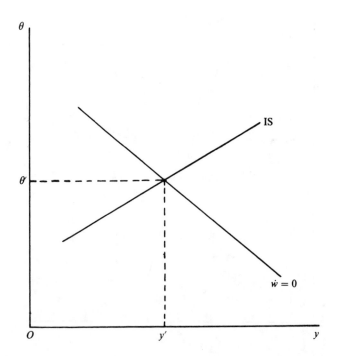

Figure 3.1

wages relative to the real wage stickiness as measured by the parameter λ. If the wage is highly responsive cyclically and real wage rigidity is nearly absent, λ tends toward infinity and the economy behaves as if it had full wage and price flexibility, which ensures rapid adjustment to full employment. Conversely, when cyclical flexibility is limited and real wage resistance is strong, λ tends toward zero. Adverse disturbances then can lead to a large impact on the price level combined with unemployment.[4]

The model described in equations (1) to (6) can be reduced to the behavior over time of money wages and the real exchange rate (see the appendix to this chapter). Figure 3.2 shows the dynamics by reference to the loci along which wages and the real exchange rate, respectively, are constant. Moving up along the $\dot{w} = 0$ schedule, an increase in the wage raises the price level and thus reduces real balances and exerts deflationary pressure, which causes wages to fall unless a cut in the real wage owing to real depreciation exerts an offsetting impact. The schedule *FF* shown in figure 3.2 represents the stable trajectory under perfect foresight. Given any initial money wage, the corresponding point on *FF*

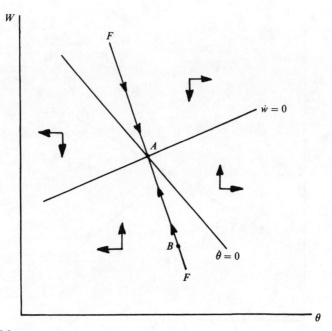

Figure 3.2

shows the equilibrium level of the nominal and real exchange rates such that the economy converges to long-run equilibrium at point A.

At point B, for example, the wage is low, and thus the price level tends to be low, which makes for high real balances and low nominal interest rates. To maintain international interest parity, the exchange rate must appreciate, which means that the real exchange rate must be above the steady-state level. At point B, as one can verify by looking at figure 3.2, the real exchange rate favors the home country; and because of real appreciation, by equation (7), the real interest rate is below the world level. Thus, aggregate demand and employment are high. High employment and the high real exchange rate or the low real wage exert upward pressure on the wage, which pushes the economy toward point A.

The framework can now be used to investigate the impact of foreign disturbances on home wages and employment. Using figure 3.3, the effect of an increase in foreign interest rates can be studied. Assume that wages increase in the long run and that the exchange rate depreciates. As figure 3.3 shows, the exchange rate will overshoot, moving immediately from the initial equilibrium at point A to a short-run equilibrium at A'.

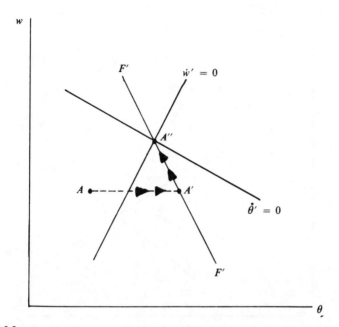

Figure 3.3

The rise in foreign interest rates creates an incipient capital outflow, which leads to exchange depreciation. When point A' is reached, home interest rates have risen somewhat, and there is now expected appreciation, which ensures a sufficient return on domestic securities. Changes in employment and in the standard of living combine to generate wage pressure that moves the economy over time to A''. In the long run, of course, there will be some unemployment.

The adjustment pattern is shaped by all the parameters, including particularly the dynamics of wages, income and interest responses of money demand, and the price elasticity of demand for goods. What is crucial to the initial behavior of the exchange rate is the long-run adjustment of money wages. If wages increase in the long run, then the exchange rate must overshoot in the short run, as is shown in figure 3.3. In contrast, if wages decrease in the long run, then there will be an immediate depreciation of the nominal and real exchange rate, but a more moderate one. In the subsequent adjustment process, the exchange rate will continue to depreciate. This case is shown in figure 3.4.

It is interesting to note that either exchange rates or unemployment *must* overshoot. As shown in figure 3.4, unemployment must overshoot, because at point A' the real exchange rate is depreciating, which means

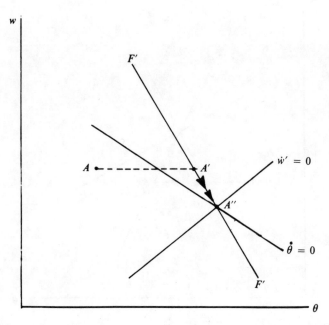

Figure 3.4

that real interest rates are above the world level, and the real exchange rate is below its long-run level. For both reasons, demand and hence employment at A' will be less than at A'', the final equilibrium. Exactly the opposite occurs at A' in figure 3.3, where employment is above the new long-run level. It is not certain, though, whether it is possible for employment to actually rise relative to the initial equilibrium at A in figure 3.4.

The overshooting of exchange rates or employment makes it interesting to ask what factors would make one or the other case more likely. As was noted previously, the outcome depends on the long-run adjustment of wages, which in turn depends on several parameters. A high price elasticity of demand implies small changes in equilibrium real exchange rates and therefore relatively little pressure on wages and output. A high price elasticity thus implies a long-run increase in wages to accommodate the reduced demand for real balances and the consequent exchange rate overshooting shown in figure 3.3. A high interest rate elasticity or income elasticity of money demand works in the same direction. In contrast, a high cyclical response of wages implies that wages could fall in the long run.[5] In the same way one can analyze the impact of foreign demand disturbances or changes in domestic fiscal policy. Again one finds that employment or exchange rate overshooting is possible, depending on the pattern of wage flexibility relative to the parameters of aggregate demand.

The effects of disturbances on domestic employment and on wages will presumably differ, depending on the direction of change. One would expect an asymmetry in the real wage resistance, in that workers accept gains in real wages but resist cuts. This extends also to the cyclical behavior of wages; wages rise more rapidly in a boom than they fall in a recession. In terms of the model, this amounts to saying that the coefficient of wage flexibility, λ, depends on the cyclical and real wage positions. Specifically, starting from full employment, a decrease in foreign demand or an increase in world interest rates will lead to unemployment and to a decline in real income. But an increase in foreign demand or a decrease in world interest rates brings about a real appreciation at full employment rather than a lasting real expansion beyond capacity.

The asymmetry issue is relevant once one considers transitory disturbances. Suppose, for example, that a transitory increase in world demand, caused by a boom abroad, leads to a real appreciation at full employment. Once the boom abroad subsides, the issue arises whether workers are willing to accommodate themselves to a cut in real income brought about by the ensuing real depreciation. There is no reason to dismiss the possibility of a ratchet effect in the operation of real wage resistance.

But if ratchet effects are present, the cyclical variability of real exchange rates, under a flexible exchange rate regime, necessitates consideration of an incomes policy that accommodates the changes in the standard of living associated with real exchange rate movements. Alternatively, active fiscal policy needs to be used to stabilize real exchange rates over the cycle to avoid the real appreciation that cannot, afterward, be undone without adverse effects on employment. But that of course raises the question whether there is more fiscal resistance than real wage resistance. In any event it is clear that transitory disturbances abound, that transitory real appreciation owing to strong demand raises the standard of living cyclically, and that instruments are necessary to dampen or to accommodate the subsequent decline.

So far, we have dealt with the case of a country that takes world demand and interest rates as exogenous. It is worthwhile to comment briefly on the changes brought about by repercussion effects. Without

going into details, this study recalls the Mundell-Fleming results specifying that with prices given, a monetary expansion in one country has
adverse employment effects abroad. Conversely, a fiscal expansion has
favorable employment effects abroad. These results depend critically on
the behavior of the real money stock in each country. They may cease to
hold the movement import prices enter the real balance deflator.
Specifically, as a fiscal expansion spreads abroad through real appreciation, it reinforces the expansion in the initiating country, but it
reduces real balances abroad, thus tending to confine the expansion. If
real wage resistance is an issue, this adverse effect of depreciation is
strongly reinforced. In contrast, a monetary expansion may, in such
circumstances, raise income abroad.

Interest Rates and Risk Premia

The discussion in the previous section was based on the assumption that
securities are perfect substitutes once anticipated exchange depreciation
is taken into account. Under that assumption real interest rates are
equalized in long-run equilibrium and in the short run can only differ by
an amount equal to the rate of change of the real exchange rate. But the
assumption of perfect asset substitution is not warranted once real
exchange rates fluctuate.

Movements in real exchange rates introduce negative correlation in the
real returns on domestic and foreign securities and thus create an
incentive for portfolio diversification. Only in a very special case, when
relative asset supplies match the minimum variance portfolio shares *and*
when there are identical consumption baskets across countries, will there
be no risk premium. In general, there is a risk premium that is related
to relative asset supplies and to the distribution of world wealth.

In the presence of a risk premium, the interest rate relationship
becomes

$$i = i^* + \dot{e} + \rho \left(\frac{V}{E\tilde{W}}, \frac{W}{E\tilde{W}} \right), \quad \rho_1 > 0 \; \rho_2 > 0, \tag{9}$$

where V and W denote, respectively, domestic outside debt and domestic
wealth, each measured in home currency, and $\tilde{W}$ denotes world wealth
measured in foreign currency. Equation (9) thus introduces a relationship between interest rates, expected depreciation, the nominal exchange
rate level, nominal wealth, and asset supplies. Where in the earlier model
nominal money was the only asset to play a role, now the supply of

domestic outside nominal assets also appears.[6]. An increase in the relative supply of domestic assets, $V/\hat{W}E$, must be accommodated by either a more rapid rate of appreciation or a higher nominal interest rate differential or else must be offset by depreciation of the exchange rate *level*.

The link between exchange rates and portfolio balance can be inferred from equation (9), taking the case of a small country, so that world wealth $\hat{X}$ is taken as given. Furthermore, assuming given interest rates and a given rate of depreciation, $i - i^* - \dot{e}$, one can find the relation between changes in domestic currency asset supplies, changes in wealth, and the corresponding changes in equilibrium exchange rates, which can be expressed by

$$\hat{E} = \hat{V} + \frac{\rho_2}{\rho_1 + \rho_2}(\hat{W} - \hat{V}). \tag{10}$$

Equation (10) shows that for a given depreciation-adjusted interest differential, an increase in domestic currency assets and wealth, in the same proportion, leads to equiproportionate depreciation. An increase in wealth, given asset supplies, leads, in contrast, to appreciation. On the one hand, an increase in wealth reduces, via domestic habitat effects, the risk premium and thus brings about appreciation; an increase in domestic currency asset supply, on the other hand, leads to a higher risk premium and thus to depreciation.

The risk premium introduces two important considerations. The first is that the composition of domestic assets, between money and debt (money being the medium of exchange for which there is a specific demand), is of importance and that open market operations therefore exert an effect on exchange rates that is independent of the effect of the change in money. This point can be illustrated in the following manner: The macro model sketched out previously determines interest rates as functions of the real money stock and real income. The model is closed by finding an exchange rate that satisfies both the macro model and the risk premium equation. An increase in debt or in home relative wealth then must affect both interest rates and exchange rates.

The second consideration introduced by the risk premium is that it constitutes a link between wealth distribution in the world, interest rates, and the exchange rate. A rise in domestic wealth leads to changes in both interest rates and exchange rates. Interest rates at home decline and/or the exchange rate appreciates. This effect is added to the macro model and provides a channel through which dynamic effects associated with the current account and the budget have implications for the exchange rate.

Intervention policy must be considered in relation to the risk premium. Intervention, viewed from that perspective, takes one of two forms. If purchases of foreign exchange are allowed to change the domestic money stock, intervention will be effective. But if there is sterilization, this has implications for the relative supply of domestic debt and thus for the risk premium. Sterilized intervention, it has been argued, is simply a reshuffling of the composition of domestic government liabilities. It has an effect on exchange rates only through the impact on the risk premium. Thus it can work only when a risk premium exists. Moreover the effectiveness—the bang per buck—depends on risk aversion being high and the variability of real interest differentials being large. Thus intervention policy works well when uncertainty is large and risk aversion is pervasive.

The risk premium has been singled out as an important channel through which the current account affects the exchange rate. Although the current account qualifies in principle as a determinant of exchange rates, it stands to reason that changes in wealth that are not included in the current account should really move to the center of attention. In particular, capital gains resulting from stock market movements certainly have a far larger impact on relative wealth than the current account does. In addition to the stock market, total domestic saving is a source of changes in relative wealth. Again the current account's share of saving is typically, though not necessarily, small. Except in special cases, the role of the current account in affecting exchange rate movements, via the risk premium, is not a large one.

Third Country Effects

The perspective we have adopted so far has been that of a country faced with external shocks. We now shift to the perspective of the system to examine the important cyclical interdependence that arises from the behavior of materials prices and import demands of peripheral countries. These countries are predominantly exporters of materials and importers of manufactures. They are also debtors.

Table 3.1 reports regressions of various measures of the *real* prices received by developing countries on the world business cycle, the real price of oil, and the real U.S. dollar exchange rate. The cyclical variable is the Organization for Economic Cooperation and Development

Table 3.1
Determinants of the terms of trade and real commodity prices, 1964-1981

Equation	Dependent variable	Constant	OECD unemployment	Real oil price	Real dollar exchange rate	R^2	D-W	ρ_1	ρ_2
(1)	Terms of trade	1.64 (0.70)	-0.01 (0.02)	-0.001 (0.0004)	-0.31 (0.14)	0.76	1.79		
(2a)	Real materials prices (Fund)	9.04 (1.58)	-0.06 (0.028)		-0.88 (0.32)	0.39	1.94	0.07	
(2b)	Real materials prices (Fund)	2.96 (1.31)	-0.15 (0.03)	0.16 (0.05)	-0.78 (0.26)	0.68	2.17	0.28	-0.73
(3a)	Real materials prices (World Bank)	2.22 (1.63)	-0.05 (0.023)		-0.64 (0.34)	0.25	1.81		
(3b)	Real materials prices (World Bank)	-1.18 (1.36)	-0.16 (0.03)	0.19 (0.05)	-0.49 (0.27)	0.66	2.02	0.29	-0.59
(4)	Real minerals and metals prices	-4.53 (1.30)	-0.20 (0.027)	0.22 (0.05)	0.78 (0.26)	0.89	1.97		
(5)	Real agricultural prices	3.71 (2.0)	-0.04 (0.03)		-0.98 (0.41)	0.28	1.85	0.15	

Note: Standard errors are in parentheses. The left-hand-side variable and the real dollar exchange rate are expressed in logs, as is the real oil price, except in equation (1). D-W denotes the Durbin-Watson statistic. ρ_1 and ρ_2 denote the coefficients for correction of first-order and second-order serial correlation.

(OECD) unemployment rate, which is taken from the OECD's *Economic Outlook*, and the real exchange rate is measured by the relative wholesale prices of manufactures of the United States (relative to trading partners), which are taken from the Fund's *International Financial Statistics*. Equation (1) in table 3.1 shows export prices relative to import prices of non-oil developing countries. The real oil price and the real dollar exchange rate are significant explanatory variables; a dollar appreciation or an increase in real oil prices leads to deterioration of developing countries' terms of trade. So does a rise in OECD unemployment, although here the coefficient is not precisely estimated. Equation (1) shows that a 1 percent real dollar appreciation would lead to a deterioration of developing country terms of trade by $^1/_3$ of 1 percent. This is of course a very sizable effect.

In equation (2a) the dependent variable is the Fund's index of the prices of all commodities (reported in *International Financial Statistics*) deflated by the dollar price of manufacturers' exports from developed countries (reported in the United Nations' *Monthly Bulletin of Statistics*). Again real dollar appreciation has a significant adverse impact on the real prices of materials. For this measure of real prices, a 1 percent real dollar appreciation leads to a nearly proportional deterioration in real commodity prices. In equations (3a), (3b), (4), and (5), it is shown that the results are not consistent, differing significantly between commodities. Equation (3a) reports the results for the World Bank's index of 33 commodities (see Grilli 1982) deflated by the dollar prices of manufactures as was done for equations (2a) and (2b). The results are substantially the same as those for equations (2a) and (2b). The index is made up of agricultural commodities (70.6 percent), metals and minerals (24.3 percent) and timber (5.1 percent). Equations (4) and (5) show that real dollar appreciation leads to an *increase* in the real price of minerals and metals, but to a *decrease* in the real price of agricultural commodities. The latter, presumably because of their predominant weight in the index, carry the results in the regressions for the total commodity group. The difference in the more disaggregated results suggests that the whole question, including the important issue of using alternative cyclical variables,[7] should be studied further.

Consider now how these third country effects operate when, say, the United States tightens its monetary policy. This would lead to increased nominal and real interest rates and to a slow down in demand in the United States. The dollar would appreciate in nominal and real terms. This paper has already discussed the direct effects on industrial countries of higher interest rates and reduced exports; they unambiguously translate into unemployment unless there is no real wage rigidity. But now there are additional effects caused by the impact of events in the United States on the material producing debtor countries. Higher real interest rates worsen those countries' current accounts. This is reinforced by the decline in demand by industrial countries for both manufactures and materials and, finally, by the effect of dollar appreciation on the real prices of materials. This combination is quite devastating for material exporting debtor countries. Typically, they will be forced to limit their own growth because of balance of payments constraints.

As seen from the perspective of industrial countries, the adjustments in material exporting debtor countries have two sides. Industrial countries as a group achieve a direct terms of trade improvement relative to material exporters, both for cyclical reasons and because of dollar appreciation. This gain may, however, be dampened, perhaps substantially, by the decline in developing countries' imports of manufactures.

Changes in the real prices of commodities during the cycle or as a by-product of changes in key exchange rates play an important role in relation to real wage rigidity. The deterioration in developing countries' terms of trade may well offset some of the real income loss an individual industrial country experiences as a result of, say, higher U.S. interest rates.

Bubbles, Pesos, and Runs

The preceding sections have focused on *actual* changes in exchange rate fundamentals, cyclical or permanent, that affect goods or asset markets and then affect the rest of the world through asset demands, demands for goods, exchange rate movements, and prices. However, many of the disturbances in the world economy are not the result of actual changes in fundamentals but rather of changes in expectations about the future course of these fundamentals. These revisions in expectations exert effects on interdependence that are as powerful as those exerted by actual changes in fundamentals.

When asset markets are dominated by expectations about the future course of fundamentals, exchange rates may move in ways that do not promote macroeconomic stability. Three ways in which this situation may come about deserve special attention. The first is familiar from recent literature on financial markets and concerns the possibility that exchange rates, in part, are determined by irrelevant information.

Market participants may have the wrong model of fundamentals, and their expectations, based on the wrong model, will affect the actual exchange rate. If there is sufficiently high serial correlation in the irrelevant variables, it may be impossible to discern the systematic forecast errors using conventional efficiency tests. But the exchange rate will be significantly more volatile than is warranted by the true model.

This point is important because market participants may be impressed by a plausible fundamentals variable, attribute explanatory power to it, and consequently make their expectations actually come true. Then, when some other variable moves, attention may shift to a different "main factor," which in turn comes to dominate the exchange rate for a while. Exchange rates carried by irrelevant beliefs are troublesome, not only because of the excess variance but also because shifting from one irrelevant factor to another will precipitate major exchange rate collapses. The possibility that exchange rates are sometimes far out of line with the fundamentals cannot be discounted. It is important to recognize this, because in the past economists may have given excessive weight to the notion that the market knows "the model" and, at the same time, is rational. It is quite conceivable that a number of fashionable factors, such as fiscal discipline, basic monetary control, long-run strength in manufacturing, and *Angebotsfreundliche Gesellschaftspolitik* (supply side policy) play a role, one at a time.

The second source of disequilibrium exchange rates is expectations about the possibility of regime changes and has been called the "peso problem." In this perspective, exchange rates are influenced not only by current fundamentals but also by agents' expectations that there are given probabilities that these fundamentals may change in specific directions. If market participants have sufficiently strong beliefs that a given course of policy will not be followed, they may in fact make it impossible for the authorities to follow that course. Under flexible exchange rates this problem may become acute because the exchange rate is so flexible a price and so much governed by expectations. It may well be argued, as was done in the discussion of the French stabilization experience under Raymond Poincaré, that speculators are the true judges of fundamentals and that a collapse of the exchange rate brought about by adverse capital flows is irrevocable evidence of a program of stabilization that was out of touch with fundamentals. But such an argument must be viewed as simplistic by anyone who recognizes that stabilization policy has a wide range of indeterminacy.[8]

The third source of disequilibrium exchange rates can be explained using the analogy of bubbles. A bubble exists when holders of an asset realize that the asset is overpriced but are nevertheless willing to hold it, since they believe there is only a limited risk of a price collapse during a given holding period; therefore asset holders expect to be able to sell eventually at a price that will provide them with sufficient capital gains to compensate them for running the risk of a collapse.[9] An analogous situation occurs when a currency has appreciated more than can be considered justified by fundamentals and overvaluation is widely thought to prevail, but appreciation is expected to continue until some disturbance causes the crash. There are no models of such a crash as yet, but it should be clear that an essential ingredient is the arrival of new information that diverts a sufficient number of speculators from keeping the bubble growing.

Bubbles, peso problems, and irrelevant information all move the exchange rate away from the particular equilibrium implied by current fundamentals. In each of these cases there is a re-evaluation of beliefs. When this occurs, exchange rates change markedly, which in turn may force an accommodating change in policies. Unless policies are very exogenous, instability of policies may be provoked by instability of expectations. That means flexible exchange rates may require, as an institutional setting, that policies be more exogenous than in fact they are today. Without such an anchor, flexibility of exchange rates may aggravate macroeconomic instability.

Coping with Interdependence

In the late 1960s discussion of international monetary arrangements centered on the idea of "flexing" the system. Exchange rates were too inflexible to be compatible with an overvalued dollar and the one-way street that overvaluation created for internationally mobile, speculative capital. Today much of the exchange rate debate starts from the recognition that it is desirable to reduce excessive fluctuations that exert undesirable interdependence effects. The quest then is for "flixed" exchange rates: the optimal exchange rate regime would prevent *persistent* overvaluation or undervaluation of a currency that would ultimately lead to protection or an undesirable monetary-fiscal policy mix. The rate system would also have to be flexible enough to yield *long-run* inflation autonomy. But, at the same time, short-run real exchange rate variability should be reduced, and the export of inflation through appreciation limited. There is little question that a flexible exchange rate system has desirable long-run features and that these should not be readily sacrificed. But, at the same time, the short-run implications of unsynchronized policy actions are sufficiently severe to raise the question whether exchange rates are too flexible at present. That question of course can be answered by comparing arrangements with a set of alternative arrangements.

Three alternative methods of reforming the present system are (1) returning to fixed or quasi-fixed rates, (2) limiting the incentives to move capital, and (3) permitting limited exchange rate flexibility. Brief comments will be made on aspects of each of these.

A return to outright fixed exchange rates appears adventurous. Such a move would be difficult because of large discrepancies in inflation rates among key industrial countries. The willingness of major industrial countries to impose trade restrictions seems striking confirmation that these countries are not disposed to abide by rules. An outright commitment to peg would yield, at best, a variety of the European Monetary System. The difficulties posed by a fixed rate system are aggravated by the economic instability in at least two key industrial countries—the United States and the United Kingdom.

An alternative to fixed rates has been proposed by McKinnon (1982). He argues that exchange rate instability and the instability of world inflation are outgrowths of misconceived monetarism. The right kind of monetarism would look at the world quantity of money. Specifically, he argues (p. 331) that

...the solution to international currency instability is straightforward: the Federal Reserve System should discontinue its policy of passively sterilizing the domestic monetary impact of foreign official interventions. Instead, a symmetrical nonsterilization rule would ensure that each country's money supply mutually adjusts to international currency substitution in the short run, without having official exchange interventions destabilize the world's money supply.

The basic premise of this prescription, and its flaw, is that it assumes that exchange rate instability is induced by shifts in the currency denomination of the public's money holdings—that is, by currency substitution. But surely international currency speculation is not carried out by shifts between different countries' M_1s (currency plus demand deposits) but by shifts between interest-bearing assets. The proposal also encounters the not negligible issue of the transition to low inflation in the United States. It certainly does not help to overlook the fact that inflation is significantly higher today in the United States than it is in Japan and the Federal Republic of Germany. As noted previously, however, monetary policy seeks to achieve a transition to low inflation, and it is the by-product of that transition that causes the real exchange rate havoc.

Proposals for more limited exchange rate flexibility take the form of intervention rules. They may either involve an exchange rate band (fixed or moving) with full intervention at the margin and none in between or an intervention rule that seeks to dampen exchange rate movements relative to some notion of a fundamentals rate.

Proponents of band proposals are reluctant to specify how the band would actually be set. They emphasize, as does Bergsten (1982, p. 11), that

there is no suggestion here of a return to fixed exchange rates, nor even to seeking "correct rates" within narrow margins. It should be possible, however, to reach international agreement on the existence of "wrong rates"—as was indeed done in November 1978, and seems largely possible today. Rates could then be pushed back toward appropriate zones through direct intervention, alterations in domestic policies and public pronouncements.

One objection to an exchange rate band is that such an arrangement actually promotes exchange rate instability within the band. The presence of a band reduces risk to portfolio holders and therefore increases portfolio shifts in response to perceived changes in mean returns. Thus, given random movements in mean return expectations, there will be more exchange rate variability within the band than there would be without such limits and the greater risk of speculation. Moreover it is not clear why a rate should be allowed to change dramatically, only to be pushed back afterward. If there can be agreement on what constitutes an excessive exchange rate change, then there can be agreement on a limiting point. But of course this question is one on which national interests may differ, as was seen so clearly in the debate over the valuation of the U.S. dollar throughout the 1960s. It also stands to reason that authorities who take a view on what an excessive exchange rate change is will also take a view on what is too rapid a correction. Thus intervention might dampen the correction of exchange rates and in this way reduce the risk of speculation, thus enhancing actual capital flows.

The basic objection to a band proposal is that it makes no sense to set limits for exchange rates but not for other key macroeconomic variables. Exchange rate targets without an accompanying, well-understood macroeconomic support program can hardly be expected to be effective. Macroeconomic policies geared exclusively to exchange rate targets rather than a broader range of targets—including real interest rates, the real value of corporate stock, inflation, and unemployment—may well lead to a deterioration of macroeconomic performance. In the absence of such a broader range of targets, one can only expect poor results from intervention policy, such as the results observed during the 1979 Carter period of overexpansion.

An alternative approach to limited exchange rate variability is based on the idea that it is possible to extract, at least approximately, from market data the sources of exchange rate disturbances. To the extent that these disturbances are portfolio shifts between currency denominations, they should be accommodated by intervention. This is the standard argument used in the literature about interest rate versus money stock targets. In that context the rule is to peg interest rates, allowing money to vary if disturbances are primarily financial. In the present context the rule is to stabilize exchange rates if disturbances are primarily portfolio shifts rather than events that require changes in the equilibrium real exchange rate. Specifically, if disturbances can unambiguously be identified as shifts between domestic and foreign currency debt, the appropriate policy is *sterilized* intervention that keeps the exchange rate as well as interest rates fixed. The same is true for portfolio shifts between home money and home securities, although in this case the maintenance of fixed exchange rates and interest rates would not require intervention.

When disturbances are both real and financial and identification becomes ambiguous, the case for rigid intervention disappears. Formal models, in these mixed cases, suggest that managed floating becomes the optimal exchange rate regime.[10] The extent to which the exchange rate would be more nearly fixed depends on the relative variability of real and financial shocks, the authorities' concern. with the composition of aggregate demand as well as the level of activity, the perceived durability of shocks, and the structure of the economy. The strong case that can be made for sterilized intervention when all disturbances are pure portfolio shifts is no longer valid, and few sturdy rules are available to guide policymakers.

Intervention policy cannot cope with the main source of exchange rate movements—namely, *divergent national monetary policies*. When money is tightened in one country to reduce inflation, the financial disturbance is, in fact, deliberately produced by the government in the hope of reducing inflation. Moreover the initial real appreciation, because it reduces inflation, is a welcome part of the disinflation process. Intervention would mean forcing the monetary contraction on the rest of the world, even though cyclical conditions abroad might not call for tight money. Of course the rest of the world might pursue tight money to stabilize the exchange rate but, at the same time, implement a fiscal expansion to maintain aggregate demand in the face of higher interest rates and lower net exports. This policy is open to the objections that fiscal policy is overused and that cyclical expansions can rarely be undone.

Concluding Remarks

The preceding discussion argues that active policy measures, as much as the business cycle itself, cannot fail to spill from one country into another, whatever the exchange rate regime. What the exchange rate regime does determine is the particular shape of the spillover—namely, whether it takes the form of a decline in employment with relatively unchanged competitiveness and inflation, or whether there are large changes in inflation and real exchange rates (and therefore in real income) but relatively smaller changes in employment. The effects of fixed and flexible rates differ markedly and are influenced by the domestic economic structure. Real wage rigidity has a particularly strong influence on exchange rate effects. It is here that one has to recognize Robert Mundell's point that the case for flexible exchange rates rests fundamentally on money illusion, in the sense that real wage rigidity must be absent.

Flexible exchange rates can work well when financial disturbances are identifiable and can be accommodated by the appropriate sterilized intervention and when, in addition, real disturbances can be accommodated by changes in real exchange rates that do not conflict with full employment. Even if neither of these two requirements is met, there are long-run benefits in using a flexible rate system. But there are also short-run costs, which may be quite high, that are brought about by the very fact that the exchange rate is too flexible. These short-run costs in turn are higher, the more fervently policymakers (mistakenly) believe that the use of flexible rates is tantamount to the achievement of macroeconomic independence. If many policymakers hold this erroneous view, the use of flexible rates may well have a destabilizing effect on the world economy. This was already recognized in the 1960s, as evidenced by the following statement made by the government of the Federal Republic of Germany in 1964:

Fixed exchange rates are an indispensable element in a world committed to integration; with a system of flexible rates the existing readiness to cooperate and integrate might be destroyed at the first appearance of serious difficulties since flexible rates would offer such an easy opportunity for isolated action.[11]

If flexible exchange rates, in the course of stabilization policy, lead to excessive real exchange rate changes, and if the latter are the source of adverse spillover effects, a reduction in incentives for international capital movements may be a remedy. The case for restrictions on international capital flows of one kind or another is old. Specifically, Modigliani argued

...there may arise a need, at least in the short run, for holding private capital movements in line with the achievable transfer of real capital. To achieve this goal, without outright limitations on the freedom of capital movements, countries could rely on general fiscal policy as one of the possible devices for influencing incentive to capital movements. But they should also be allowed to opt, just as freely, for the alternative approach relying on specific tax and related incentives, which, we have argued, is likely to be superior under most circumstances.[12]

The same view has been articulated by Tobin (1978) and Liviatan (1979).

The argument for specific taxes, often referred to as interest equalization taxes, to reduce the incentives for international capital flows, has been objected to on three grounds. The first, and most serious, is that such flows limit exchange rate movements and therefore imply a transmission of macroeconomic disturbances through the current account. A tight money policy in a large country would lead to a decline in real income worldwide, as would a regime of fixed exchange rates, thus avoiding the effects of exchange rate movements on real wages and on the price level. The second objection is that taxes on capital flows cannot work because they lead rapidly to all kinds of evasions, including the use of offshore markets. There is no doubt some truth to this argument, although its force is limited for transitory taxes, which would be appropriate during a period of divergent policy in a particular country.

The last objection to interest equalization taxes is that they interfere with the efficient operation of the world capital market. This argument is, in the opinion of the author, actually wrong. It mistakes the short-term money market rate for the social productivity of capital. Suppose a country reduces money growth and this leads (as it will) to an increase in the interest rate on financial assets. Incipient capital flows will lead to currency appreciation and a current account deterioration financed by borrowing abroad.[13] It is hard to argue that the current account deficit is a reflection of enhanced investment opportunities or increased time preference that, in an efficient and integrated capital market, would call for redirection of lending toward the home country. On the contrary, the decline in demand would reduce the profitability of domestic real capital. It therefore would not be optimal for capital to flow toward the country with a tightened monetary policy. Policy intervention in these circumstances could well enhance the efficiency of capital allocation in the world. Needless to say, not much research has been done on this topic.

Even if restrictions were imposed on capital flows, so that less adjustment took place through relative prices and adverse spillover effects on inflation, disturbances would still be transmitted through the current account. The simple fact is that whatever the exchange rate regime, real disturbances will be transmitted in *some* form. This suggests that what should be sought is a policy mix that makes disinflation less of a real disturbance. The mix that is most frequently suggested consists of incomes policy and a monetary rule. Experience with incomes policy is not encouraging by any means. Nevertheless, it is widely held that a flexible exchange rate system without a firm anchor consisting of both monetary rules and effective supply side policies severely disrupts the established liberal world order based on economic growth and openness in trade and capital markets.

Appendix: Macro Model

Combining equations (1) and (2) and using equations (3)–(5) and (7) leads to the following system of equations:

$$m - w - (1 - \beta)\theta = h(f + a\theta - br^* - b\beta\theta) - c(r^* + \theta + \dot{w}), \tag{11}$$

$$\dot{w} = \gamma(f - br^* - b\beta\theta + a\theta) + a(1 - \beta)\theta, \tag{12}$$

which defines the rates of change of wages (in equation 13) and of the real exchange rate (in equation 15)

$$\dot{w} = \{[(1 - \beta)(b\beta(\gamma - ah) - ac) - a\gamma c]\theta - \gamma cf - \gamma b\beta(m - w)$$
$$+ \gamma cb(1 - \beta)r^*\}/\Delta. \tag{13}$$

By assumption,

$$\Delta \equiv b\beta(c\gamma - h) - c < 0 \tag{14}$$

and

$$\theta = [(m - w) + (a(c\gamma - h) + (ca - 1)(1 - \beta))\theta + (c(1 - b\gamma) + hb)r^*$$
$$+ (c\gamma - h)f]/\Delta. \tag{15}$$

The slopes of the schedules in figure 3.1 are given by the following two equations:

$$\frac{dw}{d\theta}\bigg|_{\dot{w}=0} = \frac{(1-\beta)\,(b\beta(\gamma-ah)-ac)-a\gamma c}{\gamma b\beta} \tag{16}$$

and

$$\frac{dw}{d\theta}\bigg|_{\dot{\theta}=0} = a(\gamma c - h) + (ca-1)\,(1-\beta). \tag{17}$$

The long-run solutions for wages and the real exchange rate are as follows:

$$\theta = \frac{b\lambda r^* - \lambda f}{1+a\lambda} \tag{18}$$

and

$$w = m + \left[\frac{c+b(h-\gamma/a)}{(1+a\lambda)}\right] r^* - \left(\frac{h-\gamma/a}{1+a\lambda}\right) f \tag{19}$$

and are obtained by setting $\dot{w} = \dot{\theta} = 0$ in eaquations (11) and (12).

Notes

1. See Johnson (1973), p. 199.

2. This section combines sticky price, rational expectations models of exchange rate dynamics and the sticky real wage literature. See Sachs (1979), Branson and Rotemberg (1980), Dornbusch (1980), Argy and Salop (1979), Buiter and Miller (1981, 1982), Marston (1982), Modigliani and Padoa Schioppa (1978), and Obstfeld (1982).

3. The foreign price level and the full employment level output are chosen to be equal to one, and thus their logs are zero.

4. From equations (1) and (6), setting $\dot{w} = \dot{\theta} = 0$, we obtain $y = (f-br)/(1+a\lambda)$.

5. See the appendix for the long-run solutions to w and θ.

6. For references to the extensive risk premium literature, see the review in Dornbusch (1983) and Krugman (1981).

7. Regressions using residuals from a regression of the OECD industrial production index on two time trends (as the cyclical variable) performed more poorly in establishing significant determinants of the left-hand variable than the regressions whose results are shown in table 3.1.

8. See Flood and Garber (1983, 1984), Salant and Henderson (1978), Lizondo (1983), and Blanchard (1982) for discussions of regime changes.

9. See Tirole (1982) and Blanchard (1979).

10. See Henderson (1982) and Frenkel (1976).

11. Quoted in Cooper (1968), p. 233.

12. Modigliani (1973), p. 252.

13. See Dornbusch (1980) or Buiter and Miller (1981, 1982).

References

Argy, Victor, and Joanne Salop, "Price and Output Effects of Monetary and Fiscal Policy under Flexible Exchange Rates," *Staff Papers*, Vol. 26 (June 1979), pp. 224–256.

Artus, Jacques R., "Monetary Stabilization with and without Government Credibility," *Staff Papers*, Vol. 28 (September 1981), pp. 495–533.

Basevi, Giorgio, and Paul de Grauwe, "Vicious and Virtuous Circles," *European Economic Review*, Vol. 10 (1977), pp. 277–301.

Bergsten, C. Fred, *The International Implications of Reaganomics*, Kieler Vorträge, No. 96 (Tübingen, 1982).

Blanchard, Olivier J., "Speculative Bubbles, Crashes and Rational Expectations," *Economics Letters*, Vol. 3 (1979), pp. 387–389.

Blanchard, Olivier J., "Credibility, Disinflation and Gradualism" (unpublished, Harvard University, April 1982).

Branson, William H., and Julio J. Rotemberg, "International Adjustment with Wage Rigidity," *European Economic Review*, Vol. 13 (May 1980), pp. 309–332.

Buiter, W., and M. Miller, "Monetary Policy and International Competitiveness: The Problems of Adjustment," *Oxford Economic Papers*, New Series, Vol. 33, Supplement (July 1981), pp. 143–175.

Buiter, W., and M. Miller, "Real Exchange Rate Overshooting and the Output Cost of Bringing Down Inflation," *European Economic Review*, Vol. 15 (1982), pp. 83–123.

Caves, Richard E., "Flexible Exchange Rates," *American Economic Review: Papers and Proceedings of the Seventy-Fifth Annual Meeting of the American Economic Association*, Vol. 53 (May 1963), pp. 120–29.

Cooper, Richard E., *The Economics of Interdependence: Economic Policy in the Atlantic Community* (New York, 1968).

Dornbusch, Rudiger, *Open Economy Macroeconomics* (New York, 1980).

Dornbusch, Rudiger, "Equilibrium and Disequilibrium Exchange Rates," *Zeitschrift für Wirtschafts und Sozialwissenschaften*, Vol. 6 (1982), pp. 573–599.

Dornbusch, Rudiger, "Exchange Risk and the Macroeconomics of Exchange Rate Determination," in *The Internationalisation of Financial Markets and National Policy*, ed. by R. Hawkins, R. Levich, and C. Wihlborg (1983).

Drèze, Jacques H., and Franco Modigliani, "The Trade-Off between Wages and Employment in an Open Economy," *European Economic Review*, Vol. 15 (January 1981), pp. 1-40.

Flood, Robert P., and Peter M. Garber, "A Model of Stochastic Process Switching," *Econometrica* (February 1983).

Flood, Robert., and Peter L. Garber, "Collapsing Exchange Rate Regimes: Some Linear Examples," *Journal of International Economics* (September 1984).

Frenkel, Jacob A., "The Optimal Dirty Float" (unpublished, University of Chicago, 1976).

Frenkel, Jacob A., "Flexible Exchange Rates, Prices, and the Role of 'News': Lessons from the 1970s," *Journal of Political Economy*, Vol. 89 (August 1981), pp. 665–705.

Frenkel, Jacob A., and Michael L. Mussa, "The Efficiency of the Foreign Exchange Market and Measures of Turbulence," *American Economic Review: Papers and Proceedings of the Ninety-Second Annual Meeting of the American Economic Association*, Vol. 70 (May 1980), pp. 374–381.

Genberg, Hans, "Effects of Central Bank Intervention in the Foreign Exchange Market," *Staff Papers*, Vol. 28 (September 1981), pp. 451–476.

Grilli, Enzo R., ed., *The Outlook for Primary Commodities*, World Bank Staff Working Paper No. 9 (Washington, July 1982).

Henderson, Dale W., "The Role of Intervention Policy in Open Economy Financial Policy: A Macroeconomic Perspective," International Finance Discussion Papers, No. 202 (Board of Governors of the Federal Reserve System, February 1982).

International Monetary Fund, *World Economic Outlook: A Survey by the staff of the International Monetary Fund* (Washington, 1982).

Johnson, Harry G., "The Case for Flexible Exchange Rates, 1969," in his book, *Further Essays in Monetary Economics* (Harvard University Press, 1973), pp. 198–222.

Krugman, Paul, "Consumption Preferences, Asset Demands, and Distribution Effects in International Financial Markets," National Bureau of Economic Research, Working Papers Series, No. 651 (March 1981).

Liviatan, N., "Neutral Monetary Policy and the Capital Import Tax" (unpublished, Hebrew University of Jerusalem, 1979).

Lizondo, J. Saúl, "Foreign Exchange Futures Prices under Fixed Exchange Rates," *Journal of International Economics* (February 1983).

McKinnon, Ronald I., "Currency Substitution and Instability in the World Dollar Standard," *American Economic Review*, Vol. 72 (June 1982), pp. 320–33.

Marston, Richard C., "Wages, Relative Prices and the Choice between Fixed and Flexible Exchange Rates," *Canadian Journal of Economics*, Vol. 15 (February 1982), pp. 87–103.

Modigliani, Franco, "International Capital Movements, Fixed Parities, and Monetary and Fiscal Policies," in *Development and Planning: Essays in Honour of Paul Rosenstein Rodan*, ed. by Jagdish Bhagwati and Richard S. Eckaus (MIT Press, 1973), pp. 239–253.

Modigliani, Franco, and Tommaso Padoa Schioppa, *The Management of an Open Economy with "100% Plus" Wage Indexation*, Essays in International Finance, No. 130, International Finance Section, Department of Economics, Princeton University (1978).

Mussa, Michael L., *The Role of Official Intervention*, Group of Thirty, Occasional Papers, No. 6 (New York, 1981).

Obstfeld, Maurice, "Relative Prices, Employment, and the Exchange Rate in an Economy with Foresight," *Econometrica*, Vol. 50 (September 1982), pp. 1219–1242.

Sachs, Jeffrey D., "Wages, Profits and Macroeconomics Adjustment: A Comparative Study," *Brookings Papers on Economic Activity: 2* (1979), pp. 269–319.

Sachs, Jeffrey D., "Wage Indexation, Flexible Exchange Rates and Macroeconomic Policy," *Quarterly Journal of Economics*, Vol. 64 (June 1980), pp. 731–747.

Salant, Stephen W., and Dale W. Henderson, "Market Anticipations of Government Policies and the Price of Gold," *Journal of Political Economy*, Vol. 86 (August 1978), pp. 27-48.

Tirole, Jean, "On the Possibility of Speculation under Rational Expectations," *Econometrica*, Vol. 50 (September 1982), pp. 1163–1181.

Tobin, James, "A Proposal for International Monetary Reform," Cowles Foundation for Research in Economics, Yale University, Discussion Paper No. 506 (October 20, 1978).

Williamson, John, *The Open Economy and the World Economy*, Basic Books, 1983.

II

The Debt Problems of Less Developed Countries

Introduction to Part II

The LDC debt crisis by late 1984 seemed altogether solved. The major debtors had proved willing and able to service their debts, and long-term rescheduling assured that the lenders' cartel could stick together. The immediate possibility of default, which had loomed large in 1982–83, now has largely receded. Only acute domestic problems or a renewed liquidity crisis would precipitate an effort by LDCs to put together a debtors' cartel. But even as the "fundamentals" are judged to support the possibility of debt service and the IMF's managing director preaches that adjustment is a permanent commitment, with more not enough, the discussion is turning political as it should.[1]

The adjustment to debt servicing carries vast domestic costs in the debtor countries. These costs may well lead to political radicalization, which would threaten the new democratic institutions in Latin America and therefore ultimately create vast losses for the lending countries themselves. At the same time it is being recognized that if the LDCs are to service their debts, they must run trade surpluses, cutting down on imports from the OECD countries and raising their exports to our markets. In the face of continuing high inemployment in the OECD countries, we therefore face a choice of higher unemployment in our own economies or reduced debt service. Protection that is now being advocated, for example, in the Rostenkowski-Gebhardt-Bentsen bill of July 1985, cannot do away with that problem.

The political dimension of the debt problem received all the necessary emphasis in Henry Kissenger's plea for a western hemisphere development program:[2]

Major economic adjustments are required, of course, and most governments in Latin America recognize this. But in the end, sacrifice needs to be sustained by hope, by a clear prospect for improvement. The Latin American dialogue with the creditors—especially with the United States—must expand from the collection of interest to economic development.

The debt problem poses two major issues: first, whether external conditions favor servicing of debts or whether the debts, in some sense, are unviable; second, what domestic difficulties stand in the way of effective debt servicing.

The External Outlook

The external outlook is typically decided by asking whether the LDC debt problems, and especially the debt of those of Latin America, represent illiquidity or insolvency. Illiquidity means that a debtor cannot service the debt on the agreed time table but, in principle, can generate a present value of debt service equal to that contracted. Insolvency means that it is impossible to service the debts in full on *any* time table. In a domestic context insolvency is well defined by looking at the present value of new earnings of a concern, but this loses sense for sovereign debt. With a sufficient squeeze most debts are good; the only question is how much can one squeeze.

In practice, debt prospects are evaluated by assessing the impact of the world economic environment on a country's debt-export ratio. There are plausible objections to this particular indicator, but in fact it captures all the points at issue. A country's debt-income ratio will grow if the current account deficit is sufficiently large to more than offset the favorable impact of export growth on the debt-income ratio. Let d denote the growth rate of the debt-export ratio. The term D stands for the stock of nominal debt, x denotes the growth rate of *nominal* export revenue, and CA stands for the current account deficit, all in dollars. We thus have

$$d = \frac{CA}{D} - x. \tag{1}$$

Note that the debt-export ratio can decline even in the face of moderate current account deficits. This would be the case if export growth is sufficently large. Exports thus serve as the scaling factor. The formula can be further simplified by splitting the current account deficit into two components: One is interest payments on the debt, iD, where i is the nominal interest rate on dollar debts. The other is the noninterest current account deficit denoted by V:[3]

$$d = i - x + \frac{V}{D}. \tag{2}$$

Equation (2) highlights two determinants of the evolution of the debt-export ratio. The first is the world interest rate relative to the growth rate of export earnings, i-x. The second is the noninterest deficit. To improve a debtor's external position, interest rates must be low relative to the growth of export earnings. Alternatively put, real interest rates must be low relative to the growth of export volume. The second element in consolidating debts is represented by noninterest surpluses.

Table II.1 shows the IMF's outlook for Latin America's external balance and external debt. Current account deficits are petering out, and debt is declining, after the 1983 peak, relative to exports and real GDP. The driving force is primarily a large and growing noninterest surplus.

Table II.1
Latin America's external outlook

	1977–80	1981–82	1983	1984–86
External debt (% of exports)	196.2	240.8	294.1	269.1
Current account deficit [a]	20.5	42.6	11.7	6.6
Noninterest surplus [a]	− 5.5	− 4.0	26.4	32.9

Source: IMF *World Economic Outlook*, April 1985.
a. In billions of U.S. dollars.

In the IMF's forecast noninterest surpluses have to do most of the work in the 1984–86 period because export volume is predicted to grow by 5.8 percent against a real interest rate (Libor, without spread) of 5.7 percent. To work down debt ratios, it is thus necessary to run noninterest surpluses. Neither world inflation and negative real interest rates nor export booms are in the cards.

The debt projections raise the question of how much macroeconomic developments in the OECD countries affect the trade performance of LDCs. The standard view now is that OECD growth of 3 percent per year is the corner stone of a medium-term solution to the debt problem. Growth of 3 percent, combined with some decline in the dollar and stable or declining interest rates, would in terms of equation (2) work down debt ratios into the region of being acceptable.

The critical element in these calculations is the responsiveness of export volume and the terms of trade of LDCs to growth in the OECD countries. The importance of the linkage is clear from the following consideration: an extra percentage point of OECD growth will raise the growth of export earnings by 2 to 3 percentage points. In terms of equation (2) there would accordingly be a quite significant swing in the annual growth rate of the debt-export ratio.

The dollar assumes particular importance in the discussion of long-term debt prospects. This is the case because debts are primarily denominated in U.S. dollars, and hence it becomes important to know what is the rate of inflation in dollars in world trade. A dollar depreciation will influence that inflation significantly. Empirical evidence supports the view that a dollar depreciation will raise the prices of materials very significantly, almost in the same proportion.[4] Manufactures prices too would increase though not as much as the prices of commodities. For LDCs a collapse of the dollar in the manner of 1973 or 1978–80 would thus be particularly desirable.[5]

The external environment poses an interesting problem in the trade-off between interest rates and growth. The issue arose most clearly in early 1984 when record U.S. growth came hand in hand with a sharp rise in interest rates. One view is that the increased export growth, made possible by the strong U.S. growth, more than paid the extra interest bill, thus leaving LDCs ahead. But that view is correct only in the special case where export growth represents capital gains, not growth in volume. To the extent that increased OECD growth raises the growth of LDC export volume simply means hard work, or less consumption, not an increase in welfare. The correct way then to pose the question is whether the impact of growth on interest rates more than outweighs the favorable terms of trade impact.

The IMF economic outlook in table II.1 makes it clear that the working down of the debt-export ratio will not be a matter of capital gains. On the contrary, large and growing noninterest surpluses will have to do the work. It is worth emphasizing that this is a radical change in the discussion from the 1983 state where a large and rapid dollar decline and terms of trade improvements were predicted as important elements in the debt consolidation process. The need for noninterest surpluses (V/D) in terms of equation (2) makes it important to look at the domestic adjustments required for debt servicing.

Domestic Adjustment

Table II.2
Latin America's macroeconomic performance

	1977–80	1981–82	1983	1984–86
Per capita growth	2.7	−2.5	−5.6	0.8
Capital formation[a]	24.2	21.8	17.8	16.6[b]
Inflation	48.1	56.3	100.5	97.8

Source: IMF, *World Economic Outlook*, April 1985.
a. Percent of GDP.
b. For 1984.

Table II.2 introduces the domestic problems associated with adjustment. It shows the deterioration in growth, the increase in inflation and the fall off in investment.

The debtor countries must contain domestic demand and employment to reduce imports and free foreign exchange for debt service. This curtailment in demand coincides and overlaps with the adjustment of public sectors toward leaner and trimmer conditions. The results so far have been dramatic. Trade surplusses have in most cases come out well within the targets of the IMF adjustment programs; in this sense adjustment has taken place and has been successful. But it is also the case that the trade surplusses have been generated largely, if not exclusively, by demand compression and depression, rather than by export growth.

The rationing of finance, in conjunction with the 1981–83 world recession and steeply increased interest rates, has visited a depression on developing countries, in particular, in Latin America. The depression of economic activity in that region is already worse than it was in the 1930s. For Latin America the decline in per capita income over the period 1981–84 amounts to 10.6 percent. Attention therefore must turn to the way the debt problem tends to depress growth and what kind of adjustment can improve things.

There are two questions on the domestic side: how to raise fiscal revenue for external debt service and how to translate these fiscal resources into potential dollar earnings via import substitution or increased exports under conditions of full employment. Consider the case where all external debt is public and hence falls within the government's general fiscal responsibility. The need to service the external debt means that the government budget deficit is thereby increased. Extra taxes must be raised, spending must be curtailed, or money creation must finance the deficit.

It is difficult to cope with the domestic fiscal policy aspect of debt in a country where the budget, not counting external debt service, is already in a large deficit. Once no fresh money is available to finance interest charges, the debt service must come at the expense of other programs or new taxes or else it must lead to more inflation. This is highly controversial because in many instances the debt has been incurred for the benefit of the middle and upper classes, whereas the adjustment and servicing costs are borne by the public at large. For example, the debt service might be ensured by a cut in public sector wages or in food subsidies. The situation is particularly serious when the debt, as in the case of Argentina, for example, has largely been incurred to finance capital flight.

In judging the fiscal effort required to service the debt, we have to look at the ratio of debt service to GDP, which is 3 to 5 percent. Raising that fraction of GDP in extra taxes or through program cuts is an enormous task. Total tax collection typically accounts for, say, 20 percent of GDP in a LDC, and thus this requirement is to cut government spending by 15 percent or to raise revenue by that amount. The difficulty is increased because the tax structure in many developing countries remains rudimentary and relies strongly on withholding taxes on labor income. Taxation of wealth and income from capital is often negligible. Financing the debt service then likely involves yet another severe worsening of income distribution. This is certainly the case when withholding taxes and subsidy cuts are the chief way for the government to secure revenue for debt service.

translated into increased export earnings under conditions of full employment. Here the question is how to transfer the resources that are freed by the fiscal correction into increased exports or into replacement of previous imports.

It will always be necessary to change relative prices, more so the smaller the ability to shift resources. Profitability of the traded goods sector must be enhanced, thus creating incentives for the transfer of productive resources in that direction. On the demand side the fiscal tightening directly reduces demand for traded goods, thus freeing foreign exchange. But that effect must be reinforced by an increase in the relative price of tradables that discourages domestic demand. The expenditure-cutting effect of the fiscal correction must be accompanied by switching policies that move resources and demand into the right place.

Can these adjustments be achieved while maintaining employment? More specifically, what are sensible short-run policies that support the fiscal part of the transfer? The conventional argument calls for a real depreciation in order to maintain full employment in the face of higher taxes, reduced subsidies, or reduced government demand. But a real depreciation runs into three snags: first, depreciation may not be effective, second, it will decidedly be inflationary, and, third, it will cut real wages and probably with them, in the short run, employment.

Unless there are indexation linkages, the inflation shock of a devaluation will be transitory and thus will ultimately represent a minor cost. The cost is only extreme if the corrective devaluation follows after a sequence of already unsuccessful devaluations, or budget corrections, that have produced inflation without a gain in competitiveness. Inflation is not the ultimate evil, and reluctance to have a real depreciation may be much more destabilizing for real activity and financial markets than the extra inflation impact of a devaluation. Certainly the uniformly unsuccessful experiences of countries that have tried to stop inflation through overvaluation bears this out very strongly.

Available evidence from trade equations supports the view that with a sufficient adjustment time (one year or perhaps as much as 18 months) trade patterns respond strongly to real exchange rates. There remains the question of how large and rapid a contribution devaluation can make to the maintenance of employment. In the Republic of Korea, for example, matters are decidedly favorable. The export sector accounts for 40 percent of GDP, and trade is strongly responsive to the real exchange rate. In these conditions devaluation provides both relief on the external balance and, at the same time, a direct and substantial boost to output and employment. By contrast, in countries where the export sector is much smaller, devaluation mainly serves as a means of removing the external balance constraint on growth. Supplementary domestic policies are required to bring about a significant expansion of employment.

Real exchange rate adjustment brings with it some short-run contractionary effects on output and employment. Before the export expansion and import substitution get under way, there is already a cut in real wages. The real wage cut translates into a reduction in spending, a large part of which will fall on domestic goods and services. In the short run a devaluation is likely to create unemployment. This view is firmly established in theory, but there is also supporting empirical evidence. The implication for policy purposes surely is not that devaluation must be avoided. It is rather that devaluation should be accompanied by transitory fiscal policies that sustain employment. One way would be to create transitory public sector projects that have a minimal import content and are labor intensive, namely, construction.

Unless an acute liquidity problem comes in the way of external debt service, the viability of debts will be determined by countries' ability to achieve the domestic adjustment under conditions of growth. The political stability of Latin America depends largely on how Mexico and Brazil can cope with their adjustment problem. Here pessimism is warranted.

Figure II.1 shows Brazil's level of employment and the size of its labor force. The labor force is growing at 2.5 to 3 percent, but employment growth, because of increased productivity and the recession, has been

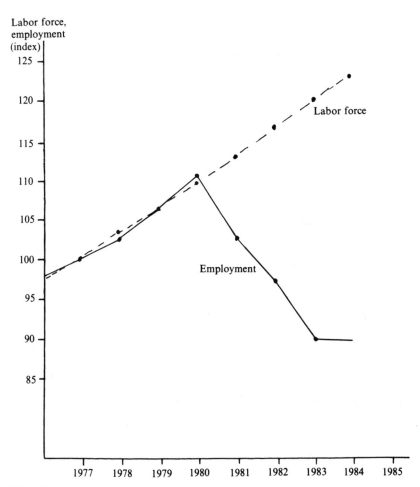

Figure II.1
Employment and labor force in Brazil (index 1977 = 100)

negative or zero. These is further an ever-widening gap between available labor supply and those having jobs. Exactly the same picture could emerge for Mexico where labor force growth is even higher. The outlook for investment and for output growth offers no comfort that the gap will be closed. On the contrary, it appears to be widening. There will not be external financing to open up the possibility of dramatically higher growth. The only serious alternatives are two: an all-out shift toward export-led growth putting Latin America at odds with the OECD, or a serious effort at regional integration to gain yet further import substitution. Either of these options is remote. In the meantime the employment outlook is deteriorating so much that it deserves at least equal place with debt service, budget cutting, and inflation.

Notes

1. See the speech by Mr. de LaRosiere reported in the *IMF Survey*, July 15, 1985, and W. Cline, "International Debt: From Crisis to Recovery," *American Economic Review*, May 1985.

2. See Henry Kissinger, "Building a Bridge of Hope to Our Latin Neighbors," *Los Angeles Times*, June 25, 1985, p. A15.

3. Implicitly direct investment is aggregated with debt.

4. See Dornbusch (1985) for details.

5. See W. Cline (1985) and R. Dornbusch (1984) for a discussion of the linkages between OECD countries and debtor LDCs.

References

Cline, W. (1984). *International Debt*, The MIT Press, Cambridge, Mass.

Cline, W. (1985). "International Debt: From Crisis to Recovery," *American Economic Review*, May.

Dornbusch, R. (1985). "Policy and Performance Linkages between Industrial Countries and Non-Oil LDCs," *Brookings Papers on Economic Activity* 2.

Dornbusch, R., and S. Fischer (1986). "The World Debt Problem: Origins and Prospects," *Journal of Development Planning*.

4   Overborrowing: Three Case Studies

This chapter explores the role of disequilibrium exchange rates and budget deficits in promoting external indebtedness and the current debt crisis. Oil, U.S. interest rates, and the 1981–82 world recession are often isolated as the chief causes of the world debt crisis. But these factors have only made much more apparent and unsustainable an underlying disequilibrium in which exchange rate overvaluation and budget deficits were perpetuated by continuing and excessive recourse to the world capital market.

Because the details of the disequilibrium differ quite a bit between countries, I will look at three different episodes: Argentina, Chile, and Brazil. In one case capital flight played a key role in the growth in debt; in the other cases the level and composition of spending assumed primary importance. These determinants are investigated for the period 1978–82, which was chosen because it coincided with major changes in the world economy and with disequilibrium real exchange rate policies in several countries.

I will start by laying out a framework and some facts concerning the debt accumulation.

Reprinted by permission from *International Debt and the Developing Countries*, Gordon W. Smith and John T. Cuddington, eds., World Bank, 1985.

Some Facts and a Framework

Latin American debt problems are not new, and only a year after the Mexican and Brazilian problems became apparent the literature abounded with references to episodes of overlending in the 1930s and before. Here is a typical quotation from 1937:

> The history of investment in South America throughout the last century has been one of confidence followed by disillusionment, of borrowing cycles followed by widespread defaults, and of a series of alternating repudiations and recognitions of external debts. Willingness to maintain service payments has certainly been less high than in the British Empire, and excesses were inevitable under the conditions which existed while the United States was investing such huge sums in these countries.... The ability of the most credit-worthy governments to avoid default must necessarily be impaired if any considerable part of the nominal value of loans has not, in fact, been put to the use for which it was intended. (Royal Institute of International Affairs 1937, p. 266.)

After the wholesale default on external debt in the 1930s there was a long gap during which current account imbalances were financed by a reduction in reserves (accumulated during the war), by direct capital inflows, by official aid, and by borrowing through international institutions.[1] Table 4.1 shows external debt data for benchmark years for several countries. The data problems, even for the very recent years, are overwhelming. But even so, the table conveys a notion of the very rapid growth of external indebtedness in the 1970s.

Table 4.1
Gross external public or publicly guaranteed debt (billions of U.S. dollars, end of year)

Country	1945	1956	1960	1970	1975	1983
Argentina	0.9	0.7	1.5	5.0	7.9	38.5
Brazil	0.4	1.5	1.8	5.5	22.2	93.7
Chile	0.4	0.3	0.6	3.2	5.3	18.7
U.S. price level (1970 = 100)	41	68	75	100	137	235

Sources: United Nations (1964) and Morgan Guaranty.
Note: The data for 1945, 1956, and 1960 include only debt in excess of one-year maturity. The price level reported in the last row is the U.S. GNP deflator. The unit value index in dollars for world trade would show a somewhat larger cumulative increase.

From the supply side the conventional explanation for the lending burst is the oil shock, which made petro dollars available for financial intermediation by commercial banks. This is brought out by the fact that

Table 4.2
Prime rate, world growth, and price inflation in world trade (average annual percentage rate)

Period	Prime rate	Inflation rate in world trade	World growth
1970–73	6.7	12.4	4.7
1979–82	15.5	4.4	1.1

Sources: *International Financial Statistics* (International Monetary Fund [IMF]) and Council of Economic Advisers, *Economic Report of the President* (Washington, D.C.: 1984).

from 1970 to 1983 the share of bank lending in total debt increased from only 25 percent to nearly 75 percent. On the demand side the reasons for the debt buildup are much less clear-cut. Oil, interest rates, and the world recession are often cited and are certainly a good part of the story in some countries.

Table 4.2 and figure 4.1 show the important differences in the world macroeconomic setting for the debtors in the early 1970s and in the 1978–82 period. The earlier period is clearly a debtors' paradise with high growth, sharp real commodity price increases, and low nominal interest rates coupled with high inflation. The 1978–82 period is just the reverse and to that extent must account for some of the debt problems. To be more precise, I will show that the degree and particular kind of openness—unrestricted capital flows, free trade in goods, both or neither—influence the way in which households and firms respond to exchange rate mis-alignment and commercial and fiscal policy.

The balance of payments accounts provide a link between the increase in *gross* external debt and the portfolio and spending decisions of the economy.

The increase in gross external debt corresponds to the sum of three items identified from the balance of payments accounts:

$$\begin{matrix} \text{Increase in} \\ \text{gross} \\ \text{external} \\ \text{debt} \end{matrix} = \begin{matrix} \text{current} \\ \text{account} \\ \text{deficit} \end{matrix} - \begin{matrix} \text{direct and} \\ \text{long-terms} \\ \text{portfolio} \\ \text{capital} \\ \text{inflows} \end{matrix} + \begin{matrix} \text{official} \\ \text{reserve} \\ \text{increases} \end{matrix} + \begin{matrix} \text{other} \\ \text{private} \\ \text{capital} \\ \text{outflows.} \end{matrix} \quad (1)$$

With respect to capital account transactions I make a distinction between direct investment and long-term portfolio capital flows on the one hand

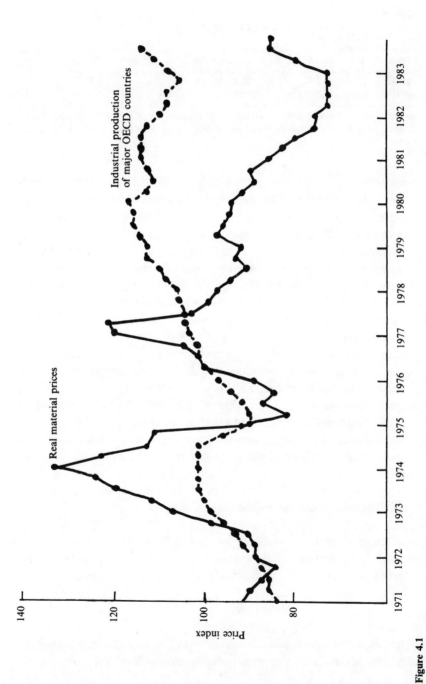

Figure 4.1
Industrial production and real material prices (1975–77 = 100). Source: *International Financial Statistics.*

and, on the other, the short-term flows, which for simplicity can be thought of as "hot money" on the way in and as "capital flight" on the way out. Equation (1) then shows that an increase in gross external debt can have three broad sources: current account deficits not financed by long-term capital inflows, borrowing to finance an official reserve build-up, or private capital flight.

The accounting identity in (1) immediately draws attention to the fact that the debt buildup does not correspond one-for-one to a resource transfer from lending countries to the borrowers. Part of the increased gross debt merely reflects capital flight and thus no change in aggregate net foreign assets. Another part reflects the capitalization through increased borrowing of the inflation component in nominal interest payments. The resource transfer is limited to the inflation-adjusted current account.[2]

The various components in (1) for Argentina, Brazil, and Chile in 1978–82 need to be identified empirically. Table 4.3 shows estimates of the components of the gross debt increase. Balance of payments and external debt data from different sources are used to try to piece together the "proximate sources" of the increase in gross external debt. The difference in data sources and the precariousness of debt and balance of payments data imply that these estimates cannot be very precise. Despite these limitations, the data give a good idea of the difference in patterns between countries.

In the case of Argentina the current account deficit is financed largely by direct investment and portfolio capital inflows. The increase in debt therefore corresponds to a large extent to the financing of capital flight—the central bank borrows abroad and sells foreign exchange to private residents, who use the proceeds to acquire foreign assets. The breakdown is of course not entirely precise because the current account certainly underestimates military imports. For Argentina it has been suggested that the underestimate may be as much as $7 billion. Underinvoicing of exports, overinvoicing of imports, and underestimates of tourism and smuggling further distort the data.

The tables makes it clear that the Argentinian case is primarily one of increased debt to finance capital flight, not current account imbalances. Thus the government incurs external debts and uses the proceeds to finance private capital outflows or private acquisition of foreign assets. The increase in gross external debt misrepresents the *net* foreign asset position of the country, since increased public debts are matched for the

Table 4.3
Components of the increase in gross external debt, 1978–82 (billions of U.S. dollars)

Country	Increase in gross external debt	Current account			Direct and portfolio capital inflow	Residual[a] (reserve gains + capital outflows)
		Total	Trade	Interest		
Argentina	26.8	−10.6	6.8	−9.3	7.2	23.4
Brazil	48.8	−58.4	−4.7	−33.7	11.5	1.9
Chile	11.5	−11.4	−3.9	−5.1	1.3	1.4

Sources : Morgan Guaranty, Data Resources, Inc., and the International Monetary Fund (IMF).
A. This column is calculated as the part of debt increase not accounted for by the current account deficit or the net capital (direct and portfolio) outflows. Interest payments are not adjusted for inflation.

most part by larger private foreign assets. But inasmuch as the latter are removed from the control and disposition of the authorities, there is nevertheless a "debt problem."

In the case of Brazil and Chile the residual item in the last column accounts for very little. The increased debt reflects current account deficits, not capital flight. In both cases direct investment and portfolio capital flows finance only part of the current account deficits, and hence external debt increases by the difference. Both countries, unlike Argentina, have a cumulative trade deficit and, of course, deficits on service account. In both cases interest payments account for half or more of the increase in debt. To explain the large cumulative current account deficits and the capital flight, I now turn to theoretical considerations. I take as given that the experience in the individual countries was highly unusual and ask in what ways policies created circumstances in which economies indulge in large current account deficits or large-scale capital flight?

Theory

It is ordinarily thought that large increases in external debt have as their counterpart large cumulative current account deficits. These current account deficits, in turn, reflect either an imbalance between private saving and investment or a public sector budget deficit. More formally, from the national accounts the current account deficit or increase in net external liabilities is

Increase in = private   − private + budget
net foreign   investment   saving   deficit.   (2)
liabilities

Episodes of current account deficits can, in this sense, be analyzed in terms of the shocks to which the economy is exposed and the impact they exert on saving, investment, and the budget. The channels through which saving, investment, and the budget are affected will be discussed within the framework of standard neoclassical macroeconomics. Transitorily high levels of investment and budget deficits or transitorily low levels of saving will be identified.

Saving

Household saving behavior takes place in the standard multiperiod framework. Saving is governed by wealth, which is the present value of after-tax labor income plus the value of initial assets, and by the real interest rate. The real interest rate is the world nominal rate adjusted for depreciation and the *domestic* rate of inflation. The latter can differ from that abroad to the extent that traded and nontraded goods or export and import prices change over time or through changes in exchange rate or commercial policy. (On this point see Bruno 1976; Obstfeld 1983; Svensson and Razin 1983; and Dornbusch 1983a.)

There are several channels through which events in the economy can lead to a reduction in saving:

- An increase in wealth because of perceived higher future incomes or an increase in the future rental on domestic real capital. Since by assumption the gains in output occur only in the future, but consumers are forward looking, the anticipations lead to higher current spending and thus to dissaving.

- The effect of expected future income gains on current spending is reinforced if these anticipated gains come together with the removal of borrowing constraints and increases in wealth that make it possible to spend at the level of normal income.

- Dissaving may be the counterpart of intertemporal resource allocation by the household in response to intertemporal relative price and hence real interest rate movements. With high intertemporal substitutability, consumption occurs in periods when interest rates are low and inflation is high.

Purchases of consumer durables are an important reason for variations in measured saving. Anticipated intertemporal variations in the real price of durables (and, even môre strongly, in the availability of durables) affect the timing of purchases. They lead to purchases in periods when the real price is low. This effect is more strongly at work the higher the rate of price increase on durables relative to interest and the rate of physical depreciation. The confidence in a strong resale market and hence increased liquidity of durables reinforces the tendency for intertemporal substitution of purchases, as does a reduction in credit constraints. (See Mishkin 1976 and Deaton and Muellbauer 1980, ch. 14.)

In the context of an open economy, a transitory real appreciation (or an overvaluation) of the exchange rate would therefore lead one to predict dissaving. Consumers would concentrate purchases of imported durables in those periods, and current account deficits would tend to be large.

A critical question is to what extent private saving behavior is affected by government budget deficits. In other words, do households, in response to deficits, build up assets in anticipation of future taxes on their own incomes and those of their heirs? It is assumed that these effects are limited to taxes borne directly by the current generation and do not extend further. Thus deficits are by and large not offset by increased current and future saving. Effects on saving result only from directly anticipated taxation or from a reduction in the value of assets that reflects future taxes on the income from those assets.

Investment

Investment is affected through three channels. The concern here is with the link between exchange rates and investment. Inventory investment is influenced by the cost of carrying inventories relative to the return on the goods being carried. Business fixed investment is influenced by changes in the desired capital stock and by changes in the adjustment costs associated with capital formation. A formal model is sketched in the appendix, but the focus here is simply on the main ideas.

An anticipated depreciation implies capital gains on imported goods, specifically on materials and consumer or producer durables. Firms would, other things being equal, purchase importables before an antici- pated depreciation and hold them to collect capital gains. But that tendency is dampened by three factors: first, there will after a point be increasing marginal costs of carrying inventories; second, there is uncertainty about the future price; and third, carrying inventories involves an alternative cost in terms of nominal interest forgone. The optimal inventory for risk-averse firms, given these considerations, will depend on the mean and variance of the expected real return on inventories, on inflation relative to interest rates, and on the marginal carrying cost. Reduced variance and increased anticipated depreciation that is not reflected in interest rates will raise inventory investment and hence imports of materials or of producer and consumer goods.

To discuss business fixed investment, it is useful to think of a standard neoclassical theory based on adjustment costs. Real exchange rates here play a role because they determine the desired capital stock by influencing the user cost of capital or by affecting the adjustment cost. Real exchange rates affect adjustment costs because investment has import content, specifically in the form of imported machinery.

What are the effects of a transitory real appreciation? While the real exchange rate is overvalued, the real price of imported goods is low and, for that reason, investment is high. During the period of overvaluation, capital is being accumulated because the overvaluation in fact constitutes an investment subsidy for those investment activities that have import content. Once the real depreciation occurs, the accumulation of capital is reversed.

A second channel through which overvaluation influences investment is via the desired stock of capital. Suppose investment has significant import content and that capital is used in the production of tradables. A transitory overvaluation and anticipated real depreciation now exerts opposing effects on investment. The low real price of tradables depresses the stock demand for capital, but the investment subsidy implicit in overvaluation tends to promote investment. The net result depends on how significant the subsidy is as a determinant of investment. When import content is important the net result will still be a transitory investment boom and hence an import boom in investment goods.

Once again the anticipated real depreciation that has been assumed is not fully matched by higher interest rates. To the extent that nominal interest rates rise in anticipation of depreciation, this raises the user cost and therefore reduces any impact on investment.

There are thus strong links between the time path of the real price of imports and the purchases of imported investment goods. Anticipation of real depreciation must produce an import bulge.

The Budget

The government, in principle, obeys the intertemporal budget constraint.

The budget constraint states that the present value of tax revenues (including the inflation tax) must equal the initial debt plus the present value of outlays. Subject to political constraints on the rate of cut in outlays or the rate of increase in taxes, the government would practice tax smoothing as suggested in Barro (1983). A permanent loss in revenues would be immediately and fully offset through increased tax rates or reduced outlays, leaving debt unchanged. Transitory shocks to revenue or to outlays would be substantially met by debt finance. The increase in debt is in turn amortized over the long term by a small increase in taxes and a small cut in outlays.

An increase in interest rates reduces the present value of the excess of taxes over outlays and hence requires an adjustment in the path of taxes and expenditures. Once again, if the shock is transitory, debt finance will bridge the gap in the short term while small changes in taxes and outlays ensure intertemporal solvency of the government. If the increase in interest rates is permanent, then immediate adjustment of tax rates relative to outlays occurs and debt remains unchanged.

The tightness of the debt finance model must be relaxed to allow for three practical considerations. First, there are constraints on the rates at which politicians can or will change taxes and outlays. Second, it may take time to identify disturbances as transitory or permanent, since all disturbances are initially assumed to be transitory, particularly when they are adverse. Third, debt default, both internal and external, is a way of ensuring the intertemporal budget constraint, although such a "policy" would of course be reflected in the interest rate required by holders of the public debt.[3]

The government budget problem is made more specific by the introduction of specific standard of living constraints. Such constraints imply that in the presence of adverse shocks to the real income of the favored group, additional outlays are required to support the standard of living. If tax adjustments or reductions in the standard of living can occur only over time, there is a built-in link between (adverse) economic shocks and the budget. Adverse shocks therefore invariably involve an early stage of deficit finance, even if they are persistent.

A failure to smooth taxes and outlays as well as benefits in the case of a permanent disturbance does need justification. Why might taxpayers prefer to see low tax rates now and pay for those low rates by higher future rates that will yield equal present-value tax collection? Why would those who receive government benefits desire a front-loaded flow of benefits rather than a steady stream of equal present value? The tax-smoothing model rejects such behavior as irrational and predicts that a government following noxious policies along these patterns would be thrown out of office for failing to maximize voters' welfare. But the moment the private sector discounts at a rate in excess of the market rate of interest the future is systematically undervalued and biased toward debt finance. The argument is reinforced when liquidity constraints lead part of the population to discount at exceptionally high rates.

There is of course an interdependence between the model of debt finance and the private sector's optimal intertemporal allocation of resources and portfolio choice. The more the government chooses debt finance, postponing required tax increases, the more the private sector can adjust to the future increased taxes or debt default by holding nontaxable assets (dollars and washing machines). This raises the cost to the government of delaying adjustment, but does not eliminate altogether the tendency toward short-run deficit finance.

In concluding on the issue of the budget, it is worth noting two important linkages between the exchange rate and government outlays. First, to the extent that there is an external public debt, a real depreciation raises the real value of debt service in terms of domestic output and hence is likely to increase the budget deficit. There is thus a potential tradeoff between international competitiveness and a balanced budget.

The second link between exchange rates and the budget arises in cases of exchange rate guarantees. If the government has guaranteed a given exchange rate sometime in the past but has since found it necessary to depreciate, the resulting exchange rate subsidy will cause the budget to deteriorate. Where exchange rate guarantees and external debt exist and it is difficult to adjust taxes, there is thus a tendency to seek overvaluation as one of the ways to minimize debt finance.

In this review of the various channels through which the current account is affected by transitory and permanent disturbances, the point is that anticipated real depreciation acts in a most forceful way to generate current deficits in the external balance. In addition, through the budget, current and transitory shocks to receipts and outlays tend to be translated into deficit finance and hence into external deficits. The next section discusses how these considerations help explain the current accounts and external debt accumulation of Chile and Brazil.

Application to Chile and Brazil

In Chile and Brazil external debt increases are the counterpart of current account deficits. They represents levels of spending and resource absorption in excess of current income. But the details of the process differ. In Chile overvaluation is *the* key, whereas in Brazil the budget deficit assumes a central role.

Chile

Following hyperinflation in the early 1970s, Chile experienced economic stabilization and a reform of fiscal and commercial policy in 1973–77. The budget deficit was moved from more than 10 percent of GNP in the early 1970s to actual surplusses in 1979–80. Tariffs were reduced from average nominal rates near 100 percent, with individual rates widely dispersed, to a uniform rate of only 10 percent by 1978. Inflation was reduced from over 500 percent a year to practically zero, and, to top it off, growth in 1977–81 averaged 8 percent a year.

Today the country's performance bears little resemblance to that performance: output has declined since 1981 by 10 percent, and unemployment stands at 30 percent. Exchange rate policy and excessive recourse to external debt finance are at the center of the explanation.

In an effort to speed up the process of disinflation the Chilean authorities decided in early 1979 to experiment with the "law of one price." The exchange rate was fixed at 39 pesos to the U.S. dollar, in the hope that the pegging would directly cut down the rate of inflation and also break inflationary expectations. At the time, however, Chilean inflation was still more than 30 percent, far above the rate in the United States. Moreover, formal indexing arrangements linked wage increases to past inflation. As Corbo (1983) has documented, the combination of inflation and indexation led over time to *growing* overvaluation as wages were pushed up relative to the prices of importables and the world prices of exportables. The growth in real wages for those employed of course implied a sharp gain in the standard of living. The loss in employment in response to overvaluation was slow to build up, and thus the period 1977–80 offered a spectacle of yet another "miracle."

The Chilean boom conditions in the early stage of overvaluation lend support to the notion that in the short run real depreciation is deflationary. Here the real appreciation, by raising real wages, has expansionary effects on aggregate demand before the employment effects and bankruptcy start making their inroads. This point has been emphasized by Diaz Alejandro (1963) and more recently by Calvo (1982) in the Argentinian context.

Table 4.4 shows the ratio of consumption and of gross fixed investment to GDP (in constant 1977 prices), as well as the budget deficit ratio. It is clear that 1980–82 is the period to focus on, since consumption sharply rises as does the investment ratio and the budget deficit. Investment and saving behavior mirror the sharp deterioration in the current account.

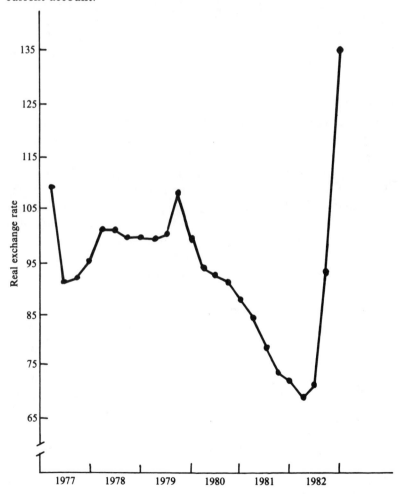

Figure 4.2
The Chilean real exchange rate (1972:2 = 100). Source: Corbo and de Melo (1983).

We now focus on the mechanism through which consumption and investment spending increased so sharply in 1980–81. Figure 4.2 shows the real exchange rate—import prices relative to the prices of non-tradables—for the period. The real appreciation, on this measure,

Table 4.4
Consumption, fixed investment, and the budget deficit in Chile (percent of GDP)

Item	1960–69	1970–79	1978	1979	1980	1981	1982
Investment	20.2	15.7	16.5	19.6	23.9	23.9	9.6
Consumption	79.7	75.8	72.4	71.1	70.5	76.2	76.1
Budget deficit	2.9	6.8	0.8	−1.7	−3.1	−1.6	2.4
Current account deficit	n.a.	n.a.	7.7	5.7	7.2	14.6	9.4

Sources: Banco Central de Chile and *International Financial Statistics*.

amounted to 25 percent by early 1982. Table 4.5 shows some of the implications. Imports of all goods increased very sharply over the period, peaking in 1981. As an example, the growth of imports of automobiles was immense both as a percentage of total imports and as a fraction of the existing stock. After peaking in 1981, imports fell off sharply.

Table 4.6 shows the same pattern in more detail and reports the quantity indexes for different groups of imports. In each case there is a sharp peak in 1981 and a decline in 1982–83. The pattern is significantly more pronounced for capital goods than for intermediates, even though in the latter category automobile parts and pieces and intermediate industrial goods, unlike primary commodities, show very high growth rates.[4]

The pattern of strongly growing imports through 1981 reflects in part the very strong performance of the Chilean economy. In addition the increase in asset prices that took place in 1977–81 implied increased wealth and hence the allocation of part of the gain in wealth to increase consumption. Harberger (1983a) in particular has emphasized this point.

In addition to the impact of growth and wealth on consumption and investment, there appears to be a strong real exchange rate effect on the composition and level of spending. By 1981 the sustainability of the increasingly overvalued exchange rate was becoming an open question. Although the government had sworn to sustain the exchange rate, the growing problems of competing export and import firms and growing unemployment made it more and more plausible that either depreciation or a return to protection, or both, would take place. Under these circumstances it is clear that a sharp increase in purchases of importables could be expected. Tables 4.3, 4.4, and 4.5 clearly bear that out. (See, too, in figure 4.3 the trade balance for 1981, which shows an all-time high deficit.) They also show that once the overvaluation came to an end•in June 1982, the import boom collapsed.

Table 4.5
Chile: imports and the real exchange rate

Item	1978	1979	1980	1981	1982
Imports (billions of U.S. dollars)	3.00	4.22	5.82	6.78	3.83
Trade balance (billions of U.S. dollars)	−0.52	−0.32	−0.45	−2.41	0.29
Real exchange rate (1978 = 100)	100	100.6	90.7	76.9	92.0
Automobiles (1,000s)					
Stock	335.8	386.0	458.7	573.8	n.a.
Imports	11.4	33.6	51.6	79.5	30.3
Production	17.1	16.5	25.2	20.6	7.9

Sources: Banco Central de Chile and Corbo and de Melo (1983).

Table 4.6
Import quantity indexes for Chile (January–June of each period)

Imports	1980	1981	1982	1983
Total	100	133	92	68
Consumption goods	100	175	125	75
Automobiles	100	226	90	38
Electric domestic	100	156	68	n.a.
Capital goods	100	134	90	38
Machinery	100	128	119	52
Transport equipment	100	140	53	20
Breeding stock	100	328	85	50
Intermediate goods	100	117	81	76

Source: Banco Central de Chile.

The real exchange rate directly affects saving and investment and hence the current account. But it also works through a separate channel. Overvaluation, once the short-run expansionary effects have passed, leads to a change in the composition of spending. Demand for domestic goods declines and demand for importables rises. The shift implies a reduction in domestic output and employment. The fall in income reduces saving of the private sector and it also leads to an increased budget deficit. Accordingly, the indirect effects cause the external balance to deteriorate.

The steep decline in world copper prices in 1981–82 further reinforced the effect of declining income on the external balance. If the decline is perceived as transitory, it leads to dissaving both by households and by the public sector and hence enlarges the external deficit and borrowing. Although the copper price decline is often cited as an explanation for the external deficit and debt accumulation, the explanation cannot be extended too far. Even in 1982 the dollar value of copper exports exceeded the 1978 level by a large margin.[5]

One further factor, which is particularly evident in the Brazilian case, is the effect of increased interest rates in the world market. For a debtor country this implies a deterioration in the intertemporal terms of trade and hence an adverse real income effect. It is estimated that the direct contribution to the deficit of higher interest rates in the world market is $3.2 billion.

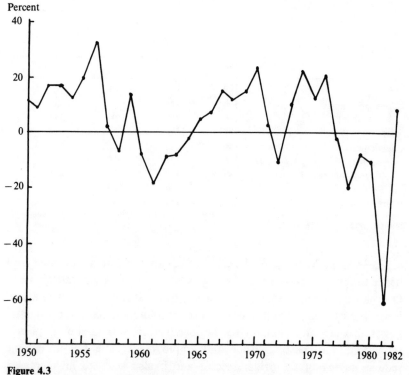

Figure 4.3
Chile: ratio of trade surplus to exports

To a large extent the increase in Chile's external debt is the counterpart of a domestic accumulation of consumer and producer capital. This invites the question whether any lack of optimality is involved in what happened in 1978–82. If so, where does the 'debt problem" reside? Did consumers and firms benefit from the disequilibrium exchange rate, and if so, at whose expense? Furthermore, assuming that the debt ultimately must be serviced, is there a welfare loss from disequilibrium exchange rate policy, aside from the implications for financial stability and economic activity?

The welfare economics of disequilibrium exchange rates appear quite straightforward. Suppose that the government borrows in the first period in the world market and uses the proceeds to finance a transitory consumption or investment subsidy on importables. In later periods taxes are collected to discharge the external debt. This represents the public finance aspects of the overvaluation policy and neglects all macroeconomic side effects. It is shown in the appendix that a subsidy of this kind will have net adverse welfare effects. This is all the more the case when the macroeconomic effects are taken into account.

The actual story is somewhat more complicated because the private capital market must be considered. Consumers and firms perceive a net subsidy only to the extent that market interest rates do not reflect the anticipated depreciation. Since the government itself did not in fact lend at negative expected real interest rates, it must be concluded that interest rates which do not fully reflect anticipated depreciation imply disagreement in the capital market about the likely timing and magnitude of depreciation. Those anticipating large and certain depreciation borrow and import; those anticipating small and unlikely depreciation are the lenders. But the government comes back into the act when a policy of bailing out troubled banks serves as a safety net and in effect makes the whole operation almost exactly like the pure finance scheme laid out above.

Brazil

The deterioration of the Brazilian external indebtedness is largely attributable to failure to adjust the budget to the combined external shocks of higher world interest rates and increased real oil prices. Higher interest rates and increased oil prices were almost automatically reflected in larger deficits through two channels: government subsidies that maintained a low domestic price of oil and government external borrowing through state enterprises to finance the increased debt service. Domestic adjustment through tight money served to raise interest rates and stop growth, but its primarily purpose was to stimulate external borrowing to finance the current account. Failure to depreciate the real exchange rate meant that the economy stagnated despite growing external deficits and debt.

Table 4.7 shows the external shocks. The terms of trade, as a consequence of higher oil prices and the world recession, deteriorated vastly. In addition, interest rates (including spreads) nearly doubled. The combined effect immediately implied a very significant deterioration in the external balance unless drastic domestic adjustment policies were pursued. Table 4.7 indicates the cumulative actual increase in debt between 1978 and 1982 as well as a calculation of the effect of higher oil prices and interest rates.

The latter calculation cumulates the difference between the cost of servicing the 1978 debt level at actual rates rather than at the 1978 Libor (London interbank offered rates) and also the difference between the actual and the 1978 level of oil import expenditures. The sum, cumulated at actual interest rates, is reported in the last row. It measures approximately the increase in debt "due to external shocks." It turns out to amount, cumulatively, almost exactly to the actual increase in external debt. The calculation supports the notion that the debt problem is due to the shocks, but it leaves open the question of the macroeconomic channels through which the shocks are translated into external deficits and debt accumulation. The budget deficit is an essential channel.

Table 4.8 shows the budget deficit as a fraction of GDP as well as the growth rate of real output. Budget data are not available before 1980. After that time, data are available for both the operational budget and

Table 4.7
External shock to the Brazilian economy

Item	0978	1979	1980	1981	1982
Libor	8.9	12.1	14.2	16.8	13.2
Terms of trade (1977 = 100)	76	79	65	55	54
Oil price (U.S. dollars, 1977 = 100)	101	127	238	275	260
Actual debt decrease (cumulative, billions of U.S. dollars)	7.4	16.7	27.1	35.2	
Oil and interest effect [a] (cumulative, billions of U.S. dollars)		3.6	11.7	23.5	34.8

Sources: IMF, Data Resources, Inc., and *Conjunctura* (Fundação Getulio Vargas).
a. For method see text.

Table 4.8
The Brazilian public sector deficit and growth (percent of GDP)

Item	1978	1979	1980	1981	1982
Public sector deficit	n.a.	n.a.	7.5	12.7	15.8
Operational	n.a.	n.a.	n.a.	6.0	6.8
Monetary correction	n.a.	n.a.	n.a.	6.7	9.0
Real diesel price (1973 = 100)	139	154	158	190	188
GDP growth	4.8	6.7	7.9	−1.9	1.4

Sources: IMF, Data Resources, Inc., *Gazeta Mercantil*, and Lauro Ramos.

the separate category, the inflation-indexation component of interest payments (or "monetary correction").

The link between the budget and current account deficits stems in large part from extensive subsidies. The government subsidizes diesel oil because the supply of merchandise to the country's interior is dependent on road transport. While the real price of oil in the 1963–82 period increased sixfold in the world market, the domestic price did not even double. Subsidies were also applied to a range of other goods, especially food products: agricultural subsidies at fixed nominal rates implied real interest rates of − 60 percent and even more.

Since the budget deficit absorbed the external shocks, there was no automatic private adjustment in response to increased world interest rates and increased real oil prices. Nor did the increased budget deficit lead to offsetting domestic saving in the anticipation of future taxes. Thus the external shocks translated fully and automatically into the current account. The increased interest costs were financed by increased external borrowing through state enterprises, as was the increased budget deficit stemming from higher real oil prices.

Imputing the increased external debt entirely to the oil and interest rate shocks may overstate a good case. Clearly there were other elements at work in the external accounts. For example, increased oil prices led to increased import spending in oil-producing countries, and Brazil was able to secure a significant share of these new trade flows, thus dampening the impact of oil on the external balance. Another favorable influence on the current account stemmed from overvaluation in other countries of Latin America. On the other side, Brazil's mispricing of tourist allowances led to a frivolous waste of foreign exchange. But these qualifications do not change the basic message that failure to adjust to the oil and interest rate shocks is the basic reason for Brazil's increased foreign debt.

Brazil is certainly not a case where the increased external deficit reflected an increase in investment. In 1965–77 investment as a fraction of GDP averaged 21.7 percent. In the period 1978–81 it averaged only 20.5 percent. The increased deficit thus reflects consumption and the budget, not an investment boom. In fact, the increasing monetary tightness that was pursued in order to raise interest rates and thus attract capital flows cut into investment.

The poor external performance of the country was not due entirely to a failure to adjust the budget for increased costs of debt and subsidized programs. A good part of the poor performance stems from a systematic overvaluation of the exchange rate. Figure 4.4 shows the real rate of exchange measured by noncoffee export prices relative to the domestic

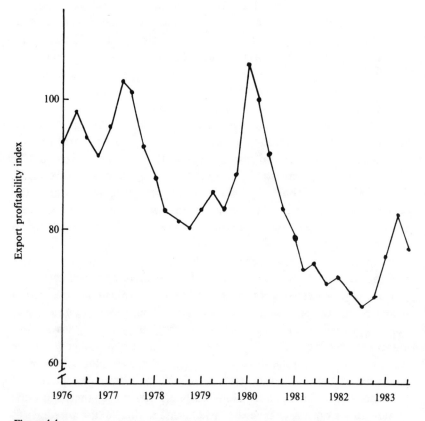

Figure 4.4
Brazilian export profitability (1975 = 100). Export profitability is measured by the price of noncoffee exports relative to the domestic price level.

price level. The exchange rate policy of the post 1968 period had been to maintain a purchasing power parity relative to the U.S. wholesale price index. But that policy of course implied that there was no adjustment for increased real oil prices and interest rates, nor for the vagaries of the dollar in terms of other major currencies.

The balance of payments consequences of the external shocks were contained by increasing domestic oil production and by correcting domestic growth, thereby sharply reducing non-oil imports. At the same time, the exchange rate overvaluation of Argentina and the growth in oil-exporting countries' imports from Brazil led to a temporary export boom. In 1979–81 export revenue grew at an average annual rate of 23 percent. The strong export growth and the poor experience with the late 1979 maxi-devaluation—inflation and no persistence of the real depreciation because of preannounced depreciation below the full, accelerated indexation—misled policymakers into maintaining a constant real exchange rate. Failure to seek a large real depreciation as the long-run adjustment to the deterioration in the external sector thus ultimately led to the 1982 debt crisis and the catastrophic collapse of activity.

Unlike in Chile and Argentina, there was no capital flight or flight into imported durables in Brazil. In part this is a consequence of the fact that the country is closed both on trade and on capital account. Imports are severely restricted, and thus a Chilean-style flight into imported durables is inconceivable. The only capital flight, aside from under- and over-invoicing, took place through the black market or through special accounts in the central bank where exchange rate guarantees are offered to capital importers. But on neither account does the capital flight lead to increased external indebtedness. In one case it is reflected in the increased premium in the black market. In the other case firms and banks have borrowed abroad in dollars and wish to repay their loans prior to maturity can liquidate their dollar debts by making a deposit in the central bank, with the central bank carrying the loan and the exchange rate risk to maturity. Hence capital flight takes the form of paying off dollar loans by making deposits in the central bank. There is no impact on foreign exchange reserves. The only effects are a monetary contraction and, should a devaluation take place prior to maturity, a future increase in the budget deficit as the central bank purchases foreign exchange to service the debt. (See Dornbusch and Moura da Silva 1984.)

In 1973–75 developing countries were generally applauded for sustaining growth in the face of world recession by running external deficits financed in the world capital market. Brazil followed that pattern at the time and again in the 1978–82 period. The experience raises the question of how a country should decide between financing and adjustment in the face of transitory shocks, such as interest rate increases, or more permanent shocks, such as increased real oil prices. Moreover, in the presence of long-term domestic energy projects—such as Brazil's alcohol program and oil production—is it sensible to sustain growth even if debt in the interim rises to a higher long-run level?

The Brazilian experience makes it particularly clear that we are only now starting to think of sensible models of the optimal *level* of external debt. So far models tell us mainly that debt trajectories are unsustainable if the trend growth rate of exports, say, falls short of the rate of interest. Brazil's case suggests that the automatic capitalization of transitory interest rate shocks or terms of trade shocks runs into risks if rolling over is not automatic. In such a model the joint probability of adverse shocks and credit rationing, and their persistence, may lead to a pattern exactly the opposite of the one in 1973–75. Debt should be retired through a deflationary strategy before the costly credit rationing occurs, or aggressive export promotion and import substitution measures should accompany the continued borrowing. The Brazilian philosophy, "debt does not get paid, debt gets rolled" is then misleading.

Argentina: Capital Flight

In the case of Argentina external debt accumulation financed primarily capital flight, not current account inbalances. Unlike Chile, Argentina had severe political instability, continuing high protection, but completely unrestricted capital flows. For these reasons, the purchase of external assets rather than imported durables was the obvious way to escape from instability and expected depreciation. Moreover, again unlike in Chile, there was clearly no sharp increase in investment. Thus the trade deterioration in 1979–80 is not a significant part of the debt story. Nor does the $1 billion deterioration in the travel account explain much of the increased debt. The large outflow of short-term capital indicated in table 4.9 is more central to the explanation of the debt buildup. Of course the trade data to not include all military imports—as much as $7 billion are missing according to one estimate—and to that extent too much of the debt increase may be apportioned to the capital account transactions.

Figure 4.5 shows the Argentinian real exchange rate, which is central

Table 4.9
Argentina: trade, capital flows, and debt

Item	1978	1979	1980	1981	1982
Trade balance	2.9	1.8	−1.4	0.7	2.7
Current account	1.9	−0.5	−4.8	−4.7	−2.5
Increase in debt	2.8	6.5	8.0	8.5	0.9
Long-term capital and direct investment	0.4	0.5	0.9	2.0	3.3
Short-term capital and errors and omissions	−1.3	1.5	−2.4	−8.5	−4.9

Source: *International Financial Statistics.*

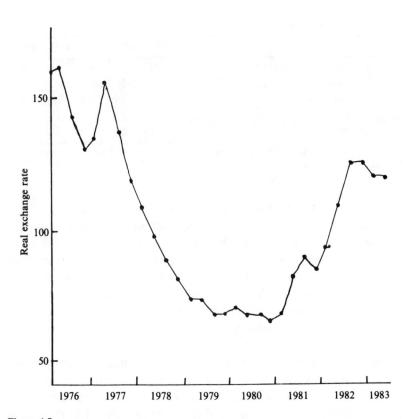

Figure 4.5
The Argentinian real exchange rate (ratio of import prices to domestic prices, 1978–83 = 100)

to an explanation of the capital flows. Under Finance Minister Martinez de Hoz the exchange rate was used systematically to stabilize inflation. Initially, until December 1978, the rate was managed by the central bank's allowing deliberate real appreciation. From December 1978 until March 1981 the rate followed a preannounced *tablita*. In 1980 the continued prefixing of the exchange rate became doubtful. Overvaluation was apparent, and the coming change in the presidency led to the fear of depreciation and instability. With no limitations on private capital outflows there was a massive shift into foreign assets. The flight into foreign assets included purchases of foreign currency, bank deposits, and securities as well as real estate, especially in the United States and Brazil.

Table 4.10
Argentinian financial instability

Item	1978	1979	1980	1981	1982
Real exchange rate (1978–83 = 100)	92	68	66	78	109
Inflation (December to December)	176	160	101	105	165
Real interest (passive rate)	−15.6	−9.5	−4.4	6.6	−26.2
Budget deficit (percent of GDP)	10.1	9.0	11.3	16.4	17.2
Excluding debt service	1.8	2.4	7.2	8.2	5.3

Sources: Cavallo (1983), Data Resources, Inc., *International Financial Statistics* and *Indicadores de Coyuntura*.

The source of capital flight was the combination of currency overvaluation, the threat of devaluation, and ongoing and increasing domestic financial instability. The domestic instability derived from an inability to bring fiscal deficits under control and stop the inflationary process in a decisive way. In fact, in 1980–81 the deficit deteriorated significantly, even when debt service is excluded, as shown in table 4.10. By 1982 the Malvinas war, and the resulting inability to tap the world capital market further, combined with domestic exchange control to end the episode.

The most interesting aspect of the Argentinian public external indebtedness is that it appears to be matched, one for one or, better, by increased private holdings of external assets. But because the authorities have no access to these assets, there is nevertheless an acute debt problem. In the aftermath of these disturbances, the question remains whether any significant portion of the capital would return following the implementation of an effective stabilization program. Experience indicates that this is not likely to be the case.

Conclusion

The popular view of growing developing-country debts is that they reflect unsound budgetary policies or unsustainable growth programs. Sachs (1981), by contrast, has argued that current account imbalances of the 1970s on average reflect high productive investment that fully justifies external borrowing. Bankers who have poured money into these countries certainly favor the view that they have supported productive investment, thus making it plausible that debts should be serviced. The present review of the debt experience of Argentina, Brazil, and Chile reveals a much more mixed story. Only in Chile does investment play any significant part in the current account deterioration. Imports of consumer goods play at least as significant a role. The burst in imports and the resulting current deterioration is due primarily to currency overvaluation.

In Argentina and Brazil increased investment plays absolutely no role in the debt increase. In the case of Brazil the budget deficit and the lack of an adjustment of the public sector to external shocks are behind the debt growth. The failure to adjust the real exchange rate in this case explains the long-term debt difficulties. In the case of Argentina, currency overvaluation in conjunction with prospects of political instability and international capital mobility explain the increased debt. Here the current account plays a small role, and capital flight is behind the rapid increase in debt.

The episodes in no way suggest that investment is unimportant in the context of current account imbalances. But whether it does play a significant role depend in part on whether trade and capital flows are unrestricted and in part on the prospects for economic stability. When trade is relatively unhampered and prospects are bright, investment may be central. In other cases public sector dissaving or capital flight are more plausible sources of external imbalance.

There are important differences in the three episodes studied. The countries differ, in the 1978–82 period, in their financial and political stability and in their openness. Argentina was the most unstable and the most open on capital account. Capital flight, therefore, was the obvious response to political uncertainty, exchange rate instability, and deteriorating expected returns on domestic assets. While some trade liberalization accompanied the overvaluation, flight into importables, other than tourism, was still minor.

Chile was at the other extreme, with domestic political stability and, at least initially, a budget surplus. The complete liberalization of trade, together with overvaluation and the initial prosperity of households and firms, led to an incredible import boom that made up for years of high tariff walls. But because there was no expectation of a financial collapse, currency reform, wealth taxes, and so forth, capital outflows never came into play in a major way.

Brazil shared Argentina's financial instability; the budget deficit was vast and any attempt at stabilization took the form of tight money, which, in the context of indexation, aggravated the condition of the financial system by causing debt to grow more rapidly, the tax base to shrink, and firms to go bankrupt. The 1979 change in the economic team signaled a drift toward fiscal irresponsibility, but even so the Chilean- or Argentinian-style flight into foreign assets or goods was impossible because the economy was firmly closed. Financial instability could be sustained only by raising interest rates to force items into the world capital market, renewing loans, and taking fresh credit, thus financing the budget and current account deficit. With the economy closed to trade flows and with high interest rates, these policies continued until the external borrowing constraints of 1982 emerged. Because there had been no timely policy of real depreciation, the country was unprepared to absorb the drying up of external credit except through a severe and lasting depression.

The experiences of the three countries studied here are by no means unique. During the 1978–82 period most Latin American countries came into financial difficulties, as did other countries around the world. This raises the interesting question of the reason for the worldwide debt problem. An obvious reason is that the world recession, dollar appreciation, and unanticipatedly sharp increase in U.S. interest rates, simultaneously converted into problem cases countries that were to differing degrees in financial difficulties. But it must also be recognized that there was a common element in the policies and events: it was not only Brazil, Argentina, and Chile that had overvalued exchange rates, import sprees, or capital flight financed by external borrowing. The same occurred in 1981–83 in one form or another in Mexico, Venezuela, and Israel, to name only a few. Indeed, it may even be occurring in the United States right now.

Appendix

Investment

Significant changes in investment can come about through two channels. The first is a transitory increase in investment as a result of an increased desired capital stock; the other is a change in the timing of investment in response to intertemporal relative price variations. A standard investment model isolates these effects.

The desired capital stock k depends on the required rate of return net of capital depreciation, $i + d - \dot{Q}/Q$, and on the real price of capital (Q/P) as can be derived from the standard arbitrage condition:

$$\frac{Pf'(k)}{Q} = i + d - \frac{\dot{Q}}{Q}, \tag{3}$$

or

$$k = g\left[\left(i + d - \frac{\dot{Q}}{Q}\right)\left(\frac{Q}{P}\right)\right], \quad g' < 0. \tag{4}$$

On the investment side we assume adjustment costs and also that imports as well as domestic output are inputs in the production of investment. We assume a proportional import requirement and an increasing marginal domestic input requirement. The solution to the investment problem then is a rate of investment that depends positively on the real price of capital in terms of imports, Q/P_m:[6]

$$I = h\left(\frac{Q}{P}, v\right), \quad v = \frac{P_m}{P}, \tag{5}$$

where v is the real exchange rate or the real price of domestic goods in terms of importables. The investment model is completed by the capital accumulation equation:

$$\dot{k} = h\left(\frac{Q}{P}, v\right) - \delta k, \tag{6}$$

where δ denotes the rate of physical depreciation.

The rational expectations equilibrium, given a constant real exchange rate and interest rate, can be visualized in terms of the conventional phase diagram. The equilibrium capital stock and the real price of capital follow a saddle path to the steady state.

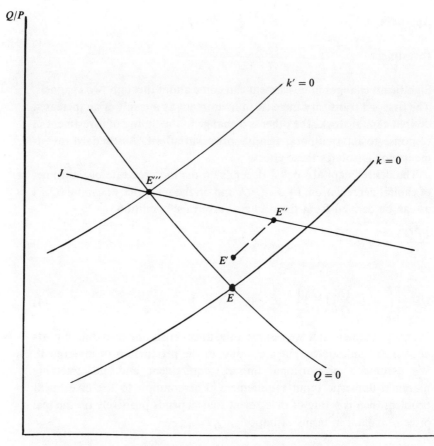

Figure 4.6
The investment effects of an anticipated real depreciation

Consider now the anticipation of an increase in the real cost of imports which acts as a temporary investment stimulus. This is shown in figure 4.6. Starting from an initial equilibrium at point E, there is an expectation that the real exchange rate will depreciate or the real price of imports in terms of domestic goods will rise in the future. There is an immediate jump in the real price of assets, and that higher real price promotes a transitory investment boom. Once the real depreciation does take place (point E'') the real price of capital keeps rising, but now disinvestment takes place. With an anticipated real depreciation, therefore, investment and hence investment goods imports are expected to be high. The obverse analysis of course applies to a transitory decline in the real price of imports.

The exposition so far assumed that capital is used to produce domestic goods but has itself import content. There is another case in which anticipated real depreciation has a significant impact on investment. In this case capital is used to produce tradables and investment has an import content. A real depreciation must in the long run raise the real price of capital, but the capital stock may rise or fall. However, with the anticipated increase in the real price of tradables, there will be an investment boom and hence a boom of investment goods imports.

Consumer Durables

Consider a much simplified model of consumer choice focusing on durables. We neglect time preference, depreciation, and resale as well as nondurables. The consumer's welfare depends on the services from durables in two periods, the second denoted by a prime:

$$U = V(S) + v(S'). \tag{7}$$

Services are given by the cumulative stock

$$S = D, \qquad S' = D + D', \tag{8}$$

where D denotes durable purchases and a prime denotes the second period. The budget constraint is:

$$Y - T = PD + P'D', \tag{9}$$

where $Y - T$ denotes the present value of income net of taxes and P' is the discounted second period price. We assume $P < P^* < P'$, where P^* is the equilibrium real price under a correctly valued real exchange rate while P is the price consumers actually face.

For the aggregate economy, tax payments are $T = (P^* - P)D$, but the individual household takes taxes as unrelated to purchases. The individual faces the budget line obtained by adding D to both sides of (9) to obtain:

$$S' = \frac{(Y-T)}{P'} + \left(1 - \frac{D}{D'}\right)S. \tag{9a}$$

Figure 4.7 shows the consumer equilibrium. The consumer views the budget line as having a slope $dS'/dS = 1 - P/P'$, which is flatter than the slope of the social budget line $dS'/dS = 1 - P^*/P'$. Consumer equilibrium, including the subsidy distortion owing to overvaluation, is at point A' on indifference curve U, with excessive purchases of durables in the first

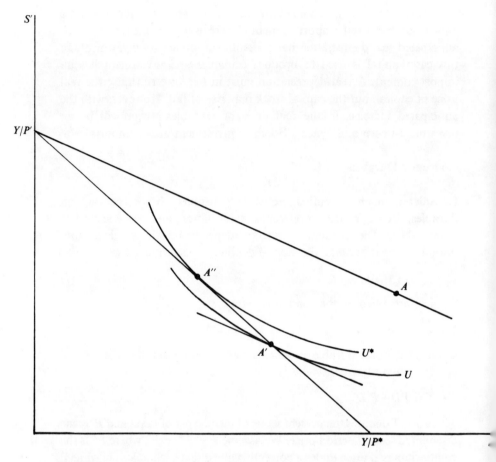

Figure 4.7
Consumer durables and disequilibrium exchange rates

period and a level of welfare lower than at A'' on indifference curve U^*. It is apparent that the larger the subsidy, the further the equilibrium lies to the southeast of A'', thus causing welfare to deteriorate further.

If the consumer does not take into account future taxes, the consumption point A would be chosen in the first period, leading to second period distress once the taxes are collected. This consideration is of interest because it helps explain the collapse of durables purchases after 1981.

Notes

1. For a discussion see Sachs (1982a), United Nations (1964), and the annual reports of the Foreign Bond Holders Protective Council.

2. Let A/P^* be net real foreign assets measured in terms of world prices. Then the change in real net foreign assets is:

$$\Delta\left(\frac{A}{P^*}\right) = \frac{\Delta A}{P^*} - \frac{A}{P^*}\frac{\Delta P^*}{P^*} = \frac{CA}{P^*} - \frac{A}{P^*}\frac{\Delta P^*}{P^*},$$

which is the inflation-adjusted current account.

3. Wealth taxes or levies as a way of responding to shocks have been insufficiently considered in the recent deficit finance literature, though not of course in the interwar writings.

4. In interpreting these numbers it is necessary to bear in mind that from 1980 to 1981 industrial production was approximately flat while from 1981 to 1982 it declined by around 20 percent. GDP growth in 1981 was 5.7 percent, -14.3 percent in 1982, and -0.5 percent in 1983.

5. The dollar value of copper exports and the real price of copper (1980 = 100) show the following pattern:

	1978	1979	1980	1981	1982
Exports (billions of U.S. dollars)	1.27	1.9	2.15	1.72	1.73
Real price (1980 = 100)	81	102	100	82	73

The real price of copper here is measured in terms of the unit value of industrial countries' exports.

6. Suppose firms in the investment business maximize the value of profits $Z = QI - aPmI - Pb(I)$ with b', $b'' > 0$. The coefficient a denotes the constant unit import content of investment. The first order condition is $b'(I) = (Q/P - av)$ or $I = h(Q/P, v)$ with $v = Pm/P$.

References

Barro, R. 1974. "Are government bonds net wealth?" *Journal of Political Economy* (December).

Barro, R. 1983. *Macroeconomics*. New York: John Wiley & Sons.

Blanchard, O. 1985. "Debts, deficits and finite horizons." *Journal of Political Economy* 93,2.

Blanchard, O. 1983. "Debt and the current account deficit in Brazil." In *Financial policies and the world capital market: The problem of Latin American countries*, edited by Pedro Armelia and Rudiger Dornbusch. Chicago: University of Chicago Press.

Borenzstein, E. 1984. "Fiscal policy and foreign debt." Unpublished manuscript, MIT.

Bruno, M. 1976. "The two-sector open economy and the real exchange rate." *American Economic Review* 66:566–77.

Calvo, G. 1982. "Real exchange rate with fixed parities." Unpublished manuscript, Columbia University.

Cardoso, E. 1986. "Stabilization in Latin America: Popular models and unhappy experience." In *Inflation, Growth, and the Real Exchange Rate*. New York: Garland.

Cavallo, D. 1983. "Deficit fiscal, endeudamiento del gobierno y tasa de inflacion: Argentina 1940–1982." *Estudios* (April–June).

Cavallo, D., and Y. Mundlak. 1983. "Real exchange rate, trade policies and sectoral growth—The case of Argentina (1946–82)." Unpublished manuscript, Hebrew University.

Cline, W. 1983a. *International debt and the stability of the world economy.* Washington, D.C.: Institute for International Economics.

Cline, W. 1983b. "International financial rescue: Viability and options." Unpublished manuscript, Washington D.C., Institute for International Economics.

Corbo, V. 1983. "An overview of macroeconomic developments in the last twenty years." Pontifica Universidad Catolica de Chile.

Corbo, V., and J. de Melo. 1983. "Liberalization and stabilization in Chile: 1974–82." Unpublished manuscript, Washington D.C.: World Bank, Development Research Department.

Corbo, V., and R. Matte. 1983. "Flujos de capitales y el rol de la politica montearia: el case de Chile." Unpublished manuscript, Pontifica Universidad Catolica de Chile.

Dagnino Pastore J. 1983. "Progress and prospects of the Latin American adjustment program." Unpublished manuscript, Buenos Aires.

Dagnino, Pastore J. 1984. "The anti-inflationary experiment, Argentina 1979–81: An assessment." In *Liberalization and stabilization: Recent experience in the Southern Cone*, edited by N. Barletta, M. Blejer, and L. Landau. Washington, D.C.: World Bank.

Deaton, A., and J. Muellbauer. 1980. *Economics and consumer behavior.* New York: Cambridge University Press.

Diaz, Alejandro C. 1963. "A note on the impact of devaluation and the redistributive effect." *Journal of Political Economy* (June).

Diaz, Alejandro C. 1981. "Southern Cone stabilization policies." In *Economic stabilization in developing countries*, edited by W. Cline and S. Weintrab. Washington D.C.: Brookings.

Diaz, Alejandro C. 1983a. "Studies of the 1930s to the 1980s." In *Financial policies and the world capital market: The problem of Latin American countries*, edited by pedro Armella and Rudiger Dornbusch. Chicago: University of Chicago Press.

Diaz, Alejandro C. 1983b. "The Brazilian debt crisis." *Brookings Papers on Economic Activity* 2.

Dooley, M., et al. 1983. "An analysis of external debt positions of eight developing countries through 1990." Unpublished manuscript, Board of Governors of the Federal Reserve.

Dornbusch, R. 1982. "Stabilization policy in LDCs: What lessons have we learned?" *World Development* (September).

Dornbusch, R. 1983a. "Real interest rates, home goods and optimal external borrowing." *Journal of Political Economy* (February).

Dornbusch, R. 1983b. "Discussion." In *Prospects for adjustment*, edited by J. Williamson. Washington D.C.: Institute for International Economics (June).

Dornbusch, R. 1987. "Argentina since Martinez de Hoz." In Guido DiTella and R. Dornbusch (eds.), *Argentina since 1945*. New York: Macmillan.

Dornbusch, R., and A. Moura da Silva. 1984. "Dollar deposits in Brazil: The 432 effect." *Revista Brasilera de Economia* (March).

Dornbusch, R., and S. Fischer. 1985. "The world debt problem." *Journal of Development Planning* 16.

Edwards, S. 1983. "Stabilization with liberalization: An evaluation of ten years of Chile's experience with free market policies: 1973-83." Unpublished manuscript, University of California, Los Angeles.

Enders, T., and R. Mattione. 1983. "Latin America: The crisis of debt and growth." Unpublished manuscript, Brookings.

Fernandez, R. 1983. "The expectations management approach to stabilization: Argentina 1976-81." Unpublished manuscript, CEMA.

French-Davis, R. 1983. "Deuda externa y apertura financeira en Chile." *Collection Estudios Cieplan* 11 (December).

Harberger, A. 1983a. "Welfare consequences of capital inflows." Unpublished manuscript, University of Chicago.

Harberger, A. 1983b. "A primer on Chile." Unpublished manuscript, University of Chicago.

Hause, J. 1966. "The welfare cost of disequilibrium exchange rates." *Journal of Political Economy* (October).

Johnson, H. G. 1966. "The welfare cost of exchange rate stabilization." *Journal of Political Economy* (October).

Martin, R., and M. Selowski. 1984. "Energy prices, substitution and optimal borrowing in the short run." *Journal of Development Economics*.

Mishkin, F. 1976. "Liquidity, consumer durable expenditure and monetary policy." *American Economic Review* (September).

Murphy, R. 1984. "Essays on macroeconomic adjustment in open economies." Unpublished manuscript, MIT.

Obstfeld, M. 1983. "Intertemporal price speculation and the optimal current-account deficit." *Journal of International Money and Finance* 2:135-245.

Rodriguez, C. 1982. "The Argentine stabilization plan of December 20th." *World Development* (September).

Rodriguez, C. 1982a. "Politicas de estabilizacion en la economia Argentina 1978-82." Unpublished manuscript, CEMA.

Royal Institute of International Affairs. 1937. *The problem of international investment*. London: Frank Cass & Co.

Sachs, J. 1981. "The current account in the macroeconomic adjustment process in the 1970s." *Brookings Papers on Economic Activity* 1.

Sachs, J. 1982a. "LDC debt in the 1980s: Risk and reform." In *Crises in economic and financial structure*, edited by P. Wachtel. Lexington, Mass.: Lexington Books.

Sachs, J. 1982b. "The Current account in the macroeconomic adjustment process." *Scandinavian Journal of Economics* 84 (2):147–169.

Simonsen, M. 1983a. "Brazil: External adjustment and economic perspectives." Unpublished manuscript, Fundacao Getulio Vargas.

Svansson, Lars E. O., and Assaf Razin. 1983. "The terms of trade and the current account: The Harberger-Laursen-Metzler effect." *Journal of Political Economy* 91, 1(February):97–125.

United Nations. 1964. *El financiamento externo de America Latina*. New York.

5   The World Debt Problem: 1980–84 and Beyond

External debt problems, like wars, are common occurrences in a broader historical perspective. They occur every 30 or 50 years, much in the same circumstances. And when they do occur, they put at odds the bond holder and the debtor and leave fundamental imprints on history. Hitler's Germany or Latin America's import substitution policy were the outgrowth of the last world debt crisis. Today Latin America is once again in a debt crisis, and the debate confronts those who call for dramatic action, including even repudiation, and others who suggest the problem is minor and can be solved by time, adjustment, and some tying-over finance—the "muddling through" strategy.

In fact not much has changed from the debt crisis of the 1930s: today the International Monetary Fund (IMF) plays the role of the League of Nations Financial Committee, the Bank Steering Committee replaces the Foreign Bank Holders Protective Council, and Bill Rhodes plays the role of Sir Otto Niemeyer.

Surprisingly, there was very little memory of debt history when the lending splurge of the 1970s got underway. Few remembered the terrible reputation of the United States in European credit markets following the defaults of the early 1840s which history relates as follows: "The vitriolic London *Times* indiscriminately denounced all Americans; and prophisied that the American name would not recover for half-a-century from the slur which had been cast upon it by the temporary or complete failure of some of the states to pay their debts."[1]

Reprinted by permission from *Third World Quarterly*, Vol. 7, No. 3, July 1985.

But closer to our topic virtually all Latin American states defaulted on their external debt in the 1920s and 1930s. Looking back over Latin credit history, Winkler wrote in 1933:

The fiscal history in Latin America, that stretch of territory lying south of the Rio Grande and housing about 110,000,000 inhabitants of various races and origins, is replete with instances of government defaults. Borrowing and default follow each other with almost perfect regularity. When payment is resumed, the past is easily forgotten and a new borrowing orgy ensues. This process started at the beginning of the past century and has continued down to the present day. It has taught us nothing.[2]

How little it has in fact taught us is apparent from a most peculiar story. In January 1983 banks joined to found The Institute of International Finance, Inc. which was intended to "improve the timeliness and quality of information available on sovereign borrowers ..." Apparently it was not even known to these good people that in 1928 they had done exactly the same thing: founding at New York University an Institute for International Finance for that very same purpose.

But there is one critical difference between the debt experience today and that of the 1930s. Today debts are continuing to be serviced, and the burden of making that possible has been placed by the international financial system, with the assistance of the IMF, squarely on the debtors. In the 1930s bond holders lost, and there was financial chaos. Today, real wage cuts in debtor countries ensure the trade surpluses and dollar earnings that keep bank stockholders in the black. One might argue (or even believe) that this is essential to maintain order in the international financial system, but that of course raises the question of in whose interest the system works. For many who are paying the bill now, there have been few benefits, and there are no obvious ones down the road.

The solution of the debt problem today is labeled economic, as if it did not have an overriding foreign policy dimension. Surely no one doubts that those who have fallen under the budget axe in the debtor countries distinguish between the IMF, the New York banks and the U.S. government. We would be wrong to believe that there is simply no politics to the immensely costly debt service that is being extracted today. This dimension is central to the call for some change in the muddling-through strategy that is being pursued at present.

Lord Lever has argued:[3]

...we must not attempt to maintain the pretence that purely commercial lending is adequate for our purposes. It is defective in that it requires premature attempts at balance-of-payments surplus by the debtor countries not compatible with our political interests or theirs. Recent net transfers of resources from the debtors have been bought at the cost of economic slack and grave risk to political stability. They are too small to restore confidence but large enough to do serious damage to the debtors' economies and societies. They are neither desirable nor sustainable.

This chapter places the debt problem first in terms of the facts: Who are the debtors and creditors, what is the size of the debts, where do the debts come from? We then proceed to identify the debt "problem," the difficulties encountered in servicing the debts. Finally, we deal with the surprise of 1984 and the medium-term prospects for relief of the debt crisis.

The Facts

We start the discussion of facts with a look at some data to establish two points: first, that the debt problem is primarily a Latin American problem and not a problem of African or Asian less developed countries (LDCs). Second, on the other side, that it is a bank problem and primarily a "big bank" problem.

Table 5.1 shows data for LDC debts both in current and constant dollars as well as the ratio of debt to exports. The table brings out that debt grew for each of the regions but that Latin America stands out by the large increase and the large ratio of debt to exports. It certainly compares strikingly with Asia where debts are large in absolute terms, but small relative to exports or GDP.

Table 5.1
An overview of LDC debts billions of U.S. dollars

	1973	1977	1980	1984
Non-oil developing countries	130.1	280.3	475.2	710.9
Debt in 1980 dollars	290.1	413.4	475.2	768.5
Long-term and short-term debt by area				
Africa (excluding South Africa)	NA	30.8	50.9	70.7
Asia	30.0	68.7	114.6	179.3
Europe	14.5	37.6	67.2	76.6
Middle East	8.7	21.9	36.3	56.2
Western hemisphere	44.4	109.1	192.6	310.5

Source: IMF.

In table 5.2 we go further to look at the debt problem in terms of debt service (interest plus amortization) and interest payments in relation to export and GDP. These are indicators of the debt burden. It is quite apparent that Latin America has a strikingly larger increase in debt burdens and a significantly larger absolute burden. The reason is twofold. On the one hand, the debt represents a larger share of exports or GDP. On the other hand, Latin America pays significantly higher effective interest rates than Asian or African borrowers. This is the case since only a small part of debt is official, at low or concessional fixed interest rates. The major part of Latin American debt is bank debt with the service linked to Libor plus spreads. In 1983, for example, the effective interest rate paid by Latin American borrowers was 10.8 percent, whereas it was only 3.7 percent for low-income countries whose debt is primarily to official lenders rather than banks.

Table 5.2
The debt burden in percent

	Low-income countries		Major borrowers		Western hemisphere	
	1977	1983	1977	1983	1977	1983
Debt Service						
Exports	12.1	13.3	19.1	29.9	29.2	44.0
GDP	1.0	0.7	3.4	6.5	3.9	8.4
Interest Payments						
Exports	4.7	5.4	7.2	18.6	10.0	32.2
GDP	0.4	0.5	1.3	4.1	1.4	6.1

Source: IMF and OECD.

The difference between the debt burdens of Latin America and the poor countries is essential to recognize. It is this difference that leads us to argue that the debt problem today is specifically one of major borrowers—particularly upper middle-income Latin American countries. It is not a problem of most LDCs, and especially not of the "poor" LDCs.

The second point to be made is that on the lending side the debt problem is one of large banks. Table 5.3 shows the Latin American debts and the part that is due to banks, and to U.S. banks in particular. For the U.S. banking system at large the Latin American debts do not present a special problem since they amount to less than 5 percent of total assets. But the problem is acute for large banks where these debts represent, for the top groups, more than 200 percent of capital. Indeed, the top 9 banks hold more than half of these debts and less than 25 banks account for almost 80 percent of the lending. The debt problem is thus very much a big bank problem.[4]

Table 5.3
The Latin American debts (billions of U.S. dollars, June 1983)

		Debt to banks	
	Total debt	All banks	U.S. banks
Argentina	37.5	25.5	11.2
Brazil	89.5	62.8	23.3
Chile	18.0	10.9	5.2
Mexico	85.6	65.5	32.3
Venezuela	31.9	26.8	10.8
Total	263.3	191.5	82.8

Source: Bank for International Settlements, Morgan Guaranty and Board of Governors of the Federal Reserve.

We now turn to the sources of the debt accumulation. Here it is important to emphasize that there are two chief sources: one is the extraordinarily poor performance of domestic macroeconomic policy in 1979–82 in virtually every Latin American country: Pinochet's move to a fixed exchange rate despite continuing inflation and indexation, Martinez de Hoz's *tablita* that led to a gigantic overvaluation and capital flight, Portillo Lopez's squandering of oil revenues and Delfim Neto's mismanagement of growth, inflation, and the external balance. The stories are not exactly the same, but they have common elements: excessive budget deficits, exchange rate overvaluation, capital flight, flight into importables, or failure to adjust to changing world prices.

Table 5.4 gives Mexico as an example. The budget deficit in 1981–82, as the Portillo Lopez administration comes to an end, moves to a vast deficit, and the exchange rate is allowed to appreciate in real terms. As a result capital flight takes place on a large scale, and the current account deteriorates under the impact of record high imports. The spending binge and capital export is financed by borrowing from banks abroad to sustain the exchange rate. Accordingly gross external debt more than doubles between 1979 and 1982.

There are differences between countries in the relative role of capital flight and trade deficits: in Argentina, capital flight was the predominant counterpart of increased (gross) external debt. This has the curious implication that Argentina's external debt position is difficult only when one looks at the government's debt, forgetting about the sizable private holdings of deposits, securities, and real estate abroad of Argentinian residents. The same applies to Venezuela or to Mexico, where private

Table 5.4
Mexican macroeconomic indicators

	1978	1979	1980	1981	1982
Budget deficit (percent of GDP)	5.5	6.0	6.9	13.6	16.3
Real exchange rate (index 1980 = 100)	117	113.5	100.0	90.6	137.9
External debt (billions of U.S. dollars)	34.0	40.4	52.5	78.9	84.6

Source: *Informe Hacendario Mensual*, November 1983, IFS and Morgan Guaranty.

dollar deposits with U.S. banks increased by as much as $4 billion between 1980 and 1982, not counting any other forms of capital flight. In Chile and Brazil, by contrast, capital outflows were of minor importance, trade deficits playing the chief role. In Chile, for example, the trade deficit of 1981 was almost three times larger than any other deficit of the last thirty years, reflecting a near doubling of previous levels of consumer durable imports.

The other source of debt accumulation is the external shock of 1980–82 in the form of dollar appreciation, sharply increased real interest rates, reduced real commodity prices and reduced demand for manufactured exports. This deterioration in the world trade and macro-economic environment is, of course, due to the U.S. inflation stabilization and the subsequent and continuing poor policy mix of tight money and over-easy fiscal policy. This shock has been particularly bad for Latin America because the debts are large, thus leading to large increases in interest bills. The effect is further reinforced because interest rates are floating rather than fixed.

Table 5.5 gives an indication of the macroeconomic problems in the world economy of the late 1970s. It compares those years to the episode of the early 1970s which was a period of debt liquidation as a consequence of a world boom. In the late 1970s real interest rates were high, growth was stagnant at the center, and an appreciating dollar increased the real burden of debt service.

How much of a contribution to the debt problem is due to the macroeconomic shock as opposed to domestic policies? One way to answer that question is to look at the debtors' deterioration in the ratio

Table 5.5
Two episodes of the world economy (annual average percentage rates)

	U.S. prime rate	Inflation in world trade	Growth of industrial countries	Dollar depreciation
1970–73	6.7	12.4	4.7	5.7
1979–82	15.5	4.4	1.1	−8.7

of debt to exports and measure the relative role in that deterioration of three factors:

- noninterest current account deficits,
- interest rates (including fees and spreads) in the world capital market,
- growth in export earnings.

The theory of debt dynamics shows that the ratio of debt to exports rises over time if a country runs noninterest current account deficits or if the effective interest rate exceeds the growth rate of export earnings.[5] If the interest rate exceeds the growth rate of export earnings, borrowing to finance interest payments makes the debt grow more rapidly than export revenue. Hence the ratio of debt to exports grows over time. Periods of high interest rates and a collapse of world trade would therefore be cases where external shocks precipitate a debt crisis.

There is a simple way of constructing a counterfactual exercise to assess the significance of the external shock.[6] Suppose that throughout the 1970s the typical debtor country had every year balanced the current account except for interest payments, the latter being borrowed at prime rate. Suppose also that export earnings had increased at the rate they actually did for non-oil LDCs in the 1970s. In this counterfactual scenario it can be shown that the debt-export ratio would actually have declined substantially below the level of the early 1970s. The debt liquidation of the early 1970s, due to negative real interest rates, would have more than compensated for the shocks of the late 1970s. In fact, of course, the Latin American debt-export ratio increased sharply. This means that noninterest current account and capital flight are an essential aspect of the debt crisis. That recognition is important because it has a bearing on acceptable policies of relief as viewed by taxpayers in the center countries.

The Debt Problem

In evaluating debt problems it is important to ask whether we are addressing liquidity problems, solvency or equity issues. Liquidity problems involve an inability to service and amortize debts *now* on the time schedule and in the full amounts initially contracted. There is no question that there is a liquidity problem. Equity problems involve the question of how the burden of large, unanticipated increases in the costs of debt service should be borne between lenders and borrowers. Finally, solvency involves the question of whether the value of a country's liabilities exceeds the ability to pay *any* time. The ability to pay, however, is in large measure a political question involving the extent to which economic activity and living standards can be depressed in order to generate the foreign exchange revenues with which to service the external debt.

The present "muddling through" strategy is becoming increasingly doubtful as massive resource transfers from debtors to creditors are made at the cost of deep recession in the adjusting countries. There is much discussion of whether the debt crisis is a liquidity crisis or a solvency problem. But the definition of solvency for a nation is not as clearcut as for a corporation: given the existing size of debts, living standards in debtor countries could be depressed to levels so low as to make it possible to service and even amortize the debts. The real issue is whether the political systems can and should be made to stand the strain.

The chief difficulty of adjustment in Latin America today, and the source of the debt problem, is that the region has been a *structural* importer of capital. Deficits in the noninterest current account were the counterpart, at least until the late 1970s, of a development strategy that used external resources to supplement domestic saving in order to finance investment and growth. It was because these countries had been structural importers of capital that the effort to rapidly generate external surpluses turned out to be so costly. In a country where deficits in the external accounts are due to a transitory overspending, correction is easy. All that is required is to stop overspending, and without much effect on employment, the external accounts return to balance. But, when development has been centered on a growing home market, a rapid return to external balance meets with short-run structural impediments that inevitably make unemployment the chief way of generating surpluses.

A second difficulty in respect to debt service is that much of the adjustment effort falls on labor whose real wage is reduced to achieve external competitiveness. But the debt accumulation in many instances primarily reflects benefits that accrued not to labor but rather to the upper middle class that engaged in capital flight or the middle class that enjoyed an import spree. Thus in Argentina, Chile, and Mexico the adjustment to service the debt involves a dramatic inequity. In Brazil this is much less obvious since the deficits that created the debt reflected oil price policies and public sector investment which also benefit the working class.

The third issue is the long-run solvency question. Can Latin American countries in the medium and long run service their debts as contracted *and* at the same time enjoy growth in per capita incomes, having made up most of the losses of 1981–84? This is the central question today and it is wide open. In part it depends on domestic policies and the scope for effective mobilization of resources in the areas of import substitution and export promotion. But it clearly also depends on the long-run external environment. If world real interest rates rapidly return to low levels, growth of world trade is strong and sustained, and protectionism is not an issue, then debt problems can be solved by some sharing of the short-run burdens.

There is no full assurance that long-run trends are favorable, but there is also no particular reason to believe that in a 5 to 15 year perspective conditions are strongly adverse. The long-run solvency question therefore is largely indeterminate and uninteresting. It is superseded by two other issues. One is the increasing urgency to see the short-run problems caused by high interest rates and a strong dollar as an equity problem. The second is the recognition that Latin America for the next decade, and beyond, will be amortizing debts: instead of borrowing on average over and above the interest bill, Latin America will have to be earning net exports to service and pay off debt. This is an implication of the fact that commercial banks are seeking to reduce their exposure in real terms and that no other major source of development finance is available. This is an extraordinary change for the international financial system, running against common sense and good economics. This long-run implication of the debt problem has been overshadowed by the short-run cyclical and financial aspects, but it deserves much more attention.

The Surprise of 1984

Even early in 1984 many observers felt that the debt crisis could not but get out of hand. Crisis management had carried the system already for more than a year, but developments in the world economy and the sharp economic setback in the debtor countries seemed to make some form of collapse of the "muddling through" strategy inevitable. It is true that there were optimists, in particular William Cline whose cheerful forecasts would even turn out to be understatements, but by and large, skepticism was the rule.[7] For the moment, and perhaps for good, the sceptics proved to be way off the mark. Latin American countries turned their external imbalances so sharply into surpluses that they paid a large part of the 1984 interest bill and, what is perhaps even more surprising, did so under conditions of recovery and political stability. The year ended with a resumption of confidence and a long-term rescheduling of the major debtors at spreads significantly below those experienced in previous years. It is worth reviewing these developments in more detail.

In 1982 unanticipated credit rationing brought about the debt crisis. Debtors had come to expect that they could roll their debt, borrowing amortization payments, interest payments, and more almost automatically. The sharp increase in interest rates and the decline in export earnings led the debtor countries to call for financing out of line with what banks were willing to advance. The moment the financing gap became obvious, general credit rationing was immediately applied, and the debtors and the banks were at a stand-off situation: banks were unwilling to lend, and debtors were unable to pay. The international financial system was actively threatened by the possibility that borrowers would simply repudiate their debts in the way of the 1930s, thus throwing into chaos a banking system that had completely irresponsible supervision and inadequate capital.

The IMF set itself up to save the system, organizing banks into a lender's cartel and holding the debtor countries up for a classical mugging.[8] The IMF was immensely successful and immediately came to be thought of as central and essential to a well-functioning international financial system. There is little doubt that the strategy protected bank stockholders at the expense of the LDCs. It is wide open to discussion whether the debtors were net beneficiaries compared to a situation of international chaos. Similarly, it is open to discussion whether the IMF should not have shifted at least some of the burdens onto the banks, forcing them to accept loan losses.

There is a lot of discussion about involuntary lending. Banks wish they could sell off part of their loan portfolio because the existing spreads do not reward them sufficiently for the perceived risk that the stock market places on their exposure. Indeed, banks may be paying higher borrowing costs, and thus experience reduced profitability on all their lending as a spillover from the pollution of their portfolio via LDC debts. In that sense banks are paying too and sharing in the adjustment. It is indeed the case that Brazil today, were she to float $80 billion in bonds, using the proceeds to pay off the bank debts, would not be able to raise all the money at Libor plus one-eighth. But it is also true that the loans remain profitable in that they pay more than 1 percent above Libor.

Table 5.6
Real per capita growth in Latin America (average annual rate)

1967–76	1977–80	1981–84	1984
3.9	3.0	− 3.0	0.2

Source: CEPAL.

In any event the process that evolved was a system of strict IMF conditionality with a counterpart of bank financing of part of the foreign exchange gap. The results were spectacular on the external balance side and dramatically negative on the domestic front. Trade surpluses of the debtor countries far exceeded expectation, and even targets, while growth turned dramatically negative.

Figure 5.1 shows the trade surplus and the service deficits of Latin America, the latter reflecting primarily interest payments; it highlights the large shift from the trade deficits of the 1970s to a large trade surplus. From 1982 to 1984 Latin America's trade balance improved by more than $30 billion thus already covering in 1984 a large part of the service deficit. Table 5.6 shows the implications for per capita growth. Whereas on average in the past decade growth was above 3 per cent adjusting for the increase in population, it averaged − 3 percent in 1981–84. Given poverty and the unequal distribution of income in Latin America, this recession implied a major reversal of social progress.

Much of the scepticism of 1983–84 concerned the external balance: how could habitual dollar spenders turn rapidly into dollar earners? The surprise may be explained in terms of four factors:

- The debtor countries went into a severe recession, induced by tight money and fiscal policies. The recession automatically reduced import spending and freed domestic output for export.
- In the adjustment process the debtor countries had undergone a very significant real depreciation that increased external competitiveness. The

U.S. dollars (billions)

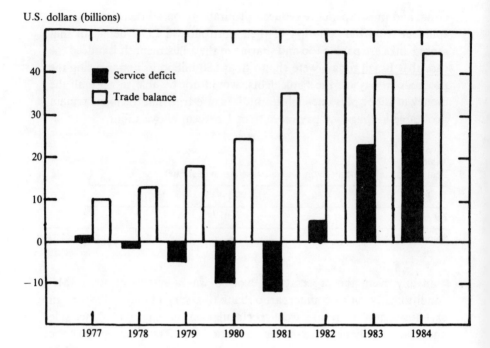

Figure 5.1
The Latin American external balance

gain in competitiveness promoted export earnings and made imports less competitive.

- The extraordinary growth of spending in the U.S. economy spilled over into imports from LDCs thus adding pull to the push of the debtors' recession and increased competitiveness.

- Finally, import substitution in the debtor countries, due to controls, earlier investment strategy, increased competitiveness, and administrative decisions made possible an enormous contraction of imports.

It is not easy to assign a precise weight to each of these factors, but it is certainly important to recognize the extend of the pull provided by U.S. growth. For example, in the year to June 1984, U.S. total import spending increased by 33 percent. Much of that increase in imports was supplied by Latin America. These cyclical effects are well understood and, in that sense, surprising only in magnitude.

The unanticipated event is the dramatic fall in imports. Figure 5.2 shows the volume of non-oil imports of Brazil as an example. Since 1980

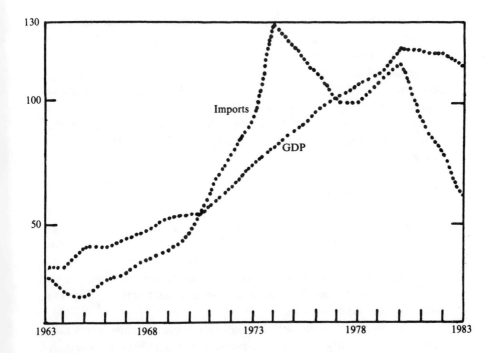

Figure 5.2
Brazil: real GDP and non-oil import volume

import volume fell by more than half. The decline reflects in part a fall in investment associated with the recession and budget cuts in public sector enterprises. The major share however is apparently a reflection of successful import substitution. It is interesting to note that the Brazilian experience is not at all atypical. In fact all of Latin America has experienced a dramatic reduction in import volume. Perhaps, just as in the 1930s, import substitution is once again providing a way for Latin America to shelter itself from external shocks.

The surprise of 1984 is not complete without a discussion of the costs of generating the external surpluses. The optimists had argued that the debt problem would not get out of hand because reduced interest rates and a collapse of the dollar would help pay the bills. Just as collapsing commodity prices, high interest rates, and an appreciating dollar had helped make the crisis, the reversal would help solve it. But in fact none of this has happened: the dollar has grown stronger since 1983, interest rates have risen above their 1983 levels, and commodity prices failed to show the typical cyclical rebound. All this is very important because it tells us that the turn around in the debtor countries' current accounts was achieved not with the aid of negative real interest rates and capital gains but entirely with hard work and forgone consumption or investment.

One cannot conclude comments on 1984 without noting that the good performance on debt and signs of recovery apply primarily to the major debtors. Indeed, there has been a division of performance. Smaller debtors, particularly Chile, Peru, and Bolivia, did not share in the prospect of getting out of trouble. Their economies are far from a course of stability.

The Medium-Term Outlook

Is there any chance that the surprising ability of the debtor countries witnessed in 1984 will carry over to 1985 and beyond? If the debtor countries can both enjoy growth and meet their debt service commitments then there simply is no debt crisis. If, on the contrary, there is an almost clear-cut trade-off between growth and debt service, then the potential for a crisis remains.

Any prediction that the debt crisis is alive must somehow show that 1984 was particularly unusual in a manner that is unlikely to recur. A sensible framework for that question is to focus on the link between import availability and growth. It is widely accepted that without growth the debtor countries will, sooner or later, explode politically. The labor force in Mexico or Brazil grows at rates in excess of 3 percent. Adding productivity growth to that number suggests that without average growth rates of 5 to 6 percent, at the least, there will be still further deterioration of social performance. Growth is thus essential.

Consider first import availability:

$$\text{Imports} = \text{exports} + \text{``new money''} - \text{debt service.} \tag{1}$$

In equation 1 import availability is interpreted as the constraining factor on growth, and the problem is that "new money" from commercial banks falls short of debt service payments. Export revenues therefore are no longer available to finance imports, limiting import volume and therefore growth.

From equation 1 it is apparent that strong export performance and low debt service due to lower interest rates and lower spreads are the recipe for the external constraint on growth to disappear. Strong export performance has three ingredients. First, there needs to be sustained growth in the center countries. The number bandied around, without much justification, is an average growth rate in OECD countries of 3 percent. Such growth would open markets for manufactures from the debtor countries and, at the same time, improve the real prices of commodities which remain the chief exports in one form or another.

But, second, it is also important how that growth comes about. The favored combination is that if growth causes the dollar to collapse in world markets, a fall of the dollar would raise dollar prices in world trade and thus, by a stroke of the pen, write down debts in real terms.

The third ingredient in loosening the external constraint is also linked to the policy mix. Since debt service is determined both by the outstanding stock of debt and the current interest rate it is essential that the policy mix be one of easy money. Debtors, not surprisingly, favor an environment of prosperity, world inflation, and cheap credit, the more the better.

Macroeconomic predictions for the near term suggest about 3 percent OECD growth, although with a significant margin of uncertainty. Interest rates are predicted to rise somewhat from their present level, though not dramatically. Dollar decline continues to be expected, but no longer predicted. The world macro outlook decidedly does not offer the prospect of easy riding: inflation, low interest rates, and a boom of the kind of the early 1970s. The LDCs may get out of their debt problems, but only by having conditions to pay, not by riding the waves of capital gains and inflationary write-offs.

The last consideration is how import availability translates into growth. The evidence in figure 5.2 is problematic in this connection. It suggests that we have no clear idea of import requirements for growth. There may have occurred in 1980–84 a once and for all decline in import requirements, both average and marginal. But the decline may also be only transitory, with no trend change in the high import content of growth that Latin America has experienced so far.

The 1984 recovery might lead us to believe that we can have both growth and debt service, suggesting that there is no painful trade-off. But that must be qualified in an important respect. In 1983–84, Brazil and Mexico transferred abroad an amount equal to 5 or 6 percent of their incomes. Chile's transfer came more nearly to 9 percent. The transfer represents the difference between the amount of output produced and income available for spending. It reflects the fact that the recovery in output in 1984 corresponds to increased employment, but not to increased domestic absorption of goods and services—people were able to find more employment by working for less. The ability to find employment is essential on the domestic side and must not be belittled. In itself it improves the distribution of adjustment and income. It also increases the chances that in the near term the situation will not blow up. But that is primarily a comfort to the creditors, not relief for the debtors.

In the near term the debt question is whether the debtor countries' domestic ability can sustain the 1984 external performance under less favorable, but at the same time not outright impossible, external conditions. That leaves on the import side the question whether controls and import substitution can be kept up. On the export side it raises the difficult issue of whether the export growth largely reflected the domestic depression of demand in debtor countries which of course would disappear in a recovery. Among the key questions is also the role of competitiveness. In 1982–84, the real wage was cut significantly, yielding reduced spending and increased competitiveness. Can these real wage cuts be sustained into a recovery? In Argentina that has proved impossible, in Brazil there is great doubt at present, and even in Mexico there are serious questions.

The debt problem has shifted to the debtor countries' domestic economies in at least three respects: first, the cuts in real wages associated with budget and external balance correction are huge and socially unacceptable. Workers now see themselves as paying for debt service on an external debt that reflects mismanagement and privilege from which they have had little benefit. For example, in Chile the real minimum wage is 30 percent below the 1981 level, and workers are clearly aware that they are paying a bill that is not their own.

The second serious issue is inflation. The adjustment to the external crisis involves, in all cases, a vast increase in inflation and with that an IMF intrusion in macro management. It is particularly clear in Argentina and Brazil that some measure for control of inflation is essential. It is much less apparent that IMF-style tight money and budget cutting is of much use in a highly indexed economy.

The third question is whether the deterioration in growth performance, compared to the last 30 years (see figure 5.3), will have strongly adverse political consequences. Few would seriously disagree with the proposition that per capita growth in the decade of the 1980s will be approximately zero. By 1990 the working-class standard of living is unlikely to be much above where it was in 1980 and perhaps not even that. This outcome is all the more likely because the growth pattern has shifted quite a bit. In the past, LDCs offset a decline in the world economy by external borrowing, thus maintaining their growth rates at

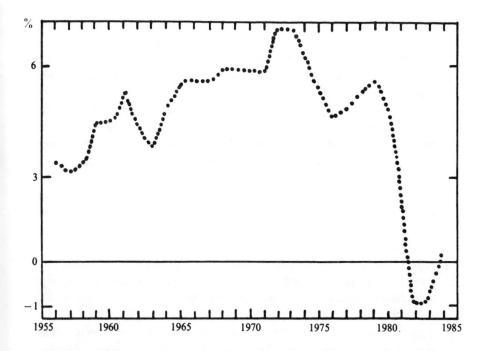

Figure 5.3
Latin American growth (GDP growth, 3-year-centered moving average). Source: IMF.

the cost of increased external debt. Now that possibility is limited and hence an external adversity will have to be borne much more by reduced growth rather than trade deficits. That fact cannot but force a reduced trend growth rate.

The optimistic outlook is that people quickly get accustomed to adversity and soon forget their previous peak real incomes or the growth rates they used to have. But that optimism may not be warranted in economies where it is increasingly perceived that poor performance is also due to a "system" that enforces, with IMF assistance, the interests of foreign banks over domestic prosperity and stability. There are also limits, as Mario Simonsen[9] has pointed out very forcefully:

To keep developing debtor countries cooperating with the international financial community, a basic question should be addressed: under what conditions rational policy makers in debtor nations would prefer cooperation to retaliation? While precise rupture points are difficult to locate, a general principle remains valid: a growing economy with expanding exports hardly would seek confrontation with its creditors. In the same line, solvency at the expense of prolonged recession may be politically unsustainable.

Concluding Remarks

Solving debt problems is mostly politics, not economics. Yet today, unlike in the 1920s or 1930s, the problem is made to look as if it were solely an issue of economics: forecasts of interest rates, growth rates, etc., are at the center of the discussion to determine what are the domestic policies of debtor countries consistent with a dramatic reduction in their external indebtedness. Only four years ago banks were falling all over themselves to persuade debtors to go yet deeper into debt. Today we are told that there is an obvious overindebtedness. The single premise of the "adjustment process" is the proposition that debts must stay intact and profitable in order to maintain the "system". Yet equity, good foreign policy, or simple long-run sense would indicate that some write-offs are in most people's interests.

The issue can be addressed simply by asking what the prospects are, thinking in terms of a decade, for Latin America. The standard view is that debtor countries will over several years work down their debts (relative to exports) by a combination of trade surpluses and export growth. One day, some day, banks will spontaneously decide that enough is enough, turn around and resume "voluntary lending." There is no assurance that this will happen and certainly no indication as to what is enough. Indeed, domestic regulators wince at the very thought that banks should think of renewed foreign lending. The priority is clearly that LDC debts should become a negligible item in both debtor countries' and commercial bank balance sheets. Until then, austerity.

But the prospect that commercial banks will seek to reduce their LDC exposure means that most of the interest will have to be earned rather than borrowed. The prospect combines with the unquestioned scarcity of official lending and the lack of significant direct investment. It adds up to the proposition that for the next decade Latin America will be a net exporter of resources. The notion that economic growth will be the same whether Latin America is borrowing resources or repaying, which is implicit in this thinking, runs against common sense and historical experience. Growth clearly will suffer simply because saving is inadequate to sustain investment levels at their historical trends. This scheme of things is somehow accepted as the inevitable short-run solution and, by extrapolation, as the medium-term outcome. The inevitability is not questioned, least of all by the IMF when it arranged for the cartelization of banks and thus provided the essential mechanism to extract resources from Latin America.

But perhaps more disappointing is the fact that policymakers in debtor countries themselves have come to accept the inevitability of this course of affairs. They have submitted to the IMF-sponsored case-by-case approach. Cartagena is remembered as an entirely embarrassing flop. They have agreed to make external debt a narrow technical problem (with vast domestic costs) rather than a burning international issue. Perhaps it is not surprising that Chile's Pinochet or Brazil's generals should avoid rocking the boat. But why did Mexico or Argentina go the same way? The answer is surely that any move on the external debt would potentially radicalize domestic politics of income distribution and property rights, perhaps beyond the precarious control of the present system?

Is the conclusion of all this that economics and politics combine to make the debt problem a dead issue? I do think that is the case, barring two possibilities. First, a major macroeconomic shock of the 1980–82 style could open up the issue of illiquidity and hence involve "impossible" adjustments. That might have happened in 1984-85 as a consequence of U.S. budget deficits colliding with tight money, but it simply has not happened. The rescuing factor presumably was skillful monetary policy in the U.S.

The other possibility, this one more plausible, is that creditor countries over the next decade find that they simply cannot live with the invasion of their home markets by exports from debtor LDCs that are required to pay the interest bill. Protection may well be the result. The protection issue of course was the main ingredient of the spreading in the 1930s of depression throughout the world economy:

When the great creditor countries reduce their exports of capital ... all their debtors must meet their obligations either in goods or in gold, instead of by fresh borrowing. Before this extraordinary situation had fully developed, however, a further check was imposed upon the capacity of the debtor countries to pay their external obligations. The increased export surpluses which they placed upon world markets caused concern in the importing creditor countries, which thereupon imposed higher tariffs and supplemented them by additional restrictions on imports. There ensued in consequence an enormous shrinkage in world trade, and the logical consequence of this shrinkage has been a series of moratoria, suspensions of payment, and standstill agreements, as a result of which the credit of many debtor countries has been gravely impaired. (League of Nations, *World Economic Survey*, 1932.)

Notes

1. R. McCrane, *Foreign Bond Holders and American State Bonds*, London, Macmillan, 1933, p. 266.

2. M. Winkler, *Foreign Bonds: An Autopsy*, R. Swain & Co., 1933. Reprinted by Arno Press, 1976.

3. Lord Lever, "Begin to write down world debt," *Wall Street Journal* (New York), 7 June 1984.

4. See H. S. Terrel, "Bank lending to developing countries," *Federal Reserve Bulletin*, October 1984.

5. See M. H. Simonsen, "The developing country debt problem," in G. Smith and J. Cuddington (eds.) *International Debt and the Developing Countries*, World Bank, 1985, Washington, D.C., for a development of this idea.

6. For details of the calculation, see R. Dornbusch and S. Fischer, "The world debt problem," *Journal of Development Planning*.

7. See W. Cline, *International Debt*, Cambridge, MSS.: The MIT Press, 1985.

8. For an account of the IMF part in solving the debt problem, see *IMF Survey*, 7 January and 21 January 1985.

9. *IMF Survey*, p. 41.

6   Stabilization Policies in Developing Countries: What Have We Learned?

You know, this new system where instead of devaluing you raise interest rates...
Paul Rosenstein-Rodan

In the first quarter of 1981, real interest rates to commercial borrowers in Chile were upward of 35 percent, they were near 50 percent in Brazil, and in Argentina they reached 135 percent. Each of these countries was in one way or another undergoing one of the new-style stabilization programs: some variant of exchange rate targeting combined with a monetarist-oriented stabilization policy. Each country had high and rising unemployment, a general dissatisfaction with the success of policies and the prospect of more trouble down the road.

This chapter sketches models of stabilization policy, old and new style, and draws some of the lessons. Old-style programs emphasize fiscal discipline and the right real exchange rate. New-style programs give prominence to purchasing power parity and the monetary approach. The former is right in the long run but does not pronounce on the dynamics. The latter turns out to be largely wrong in respect of the dynamics. Is there an alternative? Yes, but it is hard to accept, were it not for the alternatives.

Reprinted by permission from *World Development*, Vol. 10, No. 9, pp. 701–708.

The Old Paradigm

I am not sure who may have actually held the views that I characterize here as the old paradigm, but if one had to be old-fashioned, this might be as good a sketch as any of those beliefs.[1] The center of analysis is taken by fundamentals: the division of output between the private and public sectors and the financing of public sector imbalances by money creation, the symmetry between budget and payments imbalances and the role of the inflation tax.

The model focuses on the real exchange rate—traded relative to home goods or export relative to import prices—and on the budget deficit as a share of income. We denote these respectively by θ and b. In the goods market, full employment equilibrium is consistent with different combinations of the real exchange rate and the budget deficit share. The higher government spending or the lower taxes relative to income, the higher the demand for domestic goods and accordingly, the higher is the equilibrium relative price of domestic goods, $\theta = P/EP^*$. The schedule II in figure 6.1 represents internal balance thus defined. Points above and to the left correspond to unemployment, points below and to the right to excess demand.

Current account balance is defined by the schedule FF. Higher deficits due to increased government spending or lower taxes relative to (full employment) output create a deficit which needs correction via a real depreciation. Thus the schedule showing external balance, FF, is negatively sloped. Points above the schedule show a deficit, points below a surplus. Point A represents the point of internal and external balance.

The monetary sector is represented in the bottom part of figure 6.1. We assume that the entire budget deficit is money financed. Accordingly, the inflation tax revenue, $\dot{p}(M/P)$ in long-run equilibrium, is equal to the budget deficit, where $\dot{p}$ is the inflation rate, M/P denotes real balances and y denotes real GNP. With b the budget deficit ratio we have

$$\dot{p}\left(\frac{M}{P}\right) = by. \tag{1}$$

With the demand for real balances a function of real income and the inflation rate, and assuming monetary equilibrium $M/P = L(\dot{p}, y)$ in (1), we arrive at an expression for the inflation rate:

$$\dot{p} = f(b). \tag{2}$$

An increase in the budget deficit ratio raises the financing requirement.

With money demand inelastic with respect ‥ the inflation rate an increase in inflation is required to finance the deficit. This relation is shown in the bottom part of the diagram. We show the schedule as highly nonlinear to reflect the fact that deficits, as they increase, lead to sharply higher inflation rates as real money demand, at higher inflation rates, is more elastic.

The full "equilibrium" is shown at points A where there is internal and external balance, some money-financed deficit and an associated rate of inflation. If inflation is in excess of the world rate the implicit assumption is that frequent devaluations sustain the real exchange rate at the equilibrium level.

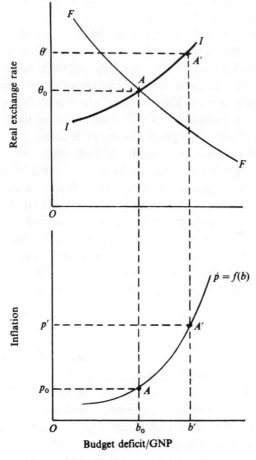

Figure 6.1
Inflation, deficits, and the real exchange rate

In this setting an increase in the budget deficit, through higher spending or reduced taxation, would move the economy to a point like A'. In the goods market, the increased real demand leads to real appreciation, which in turn brings about expenditure switching toward foreign goods and thus leads to an external deficit. On the inflation side, increased deficits require increased inflation tax collection and therefore lead to a higher rate of inflation at point A'. As long as reserves or borrowing is available, an equilibrium such as A' can be sustained. In the long run of course adjustment is required. Adjustment requires expenditure reduction or a correction of the fiscal problem as well as a real depreciation to return from A' to A. The fiscal correction is an essential part of the adjustment and it allows not only restoration of external balance, but also a reduction in inflation.

The orthodox model then suggests that *both* inflation and external deficits have (often) a common source, namely, budget deficits. Correction of the deficit and of inflation requires fiscal reform and a real depreciation. As a guidance for stabilization policy, the model is open to two important criticisms. The first is that the framework is decidely long run, focusing on comparative steady states, with no implications about the problems of adjustment that arise from inflation control in the short run. A second problem, and perhaps a more important one, is that the real depreciation that is required for long-run external balance is made to look "merely" as a gain in competitiveness rather than as a reduction in the standard of living. Given productivity, it is clear that a reduction in export relative to import prices implies reduced real incomes and therefore, in the long run, reduced real wages. Reform of the public sector budget and setting prices right are in good part euphemisms for reductions in the standard of living, replacing the older concepts of expenditure-switching and expenditure-reducing policies.

New Ideas

The old paradigm, in some respects, is structuralist.[2] It takes inflation to be a fiscal problem—and behind the fiscal problem we can choose to see conflicting social demands—and it recognizes the role of the real exchange rate in the external adjustment process. These features are decidely lost in the monetary approach with the assumption of exact or, at least, dominant purchasing power parity (PPP) and the emphasis on monetary or domestic credit rules as a mechanism of payments control and adjustment.

The new approach relegates the sources of money creation to the background by noting, first, that the choice of the rate of exchange depreciation sets the home rate of inflation. Second, given the world rate of inflation, there is a unique rate of domestic credit creation such that the real money supply grows precisely at the rate of real money demand. Stabilization policy in this model involves merely finding, establishing, and sustaining these appropriate rates.

PPP, it is often recognized, may take a somewhat milder form. It is conceded that not *all* domestic prices are in fact set in the world market. While much of the price structure is externally set, there is also some scope for domestic price movements. But these movements are subject to the discipline of competition, and any life of their own cannot take them far or for a long time away from the trend of traded goods prices. Therefore, even with these amendments, traded goods prices substantially set the pace of inflation.

It is important to recognize that PPP implies that disinflation is altogether costless. Since the country faces given world prices, the rate of exchange depreciation sets the rate of inflation with world demand perfectly elastic. The small country, in these circumstances, can experience unemployment only for neoclassical high real wage reasons, not as a consequence of monetary disinflation. Of course the presence of nontraded goods would qualify that result, but it would not alter the basic message that with a perfectly elastic world demand stabilization need not be costly.

A counterpart of the PPP tradition and the monetary approach is the belief in rules. The recognition that economic agents' expectations require an anchor leads to the belief that the announcement and pursuit of exchange rate targets provides a direct, strongly visible means for disinflation of both the actual course of prices and of the expected path of prices. Therefore fixed nominal exchange rates or preannounced target paths of the nominal rate are believed to be integral parts of stabilization efforts.

There is a final element in the analysis and this concerns the real rate of interest. With assumed perfect substitutability between domestic and foreign assets, real rates of interest are fixed at the world level. As long as capital mobility is free, real rates of interest are equalized and monetary tightness affects the price level, not the real rate of interest. Indeed, stabilization policy is seen as an effort to free domestic interest rates from their regulatory confinement and raise them to the world level, thus promoting a more efficient financial system.

Stylized facts

Suppose we called 'new stabilization programs' those experiments, whether in the U.K., Argentina, Brazil or Chile, where a good part of the new ideas are applied: monetary rules, preannounced exchange rate paths, interest rate-exchange depreciation policies aligned to be consistent with the notion of perfect capital mobility. What has been the experience? Specifically has disinflation been successful, fast, relatively costless and complete?

Certainly it can be argued that none of these countries has quite followed the recipe. Perhaps monetary policy was not right, or the interest rate policy was misaligned, or the exchange rate policy was out of line with the setting of other instruments. The fact remains that in the last 4 years we have been accumulating substantial evidence that the new stabilization programs can turn out to be quite catastrophic. It is important therefore to look for those factors which make stabilization more difficult than the "new approach" would lead us to believe.

There are, I believe, several important elements that make programs run into trouble. First, shifting from money to debt finance of an unchanged deficit leads to crowding out and is severely deflationary. Second, exchange rate targets in combination with monetary disinflation lead to real appreciation and overvaluation. Third, successful disinflation raises desired real balances relative to output which, under a monetary rule, causes excess deflation. Each factor tends to contribute to high real interest rates in the transition, low investment and unemployment. The existence of the effects relies critically on the absence of full PPP and the nonequalization of the relevant real interest rates. A fourth element is the maintenance of wage indexation, geared to lagged inflation, which in combination with monetary tightening and exchange rate targeting induces real appreciation and a squeeze on real balances.

Table 6.1 selects Chile to show some of these stylized facts. The real exchange rate index is represented by the ratio of home goods to import prices. The real interest rate is given by the rate on 30-day commercial bank loans adjusted by the CPI inflation rate. Table 6.1 reveals the steady real appreciation of the exchange rate that must be seen in the light of a growing current account deficit and domestic fiscal tightness. While the real exchange rate development is perhaps not startling, the real interest rate developments are entirely extraordinary and would certainly not allow any normal investment to proceed on a sustained basis. The real interest rates of course reflect some mixture of four

separate elements: tight-credit, risk premia reflecting the possibility of
exchange depreciation, monopolistic rents, and regulatory and tax
wedges between borrowing and lending rates.

Table 6.1
Real exchange rate and real interest rate in Chile

	1977	1978	1979	1980	1981*
Real exchange rate (1974–1977 = 100)	98.8	106.4	113.6	115.4	124.1
Real interest rate (% p.a.)	56.8	42.2	16.6	11.9	45.8

a. 1981 corresponds to the 3rd quarter for the real exchange rate.

The stylized facts suggest two important points in modelling stabilization policy. One is that PPP should not be a dominant feature and that
the real exchange rate should assume an important place. The other is the
role of the real interest rate as a determinant of aggregate demand and
international capital flows.

A Model

We now sketch a summary model that captures the main effects and
channels relevant to our analysis. In the goods market output is demand
determined. Demand for domestic goods (aggregating exportables and
home goods for convenience) is given by real income, the real interest
rate r and the real exchange rate θ, and fiscal variables represented by the
full employment budget deficit ratio b:

$$y = D(r, \theta, y, b). \tag{3}$$

In figure 6.2 we show as II the schedule along which the home goods
market clears. The schedule is drawn for a given real exchange rate and
fiscal policy.

In asset markets we assume that home securities are nontraded,
imperfect substitutes for foreign debt. Demand for home securities
depends on the nominal rate on these assets, $r + \dot{p}$, the rate on foreign
securities adjusted for anticipated depreciation, $i^* + x$, as well as on
income and wealth, w. Equilibrium in the bond market requires that real
demand equal the prevailing supply, V/P:

$$\frac{V}{P} = B(r + \dot{p}, i^* + x, y, w). \tag{4}$$

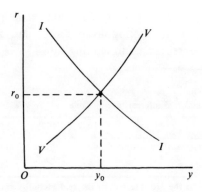

Figure 6.2
Goods and bonds market equilibrium

Figure 6.2 shows bond market equilibrium as the schedule VV. The schedule is drawn for a given rate of inflation, given returns on foreign assets as well as given wealth. The schedule is positively sloped since higher income reduces the demand for debt and therefore requires an increase in the equilibrium yield to encourage demand and restore market equilibrium.

The model is completed by an equation describing the evolution of domestic prices. The evolution of inflation is governed as shown in (5) by real appreciation and the deviation of output from full employment:

$$\ddot{p} = a(\dot{e} + \dot{p}^* - \dot{p}) + \beta(y - \bar{y}). \tag{5}$$

Equation (5) states that inflation rises whenever the rate of inflation of foreign prices in home currency, $\dot{e} + \dot{p}^*$, exceeds the prevailing rate of inflation, $\dot{p}$, or when output exceeds potential. Note that at any point the inflation rate is given or predetermined. It rises or falls in response to a changing real exchange rate or unemployment. A real depreciation leads to increasing inflation because it increases the rate of price increase of imported materials, including wage goods as well as the inflation rate of imported substitutes for domestic goods. Conversely, a reduced rate of import price inflation exerts a dampening effect, causing home inflation to fall.

The remaining variables—the stock of debt, fiscal policy and the exchange rate—are the key policy variables. Here different arrangements are possible. A given deficit can be financed by money or debt in different proportions and the exchange rate can be fixed, fully flexible or it may be set according to some rule. The rule, in turn, might be a preannounced *tablita* or it may be an activist feedback rule geared to output, the real exchange rate or the (endogeneous) growth rate of money. The evolution of the economy under a stabilization program differs of course drastically under these alternative arrangements. Little interest attaches to an exploration of all modalities. But there are some general points that can be made.

Debt Finance and Real Depreciation

A first example is a policy, such as that pursued by Brazil in 1980–1981, where deficit finance shifts from money to debt and where at the same time, in an effort to gain competitiveness, the rate of depreciation is raised relative to the rate of inflation.

Debt finance of a largely unchanged deficit means that the stock of real debt will be rising. An increase in the rate of depreciation, actual and anticipated $(x = \dot{e})$, implies that the return on home securities now is relatively lower. The combination of factors shifts the home bonds market equilibrium schedule up and to the left in figure 6.3. Moreover, the schedule keeps shifting as long as the stock of real debt grows. In the goods market the real depreciation policy shifts the II schedule up and to the right as domestic competitiveness is raised. The combination of policies leads to a path such a AA' where the economy with rapidly rising real interest rates and falling output moves into a severe recession.

What does the policy achieve? Evidently, growth of domestic credit is reduced. But of course that does not solve the problem of inflation. Inflation is reduced only due to the cyclical dampening effect of a recession and even that dampening is in part offset by the real depreciation policy. Since there is no *direct* link between money and inflation, a reduction in the growth of money and domestic credit cannot reduce inflation.

How substantial the gains in disinflation are depends on the countervailing forces of inertia (indexation) and the impact of real depreciation and unemployment as measured by the coefficients a and β. In an economy that is indexed with wages responding to past inflation, there is little flexibility in inflation and a policy of real depreciation takes substantial unemployment to avoid an increase in inflation.

What the policy mix does achieve is the following: there will clearly be a cyclical improvement in the current account, reinforced by the beneficial effects on the external balance of the real depreciation.

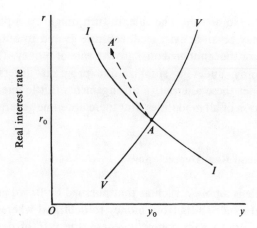

Figure 6.3
Debt deficit finance and real depreciation

Moreover the balance of payments is likely to improve since domestic credit growth is reduced through debt finance while inflation remains high.

These points are worth formulating by drawing on the standard monetary approach. From the Central Bank's balance sheet, reserves plus domestic credit equal high-powered money, $R + K = H$. Let the demand for high-powered money be proportional to prices and depend with unit elasticity on real income. Then the following relation is readily derived:[3]

$$\frac{\dot{R}}{H} \cong \left(\dot{p} - \frac{\dot{K}}{K}\right) + \frac{\dot{y}}{y}. \tag{6}$$

The equation makes the point that when credit growth is reduced below the prevailing rate of inflation (and debt growth is raised above), there is an immediate improvement in the balance of payments.

The improvement in the balance of payments is certain despite a reduction in real growth because initially inflation is very high—say 100 percent—so that a reduction in domestic credit growth from 100 to 60 percent, for example, entirely swamps the reduction in real growth which will only be a few percentage points.

Real Appreciation and Disinflation

Inflation behavior, as modeled in the previous section, implies that the exchange rate does play an important role. It is not the case that the rate of depreciation sets the rate of inflation ($\dot{p} = \dot{e} + \dot{p}^*$) as would be the case under strict PPP. Here it is the case that reduced depreciation relative to the prevailing rate of inflation leads to a falling (*not* lower) rate of inflation. What are the implications if a country were to announce and implement a policy of reduced depreciation?

In figure 6.4 we look at the case where a country announces a depreciation path, starting at time T_0, that slowly reduces the rate of depreciation to zero which is assumed to be the rate of world inflation. From an initial position of depreciation equaling inflation we how have some immediate reduction in the rate of depreciation and then a gradual, announced tapering off toward zero which is reached at time T_1.

We also show the path of inflation as the dashed schedule. Note that as depreciation is initially reduced, the real exchange rate is appreciating. This exerts a dampening effect, causing inflation to be falling. But the disinflation is very gradual with inflation staying above the rate of depreciation and hence with persistent real appreciation. The ongoing real appreciation cumulates into overvaluation and gradually reduces competitiveness causing output and employment to decline. This adds to the disinflation process leading to a more rapid falling off in inflation. Ultimately, at a point like T_2 inflation has fallen to zero and is declining further.

At time T_2, the *cumulative* real appreciation is measured by the area between the $\dot{p}$ and $\dot{e}$ schedules. This represents the loss in competitiveness that the disinflation process, led by reduced depreciation, has brought about. Of course at point T_2 output is below normal, and the current account is in deficit, the recession notwithstanding. But things are not yet at an end. It is clear to any speculator that the overvaluation cannot persist. Ultimately either inflation has to stay long enough below the rate of depreciation—perhaps aided by further outright deflationary policies—to eliminate the overvaluation or else there has to be a discrete depreciation. If the prospects for extended deflation are unreasonable, a speculative run in anticipation of the devaluation must be expected. Now the authorities are either forced into the devaluation, as was the case in Argentina, or they may try to defend the exchange rate by sharp increases in home real interest rates that favor the capital account and cyclically improve the current balance. Of course, such policies are not sustainable, and there is ultimately no way around a restoration of competitiveness.

The process of overvaluation through a reduced rate of depreciation is particularly interesting for a number of reasons. First, it is obviously a

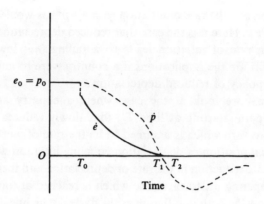

Figure 6.4
Depreciation and inflation

policy that has been followed in Chile, Argentina, and the U.K., for example. The policy is tempting because reduced depreciation immediately starts the disinflation process, even before the adverse effects on competitiveness start reinforcing disinflation through unemployment. In this sense the policy "works."

There is a second reason why the policy is appealing. In the initial phases the public will be of a divided mind: the loss in competitiveness gradually costs output and jobs, but at the same time the standard of living rises through the real appreciation. If the real appreciation moves rapidly and trade flows adjust only slowly, then it is quite conceivable that there is an early phase of euphoria—the middle class has never had it so good—falling inflation, rising real wages, and job losses only at the margin. This seems to be very much the experience of Argentina through 1980 where real appreciation raised the standard of living (in terms of importables) to unprecedented levels.

Of course the standard of living bought by the current overvaluation is only borrowed. The current account is in deficit and increasingly so and ultimately needs correction as does unemployment. The chances of doing so through a sustained deflation, as in figure 6.4, are small. But so are the chances of restoring equilibrium through a devaluation. The devaluation would certainly feed back into inflationary pressures, and the loss in real income attendant upon a devaluation would be politically hard to administer. But these facts are not appreciated when the policy is initiated; they become apparent only when it is much too late.

But even if a government chose to·sit through a period of deflation so as to regain competitiveness, there is still a major problem. The public, while often assured of the policy, will still entertain doubts. There will be some probability that a discrete depreciation could take place. The possibility of that depreciation will be reflected in home interest rates. Domestic nominal interest rates will be raised by the expectation of depreciation even though domestic inflation is reduced by the deflation policy. Thus home real interest rates are high, and quite possibly rising, while the deflation is underway. That in turn implies lower investment and productivity growth and hence a more stretched-out period to recover competitiveness.[4] The order of magnitude of the problem can be appreciated from a simple calculation: suppose at time T_2 the *real* exchange rate has appreciated by 30 percent. In case of devaluation the public therefore expects a 30 percent exchange rate adjustment, and the probability of a devaluation during the coming month is placed at 10 percent. There is accordingly an expected depreciation of 3 percent per month or 42.6 percent per year if we annualize the expected depreciation into a risk adjusted interest rate. The expectation of a devaluation of 30 percent with a 10 percent probability thus gives us a really enormous real interest rate and cannot fail to discourage demand.

Alternatives

The preceding discussion suggests that new-style stabilization programs lead to (transitorily) high real interest rates and/or overvalued exchange rates. To date there is no evidence that these programs actually succeed or that they succeed in some sense more satisfactorily than old-style fiscal discipline combined with a real depreciation.

But there is some room in between. It is now increasingly realized that inflation stabilization involves breaking the inertia arising from contracting, indexation, and expectations. The combination of wage controls *and* exchange rate targeting, along with price controls in the public sector, make it possible to synchronize the deceleration of wages and prices throughout the economy. There is nothing "wrong" with wage controls, certainly not once it is accepted that exchange rate fixing is a sensible policy.

Of course wage controls by themselves are socially unacceptable unless there is an assurance (to the extent that this is consistent with sustaining or restoring competitiveness) that prices will stay in line. Outright price control in the private sector is not a success story. It is therefore preferable that reliance be placed on excess profit taxes that discourage price increases or at least provide fiscal revenue to compensate low-income losers. At the same time of course the fixed exchange rate and the fixing of public sector prices provides in itself some discipline.

Disinflation is not complete without specifying the policy in respect to the real rate of interest. Here it is important to ensure that the real interest should not rise. Because stabilization does reduce the standard of living, it is essential that normal real interest rates should be allowed to prevail so as to encourage investment and productivity growth. Since the disinflation will raise real money demand, maintaining normal real interest rates will inevitably involve high nominal money growth.

Success at disinflation depends on a combination of two factors. Within the overall consistency of the program it is important that there be domestic slack and that there be an expectation of price stability beyond the period of the wage freeze. There are only two sources of such assurance. One is a fiscal reform that eliminates budget deficits as a source of inflation. The other is a longer-term exchange rate policy into which the government is literally locked by announcement *and* the taking of forward positions.

It is readily agreed that such a package really amounts to taking a lot of risks and involves foregoing many degrees of freedom. But—looking at Chile, Argentina, or Brazil—it is time to recognize that the alternative policies are vastly expensive and do not even succeed.

Notes

1. In the 1920s these views were certainly fashionable. An example is the Poincaré stabilization in 1926–1928 in France. Other examples are IMF programs.

2. Of course structuralist as used here differs from the Latin American notion that associates inflation with sectoral imbalances.

3. We neglect, without much consequence, the role of the interest rate in determining money demand. The exact form of equation (6) is:

$$\frac{\dot{R}}{H} = \dot{p} - \left(\frac{\dot{K}}{K}\right)\left(\frac{K}{H}\right) + \frac{\dot{y}}{y}.$$

We assume K/H is approximately unity as would be the case in a country that has only small reserves.

4. Some care must be taken to note that real interest rates differ across sectors. With the possibility of a depreciation real interest rates are perceived to be lower by import competing firms than by firms producing domestic output.

References

Baer, W., and I. Kerstenetzky (eds.). *Inflation and Growth in Latin America*. Yale University Press, 1964.

Blejer, M., and L. Leiderman. "A monetary approach to the crawling-peg system: theory and evidence". *Journal of Political Economy*, Vol. 89, No. 1 (February 1981).

Calvo, G. "Trying to stabilize: some reflections based on the case of Argentina.' Unpublished manuscript. Columbia University, March 1981.

Cardoso, E. "Inflaçao, emprego e balanca de pagamentos no Brasil." Unpublished manuscript Boston University, November 1981.

Diaz-Alejandro, C. "Southern Cone stabilization policies." In W. Cline (ed.), *Stabilization Policies in Development Countries*. Brookings Institution, 1981.

Dornbusch, R. *Open Economy Macroeconomics*. Basic Books, 1980, ch. 12.

Dornbusch, R. "Inflation, stabilization and capital mobility." NBER Working Paper No. 555 (September 1980).

The Economist (London). "French Financial Supplement," 31 July, 1926. Report of the Expert Committee.

Harberger, A. "The inflation syndrome." In J. Flanders and A. Razin, (eds.), *Inflation in Developing Countries*. Academic Press, 1981.

Khan, M., and M. Knight. "Stabilization programs in developing countries: a formal framework." *IMF Staff Papers*, No. 1 (1981).

Lizondo, J. "Precios a futuro de divisas bajo de cambio fijas com expectativas de devaluacion." Unpublished manuscript. ITAM, March 1980.

Mathieson, D. "Financial reform and capital flows in developing countries." *IMF Staff Papers*, No. 3 (1979).

Rodriguez, C. "El plan Argentino de establizacion del 20 de Diciembre," Unpublished manuscript. CEMA, July 1979.

Sargent, T. "Stopping moderate inflation: the methods of Ms. Thatcher and M. Poincaré." In R. Dornbusch and M. H. Simonsen (eds.), *Inflation, Debt, and Indexation*. MIT Press, 1984.

Taylor, L. *Macro Models for Developing Countries*. McGraw-Hill, 1980.

Williamson, K. (ed.). *The Crawling Peg: Experience and Prospects*. London: Macmillan, 1981.

III

Europe's Problems of Growth and Budget Deficits

Introduction to Part III

Europe's unemployment rate of the 1980s is twice the rate of the 1970s. The unemployment rate today stands at more than 10 percent, and forecasts show no tendency for a decline. Figure III.1 portrays this most dramatic problem of the European economies. Data for youth unemployment and for long duration unemployment reinforce the fact that Europe has lapsed into a devastatingly poor economic performance.

The policy discussion must isolate two key questions. One is whether unemployment is due to excessively high real wages and nonwage increases in labor costs or, alternatively, to lack of aggregate demand.[1] The other question is whether there is room for fiscal policy to reverse the stagnation. With that question comes the discussion of "unsustainable deficits."

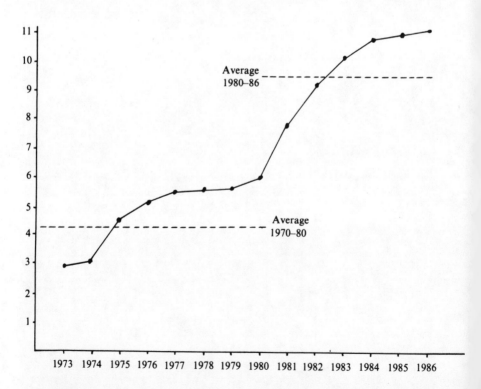

Figure III.1
The European unemployment rate. Data for 1985 and 1986 are forecasts. Source: OECD.

The Anatomy of Unemployment

There are broadly three interpretations of European unemployment. The first argues that unemployment is due to excessively high real wages. Real wages are said to have risen relative to productivity or failed to slow down in the face of adverse cost shocks. The economy is in a situation of "classical" or high real wage unemployment in the sense that at the going product wage forms are unwilling to expand.

The second source of unemployment is rigidities and nonwage labor costs, which includes tenure arrangements, severance pay, and regulation of hours, all of which work to impair a firm's flexibility in the optimal use of labor, thus raising the effective labor cost.

The third reason for unemployment is the lack of demand. Firms that cannot sell at the going prices will therefore also not hire. Figure III.2 is

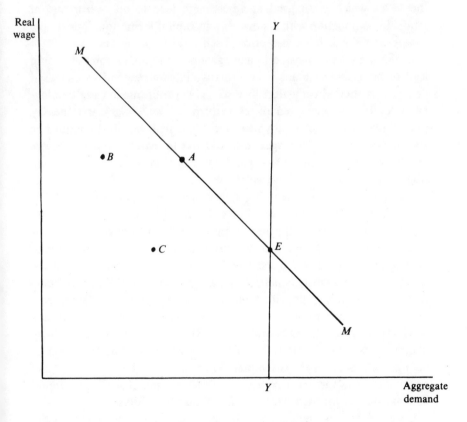

Figure III.2

the Mundell (1964) diagram, a forerunner of today's disequilibrium macroeconomics. The diagram shows along the schedule labelled MM combinations of product wages and real aggregate demand such that the output supplied by profit-maximizing, competitive firms equals the level of real spending. To meet a higher level of demand, given capital, materials prices, and technology, a lower product wage is required so as to stimulate employment and output. The vertical schedule denotes the full employment level of output.

Point E represents the classical full employment equilibrium that would be reached by a fully flexible product wage. Points on the MM schedule to the left of E correspond to classical unemployment and points to the left of MM, such as B or C, to Keynesian unemployment. The question then is whether Europe is at point A, B, or C. Those who favor the high real wage hypothesis will emphasize rising wage gaps in the 1970s which, with gradual adjustment, lead to an overpricing of labor. In conjunction with a slowdown in capital formation, jobs simply disappear because labor has priced itself out of the market.

In this view an expansion in aggregate demand, from point A, would lead to an excess demand since firms would not respond to increased demand as they already find themselves at profit-maximizing employment levels. The increased prices in turn cut real wages and thereby potentially encourage employment. But if the real wage is thought to be sticky, firms know that wages soon will rise to match the higher prices and hence do not even try to expand. Only in the case of sticky nominal wages would expansion have any benefit at all.

The alternative argument highlights increased nonwage costs. The sophisticated version runs as follows: In the 1960s firms were growing rapidly with real wages lagging on productivity. In the general atmosphere of prosperity and growth, firms could readily concede social benefits in the form of job security. But once growth turned flat in the 1970s, these job security benefits became a dramatic cost. Where before a firm would simply cope with temporary excess labor by delaying new hires by a few months, now in the absence of growth and with continued productivity gains, labor became like a Rembrandt—a major and very illiquid investment. Firms at the going real wage would find the nonwage contract terms more expensive and hence chose to hire less labor and respond less to short-term expansion. If they expanded at all, they would increase output through overtime rather than new hires.

Both reasons for higher unemployment go some way to explain the upward trend of the 1970s. It is not clear how to allocate the increase in unemployment between these two factors, but perhaps the real wage has been overdone and the nonwage labor costs has not received nearly enough attention.

But a casual look at figure III.1 will show that something special happened in the 1980s. There is a steep and sustained rise in the unemployment rate. It is not difficult to trace the increase to a sharp tightening of fiscal policy all over Europe. The example of Germany in table III.1 makes the point very clear. The actual budget deficit was in deficit throughout, but the discretionary component showed a contractionary influence year after year.

Table III.1
German fiscal policy (general government, percent of GDP)

	1981	1982	1983	1984	1985	1986
Actual budget	−3.8	−5.4	−2.8	−2.3	−1.5	−1.3
Discretionary change	+0.1	+1.4	+1.2	+0.4	+0.5	0

Source: OECD, *Economic Outlook*, June 1985.
Note: 1985 and 1986 are forecasts. A + sign designates a surplus and move toward contractioon of deficit or expansion of surplus.

The evidence for Germany, just as much as that for the United Kingdom, raises the question why governments should pursue a course of continuing fiscal tightening in the face of record high, and rising, unemployment.

The striking fact of course is to see European unemployment high allegedly for real wage reasons even at a time of record dollar over-valuation. Surely this would be the time where one would expect European employment to flourish. That of course raises the question of how Europe would cope with a major dollar depreciation. No doubt the wise course is to try to fight a dollar collapse by cuts in interest rates while at the same time offsetting the unemployment consequences through fiscal expansion.

Unsustainable Deficits

The major objection to fiscal expansion is that debts today are high and that deficits are becoming unsustainable. Table III.2 shows the extent of increase of public debt since 1970 and the burden of interest payments that accounts for a large part of budget deficits. The table brings out the advantage of negative real interest rates which are behind the erosion of British debt and which also explain that the U.S. debt as a fraction of GDP today is no higher than in 1970 despite a long string of deficits. Italy and Belgium stand out in the table with their high debt-income ratios as potential candidates for serious debt problems.

Table III.2
General government public debt and interest payments (percent of GDP)

	Net debt/GDP		Net interest
	1970	1980	1984
Unites States	28.4	27.2	2.5
Japan	−6.6	26.6	1.8
Germany	8.2	21.7	1.5
France	11.5	17.6	1.4
U.K.	75.3	49.8	3.9
Italy	39.2	81.8	8.2
Belgium	61.4	102.9	8.3
OECD	20.3	31.3	3.9

Source: OECD, *Economic Studies*, No. 3, Autumn 1984.

Although that argument is perhaps correct for Italy and Belgium, it definitely is not for the U.K. or Germany. Here is a model that clarifies some of the issues.

Suppose b is the ratio of debt to nominal income. Let the deficit in the budget (measured as a fraction of GDP) be

$$d = v - v' + ib, \tag{1}$$

where v' is the long-run noninterest surplus and v is a transitory deficit component that is being reduced over time at a rate determined by the coefficient of adjustment a as follows:

$$\dot{v} = -av. \tag{2}$$

The evolution of the debt-income ratio over time is given by the growth rate of nominal debt less the growth rate of nominal income:[2]

$$\frac{\dot{b}}{b} = \frac{v - v'}{b} + i - p - y, \tag{3}$$

where p and y are the given rate of inflation of the deflator and the growth rate of real output. Thus, using the definition of the real rate, $r = i - p$, the equation simplifies to

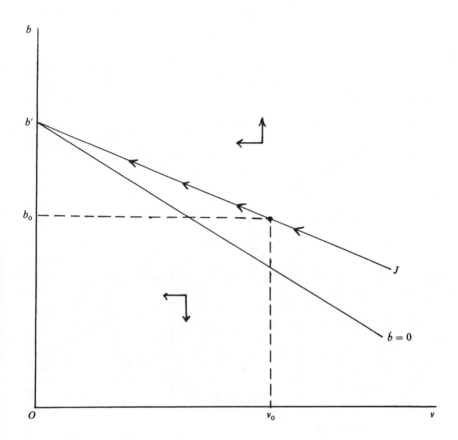

Figure III.3

$$\frac{\dot{b}}{b} = \frac{v-v'}{b} + r - y. \tag{3a}$$

Figure III.3 shows the phase diagram for the model of debt dynamics for given values of y, r, v', and the speed of correction of the transitory deficit, a. When the transitory deficit is positive, it is declining so that the arrows for v point toward the left anywhere in the positive quadrant since the $\dot{v} = 0$ schedule coincides with the vertical axis. The $\dot{b} = 0$ schedule is negatively sloped if, as we assume, the real interest rate exceeds the growth rate of output. The intercept is equal to the steady state level of the debt, b':

$$b' = \frac{v'}{r-y}. \tag{4}$$

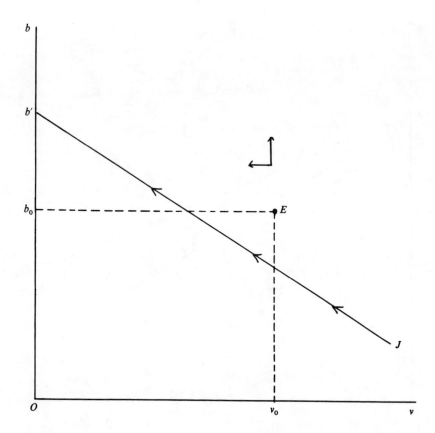

Figure III.4

Consider now the dynamics. For any initial debt b_0 there is a unique initial transitory deficit v_0 such that the system converges to a steady-state debt-income ratio as shown in figure III.3. If the transitory deficit is larger than v_0, given the real interest rate, output growth and the speed of consolidation the debt is unsustainable: there will be an evergrowing debt-income ratio.

The model can be used to discuss the problems posed by a public finance shock. Suppose, as in figure III.4, that an economy is suddenly faced with increased real interest rates and a reduced trend growth rate of output. At the same time suppose there was some initial deficit v_0. The economy at the time of the disturbance finds itself at point E which now becomes a point on a disequilibrium trajectory. Without correction there would now be an evergrowing debt-income ratio. There are a number of possible adjustments:

- The government can correct the transitory deficits at a more rapid rate. A faster speed of adjustment will rotate the solid path counterclockwise and thus accommodate stability.
- The initial deficit can be cut to a level horizontally to the left of E, on the new stable trajectory.
- The steady state noninterest surplus can be raised, thus reducing permanently the deficit and shifting upward the stable trajectory.
- The initial debt can be written down to satisfy stability.

The point is that when a government is faced with a public finance shock, something in the deficit and debt strategy must give. There is no reason whatsoever that today's deficit must be cut, but there must be a credible cut somewhere along the path. Moreover the adjustments must be larger the more persistent the adverse interest rate or growth disturbance. The difficulty is of course that cutting present deficits is politically difficult. Generating future noninterest surplusses is not only difficult but also costly in terms of resource allocation since they will have typically to come from increased taxation.

For most European countries there is simply no debt problem to speak of. Steady-state debt service ratios at normal real rates represent a small fraction of GDP. If anything governments should be alarmed about the real rates they set by inappropriate policy mixes, not about a fundamental problem of public debt. But for some countries debt-income ratios are high, and the noninterest surplusses required to service the debt absorb a large fraction of income and thus require high rates of taxation. The high rates of taxation in turn drive economic activity underground and assets abroad, thereby raising yet further the taxation falling on the smaller tax base left behind. Once taxation reaches these counterproductively high levels, it becomes worthwhile thinking about writing down the public debt. In any event the prudent asset holder thinks about the contingency long before governments start denying the possibility.

The possibility of writing down the debt was widely discussed in Great Britain, after both World War I and World War II. It has occurred of course in Germany already twice in this century and likewise in France.[3] The question is whether it should be done by a deliberate act of government in the form of a capital levy or through a surprise inflation. Interestingly there is immense public bias against the clean solution of a write-down, even if it means more financial instability, more taxation, and ultimately no assurance that repudiation will not some day occur.

In an editorial entitled "Throw Away the U.S. National Debt" Herbert Stein has called for a write-off of U.S. debt:[4]

The government should announce that, from this moment, it will not pay interest or principal on the debt now outstanding. At one stroke we would be rid of the existing debt and the interest hereafter payable on it. Elimination of that interest would reduce the deficit by $125 billion in 1985, or by about 65 percent.

Two common arguments stand in the way of a write-down. The first is that it breaches a solemn bond. This is nonsense, since an increase in the capital gains tax, the corporate income tax, the personal income tax, or a cut in food stamps just as much breaches implicit or explicit commitments, affects asset values, returns on investments and personal fortunes. Singling out the debt as a holy cow is a corner solution altogether inappropriate in public finance. The other objection is more serious: a government that writes down the debt might not be able to borrow again, or at least not at reasonable rates. That argument is not exactly correct as the German case so clearly shows. Indeed, the day after the default, however distressed the bond holders, it is clear that the defaulting government is the best debtor simply because it has no debt burden to service. And it will be so for a long while. Moreover it is very doubtful whether lenders keep track of individual countries histories or whether, more appropriately, they look at fundamentals to judge when debt becomes precarious.

With arguments so good in favor of a write-down, in the extreme cases, why do governments not in fact do it more freely? The answer is provided by the Committee on National Debt and Taxation (1927, pp. 295–296):

We do not necessarily suggest that a levy would necessarily arouse feelings of the most violent kind. We are convinced, however, that it would be strongly resented...exceptional circumstances are required to reconcile the owner of capital wealth to the levy idea. The opposition is no doubt founded partly on political suspicion and on prejudice: to impose a capital levy would be, as Mr. Keynes expressed it, to insult a set of very strong irrational feelings in men, and such grounds of opposition are exceedingly difficult to overcome. It is possible that time may bring a change of ideas.

For most of Europe, as for the U.S., there is no debt problem in sight. A policy of taking down real interest rates worldwide by a monetary expansion will immediately relieve budgetary strains everywhere. But beyond that Germany and the U.K., and of course Japan, must now go in the direction of fiscal expansion to ensure continued world recovery and some relief for the European mess. The timeliness is so apparent in early 1984 that even Paul Volcker has urged some move:[5]

...in some important countries where inflationary pressures have been success-fully contained, and where credible long-term anti-inflationary monetary policies are firmly in place, there may be scope for constructive stimulating action by measures of speeding tax reductions or otherwise.

The trick is to find the right combination of demand stimulus and supply side expansion, using fiscal expansion as a bargaining chip to secure a maximum of reduction in labor market obstacles to employment.

Notes

1. These questions have been addressed by the CEPS Macro Group in a number of pamphlets. See especially Layard et al. (1984) and Blanchard et al. (1985). The same question of course has been much discussed by international economic organizations and has received a very comprehensive treatment in Bruno and Sachs (1985).

2. Let $b = B/Y$ be the debt-income ratio. The rate of increase is given by

$$\frac{d(B/Y)}{dt} = \frac{\dot{B}}{Y} - \left(\frac{B}{Y}\right)(y+p) = \frac{(v-v')Y+iB}{Y} - b(p+y).$$

Dividing by b yields the growth rate:

$$\frac{\dot{b}}{b} = \frac{v-v'}{b} + i - p - y.$$

3. See the survey in Gottlieb (1952) and Rostas (1940).

4. See H. Stein (1984).

5. Quoted in the *New York Times*, February 28, 1985.

References

Blanchard, O. et al. 1985. *Employment and Growth in Europe: A Two-Handed Approach.* CEPS Papers No. 21. Center for European Policy Studies, Brussels.

Bruno, M., and J. Sachs. 1985. *Economics of Worldwide Stagflation.* Harvard University Press.

Gottlieb, M. 1952. "The Capital Levy After World War I." *Public Finance*, pp. 356–384.

Stein, H. 1984. "Throw Away the U.S. National Debt." *Wall Street Journal*, March 30.

Layard, R. et al. 1984. *Europe: The Case for Unsustainable Growth*, Ceps Paper, Center for European Policy Studies, Brussels.
Rostas, L. 1940. "The Capital Levey in Central Europe 1919–1924." *Review of Economic Studies*, pp. 20-32.

7   Public Debt and Fiscal Responsibility

The President denied the charge that he made a fetish of balancing the budget. He knew there were times when it should not be balanced. But he did not think those times were all the time. He believed others were making a fetish of not balancing the budget, and he was devoted to eradicating that fetish.

H. Stein, *The Fiscal Revolution in America*

Introduction

This chapter reviews the debate surrounding protracted public deficits in Europe. We note the positions that have recently been taken by public figures and institutions. We also recall our own position in previous papers. But our main concern in this chapter is not with current policy advice but with the broader question of the consequences of sustained deficits. It is widely accepted that fiscal deficits are bad; it is important to identify what the consequences actually might be and to compare them to alternatives.

We start by showing the implications of the dynamic budget constraint facing the government. Deficits cannot last forever and something sometime in the future must happen if the government is not to go bankrupt. We present illustrations of the sort of long-run noninterest budget surpluses called for by the debt stocks now in existence in Europe.

Reprinted by permission from CEPS Paper No. 22, coauthored with Olivier Blanchard and Willem Buiter, and published by the Center for European Policy Studies, Brussels.

We note in particular the problems that arise when real interest rates rise and growth declines and how this restrains the margin of maneuver of governments. We conclude that at least in *some* European countries the required noninterest surpluses have not yet been achieved. We also conclude that the moderate size of current deficits, as well as direct observation of financial markets, makes any scenario of debt repudiation highly unlikely.

We then turn to the relation of debt, deficits, and inflation. We first look at historical evidence. Often in the past, but by no means always, governments have disposed of their debt burden through inflation; the question arises whether the same is in store for Europe. We argue that inflation is no longer a way out for governments; this is because debt is now of much shorter maturity, making inflation-induced debt reduction much less effective. Inflation may, however, be an indirect way for governments to reduce their debt burden; this is because of the (largely unexplained) inverse relationship between inflation and long-term real interest rates.

This leaves crowding out in its various incarnations as the major issue associated with current deficits. We review the issues as well as recent theoretical developments and find no reason to doubt the old wisdom. Fiscal expansion increases aggregate demand and interest rates. Fiscal stabilization or fiscal contraction does the opposite.

We finally turn to the lessons that might be gained from the recent U.S. experience and point out its successes, the problems we think are genuine and those we think are not. This leads us to analyze fiscal stabilization from the point of view of public finance. We conclude that fiscal responsibility is not always synonymous with fiscal balance. Trying to achieve budget balance may sometimes make things worse, not better.

Table 7.1
Debts and deficits in Europe (percent of GDP)

	Debt EC-8	Budget deficit EC-8	Adjusted budget deficit[a] EC-8
1971–80	43.7	3.1	2.4
1984	56.7	5.4	2.0

Source: Commission of the EC, *European Economy*, November 1984, tables 6.5 and 6.7.
Note: Excludes Greece and Ireland.
a. Adjusted for cycle and inflation.

Debt, Deficits, and the Government Budget Constraint

Table 7.1 shows debt and deficits for the EC-8 (excluding Greece and
Ireland). The table brings out the fact of increased debts relative to
income. It also shows large adjusted and unadjusted budget deficits.
The evidence in table 7.1 may be disconcerting, but in itself does not give
any guidance whether the current situation is out of hand. It certainly
does not help link up with the question of sustainability. To address the
question of how debts and deficits are related to the issue of financial
stability, solvency, or *Staatsbankrott*, the appropriate framework is the
government budget constraint.

The government intertemporal budget constraint establishes the link
between the current stock of public debt and the future requirements of
debt service. The budget constraint states that the present value of debt
service must equal the value of debt outstanding. (See the appendix for
derivation.)

$$B_0 = \sum_0^\infty R_t \, V_t, \tag{1}$$

where B_0 is nominal debt outstanding at the beginning of period $t = 0$, R_t
is a nominal discount factor defined as $1/(1 + I_t)$ where I_t is the nominal
interest rate between today and time t, and V_t is the noninterest, nominal
budget surplus in period t.

There is another way of looking at the constraint, focusing instead on
the debt-income ratio and the noninterest surplus as a fraction of GNP.
We can rewrite (1) as follows:

$$b_0 = \sum_t^\infty \gamma^t \, v_t, \tag{2}$$

where b_0 is the debt to GNP ratio, v_t is the noninterest surplus as a
fraction of GNP, and $\gamma = (1 + y)/(1 + r)$ with y being the average—or
long-term—growth rate of output and r being the average—or long-
term—real interest rate.

To appreciate the implications of (2), assume that the noninterest
surplus ratio is indefinitely a constant fraction v' of income. Then,
assuming the real interest rate exceeds the growth rate of output, (2)
simplifies as follows:

$$v' = ab_0, \tag{3}$$

where $a = (r-y)/(1+r)$. Equation (3) shows that the required surplus ratio, v', stands in a relation to the debt ratio that is defined by real interest rates and the growth rate. The higher the interest rate relative to the growth rate, the higher the required noninterest surplus ratio. For example, a debt-income ratio of 0.5 combined with a real interest rate of 0.06 and a growth rate of 0.02 requires a noninterest surplus, as a fraction of GDP, equal to 1.9 percent. Note that (3) does not imply that the noninterest surplus must equal debt service. The noninterest surplus is a fraction of nominal interest payments, $a/(r+p)$. The higher the rate of inflation and the higher the growth rate of output, the smaller the required surplus ratio.

Equation (3) represents a simplification for the case of a constant noninterest surplus ratio. But the analytics are the same if the noninterest surplus is not constant. The interesting case of course is the one where the noninterest budget initially is in deficit. In that case future surpluses must be correspondingly higher, not only to average to zero but to do so including interest on the increasing debt in the initial phase.

Suppose, for example, that the noninterest budget contains the long-run surplus v'' and a transitory deficit component x such that

$$v_t = v'' - x_t, \tag{4}$$

where $x_t = \rho x_{t-1}$, $0 \leqslant \rho < 1$. With this process, using (3), the long-run required surplus becomes

$$v'' = ab_0 + \beta x_0, \qquad \beta = \frac{a}{1-\rho\gamma}. \tag{5}$$

Using the above example and assuming an initial value of $x_0 = 0.03$ with $\rho = 0.8$, the long-run surplus now must rise to 2.35 percent. If the value of ρ were as high as 0.92, the long-run required surplus ratio would increase to 2.9 percent, thus increasing by a full percentage point above the debt service requirement implied by the currently existing debt.

The example makes a critically important point: transitory deficits, if they are large and persistent, do have a significant long-run impact on the required noninterest surpluses that must ultimately be generated to sustain the government's solvency. By the same token, if the transitory deficit is small and is not persistent, the long-run impact is approximately negligible.

Debt difficulties and financial instability arise when the public no longer believes that there is a course of policies, economically and politically feasible and plausible, such that (2) or (5) are satisfied. There are two major kinds of disturbances that can lead to such fiscal instability.

The first is the emergence of a large, persistent deficit due to wars, populism, or the like. In such a case x assumes a large deficit value which, looking ahead, is not going to disappear for quite some time. Debt therefore is accumulating and government solvency is being put in question unless there is no doubt that future noninterest surpluses can be raised in a compensating fashion.

The second kind of disturbance is a change in economic structure which changes the relative magnitudes of growth and the real interest rate. Of particular relevance here is the case where the changes are negatively correlated: the real interest rate rises, and the trend output growth rate declines. This represents a dramatic impact on the budget and the required surplus, as the following calculation makes clear.

Suppose the real interest rate rises permanently from 4 to 6 percent and output growth falls from 2 to 1 percent. The long-run noninterest surplus ratio would have to rise from 1.0 to 2.4 percent, more than a full percentage point. But this negative correlation is, of course, not a special case but rather the rule. It certainly is a very important part of today's debt difficulties.

In the last six to eight years growth has been sharply reduced, and the real interest rate has sharply increased, thus putting an end to declining debt-income ratios and opening the prospect of fiscal trouble. The point remains valid even when it is accepted that the deterioration may not be permanent. It remains valid because the deterioration will in all likelihood be accompanied by noninterest deficits that persist for some time.

Table 7.2
European debt and budget conditions, 1984 (percent of GDP)

	Debt	Noninterest deficit	
		1984	1985[a]
EC-8[b]	56.7	1.2	0.6
France	33.3	1.0	1.2
FRG	41.0	−0.7	−1.5
Italy	92.7	4.5	2.8
United Kingdom	55.3	−0.2	−0.5
Belgium	113.1	2.0	0.5
Denmark	68.2	0.0	−2.1

Source: Commission of the EC, *European Economy*. November 1984, table 6.7.
a. Forecast.
b. Excludes Greece and Ireland.

Therefore the favorable impact of the fact that ultimately output and growth return to normal must be matched against the adverse effect of the initially larger deficit, leaving on balance the previous conclusion.[1]

With this framework in mind we can return to the data for Europe. Table 7.2 shows the debt/GDP ratios for individual countries as well as the noninterest budget deficit ratios for 1984 and those forecast for 1985. Noninterest deficits are still positive for most countries. Although the picture is markedly better for 1985, many countries and the EC-8 average are still shy of the 1 or 2 percent surpluses as a proportion of GNP that they need to achieve eventually.

Does this mean that government bankruptcy and debt repudiation are serious possibilities? Suppose they were. Financial markets would start taking into account the probability that the government is not going to make good on its debt. Public debt would most likely start carrying a premium, thus making it even harder for the government to meet its intertemporal constraint. There might also be capital flight as property owners attempted to protect themselves from special taxation or repudiation.

We do not observe anything like this, even in countries that have the most serious deficit and debt problems, such as Belgium and Italy. For example, there has been no increase in the (usually negative) premium required of public as opposed to private bonds in either of the two countries in the past few years. This strongly suggests that the meeting of intertemporal constraint is not at issue in Europe at the moment.

Debt, Deficits, and Inflation

It has long been argued, however, that even in the absence of explicit repudiation or special taxation, governments often meet their intertemporal budget constraint through inflation. Keynes[2] made the point in predicting devaluation-induced inflation as an inevitable consequence of the large French public debt:

The level of the Franc is going to be settled in the long run, not by speculation or the trade balance, or even the outcome of the Ruhr adventure, but by the proportion of his earned income which the French taxpayer will permit to be taken from him to pay the claims of the French rentier.

The discussion was taken much further by Colin Clark.[3] He argued that any time when taxation reaches 25 percent of income, there is pressure for inflation to reduce the real value of the public debt and thus to lighten the burden of debt service. Clark reviewed the fiscal history of various countries in the twentieth century and found the evidence to support his debt burden theory of inflation. Specifically he argues:[4]

But excessive taxation, levied for payment of interest on public debt, and capable therefore of being relieved (in real terms) by a general rise in prices, may cause a temporary transfer of allegiance from the deflationary to the inflationary side on the part of politicians, bankers, economists and others, sufficient to alter the balance of power. The parliamentarian, banker, or administrator, confronted with what he considers excessive taxation (or with a large deficit which holds out prospects of higher taxation in the near future) becomes, consciously or unconsciously, more reluctant to erect those barriers which in more normal times, he would erect against rising wages and prices....When the value of money has been reduced sufficiently to make the burden of the budget bearable, there will be a retransfer of allegiances: government authorities and bankers will resume their normal opposition to all proposals which they think would have an unduly expansionist effect....

The Keynes-Clark Model

The Keynes-Clark model of debt liquidation assumes that a deliberate inflation policy can succeed in reducing the real value of public debt. Moreover such a policy is claimed to be an empirical regularity and therefore would be expected by bond holders should the conditions under which debt liquidation takes place materialize. It is useful at this point to review the connection between inflation and debt reduction.

Suppose that governments could overnight and unanticipatedly increase the price level. Then, as long as debt was denominated in nominal terms, the real value of debt as well as that of interest payments on the debt would be reduced in proportion. This option, however, is clearly not available. Increasing the price level sharply and quickly is not easy; the most obvious way of accomplishing it, namely exchange rate depreciation, still takes a while to translate into higher prices. Furthermore, if devaluation appeared to be the only way out for the government, all that would be unanticipated would be the precise timing of the devaluation. Bond holders would be taking into account the possibility of the devaluation and requiring correspondingly higher rates on government nominal assets to compensate for the probability of depreciation-induced inflation. This is the "peso problem" addressed in the international finance literature.

Ruling out price level jumps, we may limit ourselves to the effects of changes in the rate of inflation. Let us keep for the moment a few unrealistic assumptions. Let us assume that the government can still increase the rate of inflation overnight and unexpectedly and that the real rate of interest is unaffected by the rate of inflation, so that nominal rates increase one for one with inflation. What then is the effect of this higher rate of inflation on debt and deficits? The answer depends on the maturity of the debt. If, for example, all bonds are consols, the effect on the market value of debt is given by

$$\frac{(dV/dp)}{(V/p)} \cong -\frac{p}{(r+p)},$$

where V is the market value of the debt, p is inflation, and r the real rate of interest. If the real rate is, say, 3 percent, an increase in the inflation rate from 5 to 6 percent decreases the market value of debt by approximately 12 percent. The effect, however, decreases as the maturity of the bonds shortens. If the average maturity of the debt is shorter, say five years, the same increase in inflation decreases the market value of the debt by only 5 percent.

How does the decrease in the market value of debt translate into lower deficits? Nominal interest payments on existing debt remain the same while the value of nominal debt decreases at the higher rate of inflation. Inflation corrected deficits decrease. However, as old debt matures and the government must issue new debt, it is forced to offer higher nominal

Figure 7.1
The real value of French 3 percent rentes (1913 = 100). Source: *International Abstract of Economic Statistics*, International Economic Conference, London, 1934.

interest payments. Once old debt has disappeared, the beneficial effects of inflation on the deficits also disappears. Again, the shorter the maturity of debt, the faster old debt disappears and the more short-lived the deficit reduction effect of inflation.

When we remove some of the unrealistic assumptions made earlier, the scope for inflation as a solution to the debt problem becomes even smaller. There is no such thing as an overnight unanticipated increase in the rate of inflation. Again, as the debt problem mounts, bond holders will start thinking about the possibility of inflation and require an inflation premium, to compensate both for higher expected inflation and the uncertainty about inflation. Even if the government chooses the inflation route, it takes some time for inflation to build up; during that time bond holders will also require an inflation premium. What matters in the end is the maturity of existing debt compared to the time between which bond holders start taking into account the possibility of inflation and inflation actually occurs.

The point concerning the maturity of debt is in many ways the most central. At the time Keynes wrote, debt was primarily longterm; today it is at the other end of the spectrum, very much concentrated on short maturities. Inflation unanticipated at the time of bond issue will not be reflected in the coupon rate of a long-term bond issue and hence serves as a levy on bond holders. That levy is the relief on the budget in the form of a reduced value of real debt service.

Figure 7.1 shows the real value of 3 percent Rentes Perpétuelles in France in the 1920s. The figure shows an index with a base of 1913 = 100. It is apparent that at the end of World War I the real value had already declined to 30 percent of the pre-war level. The stabilization at depreciated levels of the exchange rate reduced the real value by yet another 50 percent. While the experience is less drastic than during the German pre-WW II hyperinvlation, the reduction in the real value of public debt comes practically to the same thing.

Consider now a comparison of the maturity structure of public debt in the 1920s and today. We look at a comparison of France then and the United States today:

France: 1925	Percent	United States: 1983	Percent
Perpetuities	41.5	Maturity above 6 years	19.4
Other long-term debt	20.7	Maturity of 3 to 6 years	11.5
Short-term debt	19.1	Maturity of 1 to 3 years	23.7
Floating debt	18.7	Maturity of 1 year or less	45.5

The difference in maturity structure is further emphasized by noting that the category "short-term bonds" in France includes some maturities of up to ten years.[5] Figure 7.2 shows the average maturity reported for the U.S. debt. It is clear that there has been a fundamental change in the direction of shortening the U.S. debt and that implies less effectiveness (per unit of social aggravation) in solving fiscal problems by inflationary debt liquidation.

Without further information we assume that the same process occurred in Europe. Suppose then a country where the debt-income ratio is 0.5 and the real rate of interest is 0.05, so that 2.5 percent of GDP is devoted to debt service. If all the debt were represented by perpetuities, there is a reduction of debt service equal to 0.5 percent of GDP for every 20 percentage point cumulative (even anticipated) increase in the price level. A dramatic devaluation and its implied inflation consequences would clearly achieve the purpose. A process of anticipated inflation can achieve this only for long-term debt. In France the price level rose between 1921 and the stabilization in 1926 by approximately 90 percent. Clearly that rise in prices must have been the major part of the Poincaré stabilization. Similarly it is clear that with a maturity structure that is heavily biased towards short maturities, an inflation adventure is a very ineffective way of restoring budget balance.

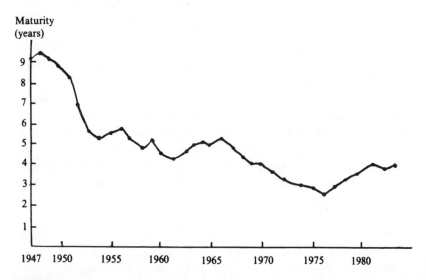

Figure 7.2
The average maturity of the U.S. public debt. Source: *Economic Report of the President*, various issues.

Figure 7.3
The U.K. ratio of debt service to GNP, 1811–1950s. Sources: P. Deane, *British Economic Growth*, Cambridge University Press, 1967, and B. Mitchell, *Second Abstract of British Historical Statistics*, Cambridge University Press, 1971.

Lest the reader conclude from the French and German examples that major debt build-ups always ended in inflation, it is worth reviewing the English 19th century experience. Figure 7.3 plots averages of the debt service ratio in the United Kingdom over the past 140 years and shows the enormous debt service build-up at the end of the Napoleonic wars. The reduction in debt over the following 60 years was not accomplished by inflation but by taxes. Quoting from the 1927 U.K. Committee on National Debt and Taxation:

... for some years after the Napoleonic wars, debt and taxation were far more burdensome to the nation as a whole than they are now. They came in the Victorian era through an unprecedented advance in industry and transport and in the development of the credit system, accompanied by rapid growth in population. The burden of debt was spread over a body of taxpayers growing in number and prosperity. It is true that the dominant changes in the price level were falls ... so that greater purchasing power had to be transferred to the debt holder ... nonetheless the necessary taxes were provided with increasing ease.

Inflation and Real Rates of Interest

The preceding discussion concludes that inflation is no longer an easy way out for governments to expropriate debt holders. Thus, *ceteris paribus*, debt accumulation does not portend future inflation. (The *ceteris paribus* clause is important here. Look at Israel and Brazil: both have issued indexed debt but nevertheless are experiencing very high inflation.) However, the argument has proceeded under the assumption that real interest rates are unaffected by inflation. This is not right.

Whether achieved through devaluation or through higher money growth, higher inflation is likely to be associated with lower real interest rates. Even if transitory, the implied reduction in inflation-adjusted deficits may be far from negligible. Two or three years of negative real rates would considerably alleviate the debt problem in many European countries.

How transitory is the effect of inflation on real interest rates, however? Theory strongly suggests that, as prices catch up with money, nominal rates rise by the rate of inflation. This is the wellknown Fisher proposition. Adjusting for taxes suggests that the effect of inflation on nominal rates may be even greater than one.

Empirical evidence is, however, quite at variance with the theoretical proposition. Figure 7.4 plots decadal averages of inflation and realized real rates in the United States for the last twelve decades. There is an obvious and strongly negative correlation between the two.[6] Nothing implies that this relation is a causal one running from inflation to real rates; other factors could be responsible for both, although it is hard to identify what they might be.

If the relation is stable, however, it implies that inflation may, through this channel, be a way out of the debt problem. Assuming, for example, that an extra point of inflation decreases the real interest rate by 50 basis points (if anything, this underestimates the trade-off implicit in figure 7.4), 10 percent more inflation would reduce the real rate to approximately zero. This link between inflation and debt service may well, in the end, be the most relevant.

The Minnesota School

Quite a different theory of the relation between debt and inflation arises from the work of the Minnesota School. This theory of the link between

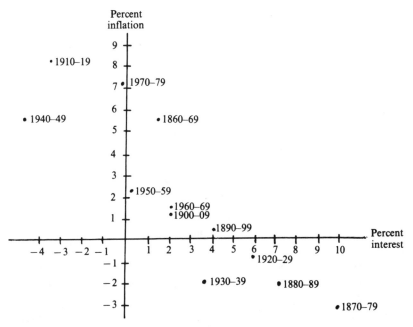

Figure 7.4
U.S. inflation and real interest rates, 1860–1979 (percent, decadal averages). Source: Data
is from L. H. Summers, "The Non-Adjustment of Nominal Interest Rates," *Essays in
Honor of A. Okun*, Brookings Institution, Washington D.C., 1983.

debt finance and inflation is at the center of the work by Sargent and
Wallace.[7] Their argument concentrates on the ultimately inflationary
effect of a shift from money to debt finance of a given deficit, but it can
be taken more generally to apply to deficit finance.[8]

Stripping the argument of some of its flair, it goes as follows. A
government finances a given deficit with debt and money, but once a
given point in time T is reached, the real per capita public debt can grow
no further. Monetary policy at that time must become endogenous to
finance the deficit. Let the real interest rate be fixed and exceed the
growth rate of population. The per capita noninterest deficit is fixed and
equal to v. The government budget constraint then implies that the rate
of money creation (and inflation) must be higher the higher the stock of
debt per capita. In the long run, the seignorage from money creation (the
growth of nominal money times the stock of real balances or um) must be
sufficient to pay not only the noninterest deficit but also debt service
adjusted for population growth:[9]

$$um = v + (r - n)b. \tag{6}$$

The sketch of the model already makes it clear that this is a far-fetched story about inflation. It is far-fetched not only in assuming a fixed real interest rate and a fixed date for the end of debt finance but also because seignorage is assumed to be the ultimate method of budget finance.[10] It is more plausible, given the high marginal political cost of collecting fiscal revenue through seignorage, that taxes, outlays, or indeed the terms of the debt might give.

Consider now the increased inflation required to service a 10 percent increase in the debt-income ratio. Suppose the real interest rate exceeds population growth by two percentage points, and let the ratio of the money base to income be 5 percent. Then, from (6), an extra ten percentage points in the debt ratio require an extra four percentage points in the long-run inflation rate to service the debt. The model is consistent, but it strikes us as implausible that policymakers prefer an extra 4 percent inflation to an extra 0.02 percent income tax rate.[11]

To summarize, the connection between debt, deficits, and inflation is a loose one. In the current European context, there is little reason to expect renewed inflation as a result of deficits. The only danger lies in the temptation that governments may have to reduce real interest rates through inflation; the temptation will indeed be stronger the higher the level of debt.

Crowding Out

This leaves crowding out as the main problem generated by sustained deficits. There are many new controversies surrounding crowding out. It is now sometimes argued, for example, that multipliers are negative, so that deficits are contractionary, surpluses expansionary. This section reviews the discussion surrounding the crowding-out issue.

Old-Fashioned Crowding Out

Crowding out of the 1960s variety uses the IS-LM apparatus to discuss the implications of debt-financed changes in spending or taxes. A fiscal expansion raises aggregate demand and output. But the increase in output also raises money demand. Given the money stock, the equilibrium interest rate will increase. This increase in interest rates in turn dampens the extent of income expansion associated with expansionary fiscal policy. In other words, the fiscal multiplier is smaller the larger the increase in money demand associated with higher income, the lower the interest response of money demand, and hence the larger the rise in interest rates and the effect of these higher interest rates on aggregate demand.

In this analysis crowding out takes place via the effect of higher interest rates on the interest-sensitive components of aggregate demand. Investment, residential as well as business fixed investment, would be especially sensitive to the increased interest rates. It is important to recognize, however, that this analysis applies to an income tax cut, not to investment subsidies. If the fiscal expansion takes the form of investment subsidies, then there can be no issue of crowding out. The incentive to investment more than offsets the effect of higher interest rates on the user cost of capital, and hence output expands, interest rates increase, and—in the new equilibrium—investment is higher.

Figure 7.5 outlines this point in the standard IS-LM diagram. The subsidy to investment leads to an upward shift of the IS curve, also shown in the right-hand panel in terms of the investment schedule. Given the real money stock, the LM schedule is not affected by the fiscal policy. Equilibrium income rises, the interest rate rises, and investment increases as the economy moves from A to A'.

The point is obvious, but it represents an important qualification in the crowding-out debate. If investment performance is an issue, it clearly makes the case for investment-based fiscal policies. If there is sufficient

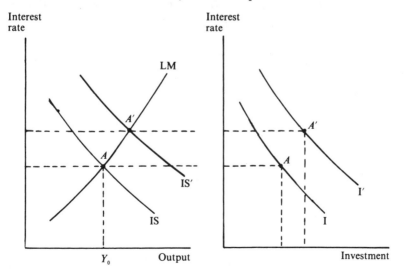

Figure 7.5
An investment subsidy

slack for output to be responsive to demand, then there need be no opposition to fiscal expansion on the grounds that there is a trade-off between employment and investment. Moreover the fiscal expansion can take place even without monetary accommodation.

Negative Multipliers

The previous analysis assumes that a fiscal expansion indeed translates into increased output and employment. But there is now an entire literature questioning whether such a stimulatory effect will prevail for any significant length of time under conditions of constant money. Here are two of the arguments:

Suppose money demand depends on expenditure, not GNP. Then a tax cut, by raising spending relative to output, leads to an increase in both aggregate demand and money demand. With a fixed money stock interest rates must rise, but output need not even increase. Mankiw and Summers[12] argue this point, making the assumption that consumption, not income, is the right transactions variable in money demand. They conclude that income tax cuts are likely to be contractionary. Whatever the merits of their argument, it is clear that accommodating monetary or fiscal policy concentrating on investment dispenses with the difficulty.

Feldstein[13] has argued that income tax cuts exert a net contractionary effect in a disaggregated model of the economy where prices are upwardly flexible. Because tax cuts lead to increased prices of consumption goods, they reduce the real money supply. Hence they force interest rates above the level of crowding out operating via the effect of higher income on money demand. Under certain conditions the net effect may be contractionary—supercrowding out.

As before, the problem lies in the constancy of money. Note further that contrary to what might be suggested in Feldstein's analysis, the effects he discusses have nothing to do with *budget deficits*. An increase in government spending has expansionary effects, (because it does not affect the LM curve) while a tax cut does not, even if both have the same impact on the budget. Moreover a balanced budget fiscal expansion would have super multipliers if it were financed by increased income taxes.

Either of these arguments primarily cautions us to pay attention to the precise determinants of money demand; they are really not serious objections to fiscal expansion. If there is assurance of economic slack that is responsive to aggregate demand, the only issue is the right monetary-fiscal mix or the right composition of tax cuts to address the double target of the composition and the level of output.

This first line of argument assumes that there is one interest rate common to all financial assets, or that there is a fixed structure of rates. Some recent work, following the early lead of Tobin,[14] has re-examined the degree of substitutability between assets (especially between stocks and bonds) to see how the large increases in government debt might affect the relation between asset returns. If government bonds and equities are imperfect substitutes, then an increase in the proportion of wealth held in the form of bonds is likely to lead to an increase in the required rate of return on bonds compared to stocks. Although this is bad news for the government because it further increases the cost of servicing the debt, this also tends to decrease the amount of crowding out. If firms are mostly equity financed, the increase in their cost of capital will be smaller than the increase in rates of return on bonds.

A recent study by Friedman[15] concludes that an increase in the share of government bonds will indeed increase their required rate of return over the riskless rate, but will have a small effect on the required rate of return on equities. However, more recent work by Frankel,[16] which looks at the magnitudes of the changes in premia associated with changes in relative proportions, reaches a strikingly different conclusion: namely that all proportion effects are extremely small and practically irrelevant. In effect, in his econometric study he finds that in the U.S. case the impact of increased public debt on the required premium on debt is negligibly small—a 1 percent increase in the public debt raises the required premium by less than 0.01 percent! Moreover the impact on the required rate of return on capital is negative, though insignificantly different from zero. The importance of his finding for the crowding-out issue is conveyed by his conclusion:[17]

Perhaps it would be best to describe the finding by arguing that evidently we are not far from the borderline case in which we can ignore any portfolio effects of debt financed government deficits on the expected return on capital.

Anticipations

In several contexts current anticipations of future budget deficits have been shown to have adverse effects on output and employment. One prominent channel is through the long-term real interest rate that immediately rises in response to future crowding out. In Blanchard and

Dornbusch[18] it is argued that future deficits, at full employment, bring about an increase in short-term real rates and hence a rise in the present, forward-looking, real long-term rate. Since aggregate demand has not yet risen, the rise in the long-term rate exerts a deflationary effect. But it is worth bearing in mind that there may be offsetting effects under conditions of less than full employment. It is possible, for example, that the stock market rises in response to the future increase in aggregate demand. The increased profitability of investment could actually promote an expansion in investment as firms build ahead of demand.[19]

A second channel through which anticipation works is the real exchange rate. In a small open economy a fiscal expansion at full employment will lead to an appreciation of the real exchange rate, at least while current account effects on wealth and portfolio composition have not occurred. The anticipation of future deficits would therefore lead to some immediate appreciation. The exchange rate appreciates ahead of aggregate demand and this causes a recession.[20]

In each case the future fiscal expansion exerts negative current effects on output and employment. But it is important to bear in mind that these effects are associated only with growing (full employment) deficits and that they are transitory, pending the actual implementation of the anticipated policy.

A final version of negative multipliers is associated with adverse confidence effects. The argument appears mainly in the financial press and runs typically as follows.[21] Certainly a fiscal expansion exerts direct effects on spending and income. But soon the expansion turns sour as anticipated inflation raises interest rates and causes the currency to depreciate. Business confidence is weakened as is the profitability of investment. The expansion turns into recession and inflation. We are only mildly uncertain as to what to make of this argument.

Full Employment Capital Accumulation

A last strand of literature considers the effects of debt-financed deficits in the full employment growth setting.[22] In this literature increased absorption by the government, not fully offset by a reduction in private spending, reduces the sustainable level of output and private spending.

At full employment increased public sector deficits absorb private savings, and public debt—by increasing perceived wealth—decreases private savings. Private fixed capital formation is crowded out on both counts. The capital/labor ratio will decline. This is the standard result of most neoclassical money-capital-bonds growth models. We see no reason to doubt that it holds in the long run.

Lessons from the U.S. Experience

The United States has enjoyed a strong expansion as a consequence of massive, broad-based fiscal expansion. The combination of tight money and expansionary fiscal policy has allowed a recovery without significant increases in inflation. The distribution of tax cuts between households and firms ensured that investment as well as consumption shared in the expansion. Crowding out on the investment side was decidedly not an issue. Despite large and continuing deficits, there is no suggestion of capital levies, asset taxation, repudiation, or inflationary debt liquidation. These issues are simply not in sight.[23]

Everything considered, there are still two serious issues raised by the U.S. experience. The first is that crowding out has been taking place on the external side. The trade balance as a fraction of GNP has shifted from a small surplus to a nearly 3 percent deficit. To some extent this represents a cyclical deterioration due to the relatively faster U.S. growth. But primarily it must be attributed in the deterioration in external competitiveness associated with the dollar appreciation.

The dollar appreciation has had the benefit of containing the cyclical rebound of inflation. It has strongly contained cost pressures for firms via depressed real prices of commodities and via gains in real wages rather than product wages. The dollar appreciation has been an essential part of the low-inflation/strong-recovery success. The question now is how to manage the unhooking of the dollar without experiencing a deterioration of macroeconomic performance of the kind seen in 1978.

The second difficulty and puzzle for the U.S. economy resides in interest rates. U.S. rates are unusually high by the standards of the 1970s, though of course not in a broader historical perspective (see figure 7.3). So far the high real interest rates have not impaired investment because there have been offsetting tax advantages that maintained the user cost of capital, at least in the business equipment sector. But the high rates have had adverse effects on construction, where interest rates matter more and tax advantages have not been compensatingly increased (see figure 7.6).

The interest rate puzzle is whether these high rates are to be attributed to the fact of deficit finance and accumulating public debt, or whether other plausible explanations can be offered. One view is that the increase

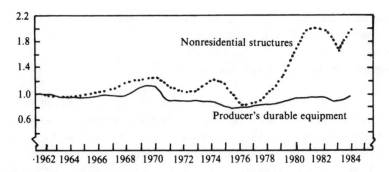

Figure 7.6
User costs of capital in the United States, 1962–84 (index: 1962 = 1). Source: Congressional Budget Office.

in interest rates is almost entirely due to relatively tight money. The strong expansion in demand and income has pushed up money demand relative to a non-accommodating path of the money supply, thus leading to an increase in interest rates. In this view, exactly the same rise in rates would have occurred if the growth had been the result of an export boom. It would also have occurred with a massive balanced budget fiscal expansion.

A second view is that the rise in rates reflects—in addition to tight money, or even predominantly—an increase in the profitability of investment. The sources of the gain in profitability may be diffuse, but the strong performance of investment, even making cyclical adjustments, would certainly be supportive of the argument. These two views of interest rate determinants are largely complementary.[24]

Each of the interest rate interpretations is plausible. By contrast we do not believe that any evidence has been offered that deficit finance *per se*, as opposed to strong growth and tight money, has had any effect on interest rates. With these conclusions in mind, what recommendations emerge from the United States experience?

First, there is absolutely no doubt that fiscal expansion with tight money promotes strong, durable expansion in demand, output, and employment. Second, if the policy looks after investment, there is no reason to be concerned with crowding out. Third, in the midst of stagnation, promotion of investment is animated above all by strong demand. That means fiscal austerity and bootstrap recovery is a very unlikely pattern. By contrast, the drastic U.S. fiscal push leaves no doubt that it works, and thus generates significantly stronger confidence in demand and hence expansion in employment and capacity.

However, the U.S. expansion also leaves a further concern. The high real interest rates are largely offset by tax deductions or investment subsidies and to that extent the impact on capital formation can be discounted. But the same cannot be said for the effect of the dollar on the composition of production and on inflation. In the same way that the United States has borrowed good inflation performance from Europe, Europe has borrowed growth from the United States.

When to Balance the Budget

The European policy, especially in the Federal Republic of Germany, has been to attach great importance to the debt and deficit issue. Fiscal policy has taken a severely restrictive drift in an attempt to turn deficits around, even at a time of record high and even mounting unemployment. The other European countries have followed the German example in varying degrees. But the case can be made that inappropriate haste in redressing deficits in fact worsens the fiscal position. The optimal policy is to rely on a prosperous economy to generate the tax revenues to finance debt service; the risk is that overtaxation shrinks the tax base on a course of ever increasing fiscal difficulties.

The case for a fiscal expansion as a debt stabilization tool in a depressed economy can be argued as a simple application of optimal debt stabilization policy when fiscal initiatives today have an important effect on income and the income tax base in the future. A government paying attention to intertemporal solvency will still have to plan when to accumulate debt and when to retire debt. The higher the debt, the more conservative the fiscal policy and the more directed it should be towards raising taxes. But that direction is modified by the state of the economy and the tax base.

Increasing taxation reduces income and therefore deteriorates tax collection over time. By contrast, tax cuts encourage growth in the tax base and reduce future costs of tax collection. Table 7.3 shows alternative states of the level of taxes and of the level of output relative to potential. The body of the table shows the optimal policy responses.

The point that emerges from this classification is that countries where output is depressed and taxes are high should first invest in recovery before using the higher level of activity to achieve more easily a stabilization of debt. With a rising or a falling tax base, of two strategies of balancing the budget only the former strategy may be stable.

In Europe the very attempt to balance budgets has cut into employment; moreover tax collection shows in the end little fiscal advantage and an ongoing deterioration in economic performance. In this respect

Table 7.3
Optimal debt stabilization policy, with high initial debt

	Output relative to potential	
	High	Low
Tax rate high	Raise taxes	Lower taxes (Germany)
Tax rate low	Raise taxes	Raise taxes?

the U.S. experience has been radically different and better. Of course, it might be argued that over the past two years the U.S. debt-income ratio increased by 8 percentage points, whereas in Germany it only increased by 2.7 percent. But does that really constitute evidence to the effect that five years out the U.S. experiment will not prove to have been the best policy for that country to have undertaken?

Appendix: The Government Budget Constraint

The dynamic budget constraint links debt accumulation to the level of debt, interest rates, and the noninterest budget surplus:

$$B_{t+1} = (B_t - V_t)(1 + i_t), \tag{7}$$

where B_t is nominal debt at the beginning of period t, i_t is the nominal interest rate from t to $t+1$, and S_t is the nominal primary surplus.

We can rewrite this as

$$B_t = V_t + \left(\frac{1}{1+i_t}\right) B_{t+1}. \tag{8}$$

Starting from the time zero and solving recursively forward in time gives:

$$B_0 = S_0 + \frac{1}{1+i_0} V_1 \cdots \frac{1}{(1+i_0)\dots(1+i_{t-1})} V_t \tag{9}$$

$$+ \frac{1}{(1+i_0)\dots(1+i_t)} B_{t+1}.$$

The intertemporal budget constraint is then obtained by using a transversality condition. This condition is that nominal debt does not grow faster than the nominal interest rate forever. Equivalently it says that at least some of the debt service must be earned through noninterest surpluses rather than entirely borrowed. So

$$\lim_{t \to \infty}[1+i_0]\ldots[1+i_t]^{-1}\,B_{t+1}=0. \tag{10}$$

Note that this does not imply that debt is ever repaid or even remains constant. Using (10) in (9) and defining $R_t=[1+i_0]\ldots[1+i_t]$ gives equation (1) in the text:

$$B_0=\sum_0^\infty R_t\,V_t. \tag{11}$$

To get equation (2) in the text, we start from

$$Y_{t+1}=(1+y_t)\,(1+p_t)\,Y_t,$$

where Y_t is nominal GNP at t, y_t is the growth rate of output, and p_t is inflation. Dividing both sides of (8) by Y_t gives

$$b_t=v_t+\left[\frac{(1+y_t)\,(1+p_t)}{1+i_t}\right]b_{t+1},$$

where is b is the debt to GNP ratio, and v_t the surplus to GNP ratio. Going through the same steps as before gives

$$b_0=\sum \gamma_t'\,v_t$$

where

$$\gamma_t'\equiv\left[\frac{(1+y_0)\,(1+p_0)}{(1+i_0)}\ldots\frac{(1+y_{t-1})\,(1+p_{t-1})}{(1+i_{t-1})}\right].$$

This gives equation (2) in the text. If v is constant, then

$$b_0=[\sum \gamma']v=\frac{1}{1-\gamma}v.$$

Thus v must be equal to

$$(1-\gamma)b_0=\frac{r-y}{1+r}b_0.$$

We present next the derivation of equation (6) in the text. From the government budget constraint we know that money plus debt creation, in real per capita terms, equals the noninterest deficit plus debt service:

$$\frac{\dot M}{NP}+\frac{\dot B}{NP}=v+ib, \tag{12}$$

$$\frac{\dot B}{NP}=(n+p)b, \tag{13}$$

where N and n are the population and its growth rate and where (13) is the condition for constant per capita real debt. Using (13) in (12) yields the growth rate of money, u, as an increasing function of the stock of debt implicitly defined by the equation:

$$um = v + (r-n)b. \tag{14}$$

It follows that any policy leading to increased debt accumulation must ultimately lead to more inflation, assuming of course that money demand is less than unit elastic with respect to the interest rate. The argument is stated in terms of the debt to population ratio. It could readily be cast in terms of the debt to income ratio.

Notes

1. Needless to say, the remarks applying to domestic debt difficulties apply in exactly the same manner to external debts and provide an interpretation of the recent debt crisis. There, of course, growth refers to the growth rate of real export revenue.

2. J. M. Keynes, *A Tract on Monetary Reform*, Macmillan, 1924, p. 105.

3. Colin Clark, "Public Finance and Changes in the Value of Money," *Economic Journal*, December 1945.

4. Ibid., pp. 272–373.

5. See E. Dulles, *The French Franc 1914-28*, Macmillan, 1929, p. 498, and Congressional Budget Office, *The Economic and Budget Outlook: An Update*, August 1984.

6. The evidence is reviewed in L. H. Summers, "The Non-Adjustment of Nominal Interest Rates," *Essays in Honor of A. Okun*, Brookings Institution, Washington D.C., 1983.

7. T. Sargent and N. Wallace, "Some Unpleasant Monetarist Arithmetic," Federal Reserve Bank of St. Louis, *Quarterly Review*, Fall 1981.

8. See, too, P. Miller, "Budget Deficit Mythology" and "Higher Deficit Policies Lead to Higher Inflation," Federal Reserve Bank of Minneapolis, *Quarterly Review*, Fall and Winter 1983; M. Darby "Some Pleasant Monetarist Arithmetic," Federal Reserve Bank of Minneapolis, Spring 1984; and B. McCallum, "Are Bond-financed Deficits Inflationary?" *Journal of Political Economy*, February 1984.

9. The derivation is given in the appendix.

10. Note that if interest rates rise with the level of debt, the ultimate inflation would be even higher.

11. We assume a flat income tax applicable to all of GNP. If only half of GNP were taxable, the increase in the income tax rate would still be less than one half percentage point.

12. G. Mankiw and L. Summers, "Are Tax Cuts Really Expansionary?" NBER Working Paper No. 1443, National Bureau of Economic Research, Cambridge, Mass., 1984.

13. M. Feldstein, "Can an Increased Budget Deficit be Contractionary?" NBER Working Paper No. 1433, 1984.

14. J. Tobin, "Money, Capital and Other Stores of Value," *American Economic Review*, May 1961.

15. B. Friedman, "The Substitutability of Debt and Equity Securities," NBER Working Paper No. 1130, 1983.

16. J. Frankel, "A Test of Portfolio Crowding Out and Related Issues in Finance," NBER Working Paper No. 1205, 1983.

17. Ibid., p. 22.

18. See O. Blanchard and R. Dornbusch, *US Deficits, the Dollar, and Europe*, CEPS Papers No. 6, Centre for European Policy Studies, Brussels, 1984.

19. This argument is developed in O. Blanchard, "Output, the Stock Market and Interest Rates," *American Economic Review*, 1981, pp. 123-143.

20. See O. Blanchard and R. Dornbusch, 1984, op. cit; R. Dornbusch, "The Experience with Flexible Exchange Rates: Comment," *Brookings Papers on Economic Activity*, I, Brookings Institution, 1983; and A. Burgstaller, "Contractionary Effects on an Anticipated Fiscal Stimulus in the Flexible Exchange Rate Economy," unpublished manuscript, Columbia University, 1983.

21. See, too, the intervention by Sir A. A. Walters at the Conference on Deficits and the World Economy, The World Bank, Washington D.C. 1 October, 1984, to be published shortly.

22. See E. Burmeister and E. Phelps, "Money, Public Debt, Inflation and Real Interest," *Journal of Money, Credit and Banking*, May 1971; D. Foley and M. Sidrauski, *Monetary and Fiscal Policy in a Growing Economy*, Macmillan, 1971; R. Dornbusch, "Inflation, Capital and Deficit Finance," *Journal of Money, Credit and Banking*, February 1976; W. Buiter and J. Tobin, "Debt Neutrality: A Brief Review of Doctrine and Evidence," in G. Furstenberg (ed.), *Social Security Versus Private Saving*, Ballinger, 1979; J. Tobin and W. Buiter, "Fiscal and Monetary Policies, Capital Formation and Economic Activity," in G. Furstenberg (ed.), *The Government and Capital Formation*, Ballinger, 1982; and J. Tobin, *Asset Accumulation and Economic Activity*, Blackwell, 1980.

23. See, however, the editorial by H. Stein, "Throw Away the U.S. National Debt," *The Wall Street Journal*, 30 March, 1984.

24. An additional hypothesis, specifically relevant for long-term rates, considers the implications of uncertainty about the future course of inflation. We observe high long-term rates but we are not certain whether they reflect the safe real rate.

Conversely, an asset with a real return that is high when consumption is low will be held even at a discount relative to the safe rate.

An increase in long-term interest rates in this model could be explained by a shift toward scenarios where real bond returns and consumption move together: sharply increased inflation combined with a recession. Such a scenario could emerge from supply shocks, specifically from a collapse of the dollar.

8
Sound Currency and Full Employment

"The British Experiment" is the unfortunate title the Chancellor of the Exchequer, Mr. Lawson, chose for his Mais Lecture last June. The title reflects the detachment with which policymakers in Great Britain have fought to transform British society and to stop inflation. There is no question that the Thatcher government has changed the country. The most striking achievements are the reduction of inflation to surprisingly low levels (by the standards of the 1970s) and, to a lesser extent, the consolidation of public finance. These two strategic victories return the country to the position of the early 1970s, undoing the extreme instability of the past decade. But they have not been achieved without costs: unemployment conditions today resemble those of the 1930s. Unemployment, far from being transitory, is becoming a way of life for an increasing number of people.

The increase in unemployment, and the absence of any policy commitment or conception to cope with the problem, must leave any observer in awe. What is there to assure society that the "experiment" will be called off in time if it becomes evident that the present course cannot achieve a reintegration of the unemployed into normal social conditions? The rules of the experiment, for maximum success, call for stone-walling the very idea of concession. But the policy stance of nonnegotiability of course also means that failure can be total. Gains, rather than being locked in by a judicious and timely shift in policy, may be sacrificed in an ideological quest for total victory. To convey a sense

Reprinted by permission from The Employment Institute. An extended version of a public lecture delivered on May 29, 1985, in King's College, London.

of the problem, here is an excerpt from Mr. Lawson's above cited speech:

Stable prices are a blessed condition, but one that we in this country have not experienced other than very fleetingly for 50 years. To achieve stable prices thus implies fighting and changing the culture and the psychology of two generations. That cannot be achieved overnight. But let there be no doubt that is our goal.

One cannot but note the difference between the approach pursued in the U.S. and conditions in Britain. I am not only thinking of Paul Volcker, the chairman of the Federal Reserve, who has combined a pragmatic policy approach with a basically uncompromising commitment to disinflation. In the White House too, where the free market philosophy runs at least as high as it does with policy makers in Great Britain, amid union-busting and deregulation there is a keen appreciation of the merits of prosperity. And, for the time being, prosperity is on the move.

The single most important question for Great Britain today is whether an argument can be made for a prosperity policy to build employment opportunities, without threatening the double achievement of disinflation and consolidation of public finance. If so, is this the time to move, or are there further important gains to be reaped from the current course of action?

I do not believe that many thoughtful observers would opt for expansion at any price. That philosophy is bankrupt today, whatever its merit and appeal may have been on past occasions. Today the public would want assurance that a shift in policy is in fact sustainable and does not involve throwing away the gains of the past few years. At the same time it must be clear that the deterioration in economic performance, as evidenced by high and rising unemployment, cannot go unchallenged. Of course it might be argued that it would be a big mistake to deviate from the set course of policy just as the rewards for steadfastness are about to be reaped. But credibility cuts two ways: the assertion that steadiness of policy will reap rewards in terms of falling unemployment and rising prosperity is still just an assertion. There is little favorable evidence of success so far. On the contrary, it looks as if Mrs. Thatcher's Financial Squeeze (MTFS for short) might turn out to be the big blunder of the 1980s, on a par with the mistakes of over-optimistic Keynesian policymakers in earlier episodes. Indeed, unless there is a really big surprise around the corner, that must be the verdict.

Much the same problem, though on a more moderate scale, is faced in all of Europe, but few countries have achieved the consolidation that the United Kingdom can point to. The closest comparison is Germany where fiscal stabilization and the fight against inflation has been pursued with less rhetoric but with as fierce a commitment and determination. Significantly in Germany there is now much public support for a program of fiscal expansion to promote more rapid recovery.

In light of the obstinacy of British policymakers in the face of a dramatic unemployment problem, it is worth remembering some comments of John Maynard Keynes under very similar conditions in 1929.[1]

Except for a brief recovery period in 1924 before the return to the gold standard, one-tenth or more of the working population of this country have been unemployed for eight years—a fact unprecedented in our history . . .

Was there ever a stronger case for a little boldness, for taking a risk if there be one? It may seem very wise to sit back and wag the head. But while we wait, the unused labour of the workless is not piling to our credit in a bank, ready to be used at some later date. It is running irrevocably to waste; it is irretrievably lost. Every puff of Mr. Baldwin's pipe costs us thousands of pounds . . .

It is not an accident that the Conservative Government have landed us in the mess where we find ourselves. It is the natural outcome of their philosophy:

"You must not press on with telephones or electricity, because it will raise the rate of interest."

"You must not hasten with roads or housing, because this will use up opportunities for employment which we may need in later years."

"You must not try to employ everyone, because this will cause inflation."

"You must not do anything, because this will only mean that you can't do something else."

"Safety first! The policy of maintaining a million unemployed has now been pursued for eight years without disaster. Why risk a change?"

Table 8.1 offers a perspective on key economic indicators in the past 15 years. The striking success at disinflation is quite obvious as is the reduction in the budget deficit. The counterpart is the huge increase in unemployment. Figure 8.1 shows inflation and unemployment to document the pattern since 1970. The figure reminds us that twice in the past decade the inflation rate was at or above 20 percent. The return to

Table 8.1
Main economic indicators

	1971–80	1980–84	1985 (forecast)
Unemployment Rate (percent)	4.1	9.8	13.0
Inflation rate (RPI, percent)	13.3	9.2	5.2
Budget Deficit (percent of GDP)	3.3	3.7	2.6
Public Debt (percent of GDP)	57.4	48.6	NA

Source: EC, *European Economy* November 1984 and OECD, *Main Economic Indicators*.

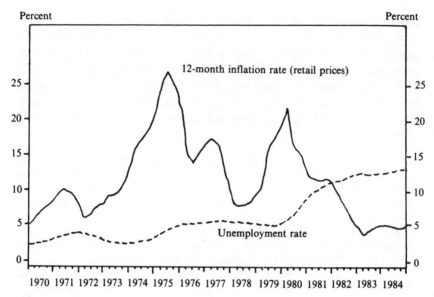

Figure 8.1
Inflation and unemployment. Source: *Dept. of Employment Gazette* and CSO database.

such instability is an important objection to any ill-considered policy. But the figure also documents the relentless rise in unemployment. The rate of unemployment today stands at over 13 percent, and nobody would predict that there is a chance, on the present course of policy, of a return to even 8 percent as far as the eye can see.

The budget and public debt figures in table 8.1 deserve special attention. In 1970 the public debt amounted to nearly 75 percent of GDP, whereas now it is around 50 percent and will decline on present policies. The budget deficit has been cut since 1979–80. That reduction, while aided by North Sea oil revenues, is striking since it occurred in the face of a poor macroeconomic performance which meant a reduction in the effective tax base. Furthermore the sharp cut in inflation did not help cure debt problems because it stopped the inflationary erosion of debt burdens. If adjustments are made for the effect of inflation on debt service and for the effect of economic slack on revenues and unemployment benefits, the budget figures on an adjusted basis now show a surplus. If the economy were using all available resources at reasonable capacity levels, the impact on budget revenues would be more than sufficient to balance the budget.

The impressive results in the area of fiscal consolidation are offset by extraordinarily poor performance in other areas. The youth unemployment rate is over 25 percent. The extremity of the unemployment problem shows up similarly in statistics on the fraction of the unemployed who have been out of work for more than 6 months or even a year. Already in 1983 more than half of the unemployed had been out of work for more than 6 months, and more than a third for as much as a year or more. Since then the position has of course deteriorated further.

Where Does the Unemployment Come From?

Since 1978–79 unemployment has risen by nearly eight percentage points, from just above 5 percent to over 13 percent. It is certainly an important question to know why unemployment in the late 1970s was nearly double the level of the early part of the decade, but that is not the immediate concern of current policy options. There is wide consensus that supply side factors account for a significant part of that increase. In the period to 1980 increased real labor costs because of labor taxes and unwarranted real wage increases reduced employment. Increases in structural rigidities and regional problems aggravated the reduction in labor demand. The existence of an improved level of unemployment benefits and perhaps the fostering of an "unemployment culture" may have worked to raise the fraction of the labor force that "chose" to be unemployed. These microeconomic factors are important, but they share the characteristic that they accumulate over time, sometimes even in an offsetting manner, so that their net impact over a short interval is in fact difficult to document.

Careful studies of unemployment since the 1950s have singled out and documented the role of microeconomic factors. I would not challenge the common belief that microeconomic factors account for a good part of increased unemployment. But the interesting finding is that whereas demand factors explained less than one-third of the change in unemployment in the period 1956-1979, in the period since 1979 they account for 70 percent.[2] In the last six years, macroeconomic factors have simply swamped all the microeconomic determinants of unemployment. Our focus here is primarily in the dramatic rise in unemployment in the 1980s which has occurred simulateneously in the United Kingdom and all over Europe. The important issue is to understand the massive rise in the past six years where (counting discouraged workers) perhaps as many as 15 out of every 100 people cannot get jobs. Here macroeconomic developments are the explanation.

The rise in unemployment in the United Kingdom over the past six years can readily be explained by the decline in employment which in turn can be traced to the combination of slow growth in real demand for goods and services and growth in productivity. Spending growth has been slow because monetary and fiscal policy, the exchange rate, and growth abroad combined into an unfavorable setting for spending on British goods. The growth in productivity, with both labor shedding and genuine improvements in production, has reinforced the impact of slow demand growth by making it possible to produce the same amount of output with less labor.

Econometric evidence leaves little question about the influence of four key factors on changes in the unemployment rate:

- Real appreciation of the exchange rate, or a loss of external competitiveness, shifts demand from U.K. goods to those produced abroad. Hence real appreciation leads to a rise in unemployment.

- Fiscal policy has an important effect on real demand, employment, and hence unemployment. Specifically, an increase in the cyclically adjusted budget surplus via increased tax rates or cuts in public spending will raise unemployment.

- Growth of the world economy is also a significant, though quantitatively small influence in determining employment. Stronger growth of the world economy expands foreign demand for U.K. goods and thus helps create employment.

- Monetary policy is one more critical determinant of employment and hence unemployment. It is difficult to assess the various channels through which monetary policy works. But there is little disagreement that tight money would find its expression in increased real interest rates and reduced real credit availability. Through both channels there would be a reduction in spending by households and firms and hence reduced production and employment.

The Role of Output

There are two strong facts that emerge from a study of unemployment behavior. First, growth of real spending and income must be sufficiently high for unemployment not to increase. Growth of productivity, among other factors, reduces labor demand over time at each level of production and hence raises unemployment. To overcome this adverse trend, output growth must be sufficiently strong to create a demand for labor that matches the growing labor supply. If growth falls below this threshold level, unemployment will be rising because the growth of labor demand is simply not sufficiently high.

The second fact is that, following a shock, unemployment does not tend to return automatically or spontaneously to a normal level, whatever that level might be. Following an increase in unemployment due to some disturbance, only growth above trend can bring down the unemployment rate; it will not decline spontaneously, at least not over a span of a few years.

These two facts have important implications for unemployment policy and in other countries are well appreciated as lesson number 1 of the political or election business cycle. The lesson is this: to reverse the impact of a recession that has raised the unemployment rate above its normal level, growth must *exceed trend* for some time. The extra growth is required to drain the unemployment pool by an extra dose of labor demand. Failure to have growth above trend simply means that the unemployment rate will stay higher permanently or at least for quite a few years. The reason is, in simple terms, that the market for labor is very different from the market for fresh fish. In the fish market price adjusts so that all fish finds its way into the frying pan. Not so in the labor market. Workers need not take any pay cut just to remain employed: the social arrangements today provide for unemployment relief that has as a cost reduced the flexibility of real wages and thus increased the risk of unemployment. Collective bargaining adds a distinction between those who have jobs and therefore have an interest in protecting their standards of living, and those who are unemployed and hence do not sit at the bargaining table.

If the trend growth of output were 2 percent and for some years the economy fell below that growth trend because of a recession, then it will never return to trend output unless there are a few years of *catching up*. Failing the extra growth, the economy will simply be growing at the trend rate, but at a lower output level than potential. The difference between potential output or trend output and actual output reflects unemployment and the unused capacity that has not been wiped out. Everything else aside, it is obvious that such a policy amounts to wasting scarce resources.

The point can be best appreciated in terms of figure 8.2. Here we show the level of actual real GDP (*including* oil) and the level of trend output or potential output. To calculate trend output it is assumed that the first quarter of 1977 reflects a normal level of employment and output and that the trend growth rate is a modest 2 percent per year. The discrepancy between trend output and actual output is the GDP gap—the loss of output due to macroeconomic policy. Corresponding to the output gap there is a gap for employment. If, in 1985, output were at the trend level, capacity utilization and profitability would be higher,

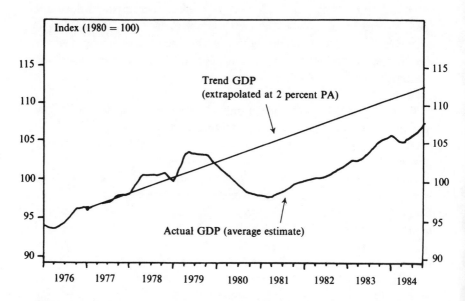

Figure 8.2
Actual and trend real GDP. Source: *Economic Trends* and CSO database.

employment higher, and unemployment lower. In fact in 1984 the output gap was 6 percent even on the very modest 2 percent trend growth assumption. If trend growth were reckoned at the more realistic rate, given the expansion of North Sea oil production, of 2.25 percent per year, the gap would be 8 percent.

Figure 8.2 shows at once the problem of never making up for the 1979–81 decline in output. The British economy since mid-1981 has grown at about 2.4 percent per year (including the effects of North Sea oil), slightly above the trend, but the loss in output accumulated before is still around today and, indeed, unemployment is even higher because the growth of 2.4 percent has not been enough even to keep unemployment constant at the high level to which it had been driven.

Explaining the decline in real activity in 1979–81 is easy: there was a massive correction in the cyclically adjusted budget in the direction of restraint, the real interest rate was pushed up strongly, external competitiveness deteriorated, and world growth slowed down sharply.[3] The combination caused a recession. Subsequent easing of monetary and fiscal policy in 1982–84 and the real depreciation of the currency restored growth, but not sufficiently to wipe out the accumulated unemployment. Growth since 1982 has not been much above the trend rate, leaving the gap unfilled. Hence the problem that we can look backward and say: yes, there has been reasonable growth, and yet we know that something is wrong because unemployment remains at record levels.

The basic point that the recession of 1980–81 was never made up by extra growth is so obvious that one would expect even people unacquainted with macroeconomics to have seized on that point. Yet Sir Alan Walters, in his assessment of the British economy, paints an altogether different picture:[4]

... Britain's monetarist policies have been associated with increasing GDP since the second quarter of 1981 at an average rate of about 2.5 percent a year. As a "small" locomotive, Britain led Europe and most of the OECD countries out of the severe recession of 1980–82 ... Since early 1983, employment has increased by 613,000 jobs. It is difficult to see how "inadequate aggregate demand" could be responsible for the continuing high level of unemployment.

Perhaps it helps to think of the question in terms of the Great Depression in the United States. From the trough of the depression in 1933 real output grew at the average rate of 10 percent per year over the next four years. Even so the unemployment rate was still 14.3 percent by 1937, down from 25 percent. Does anyone doubt that unemployment remaining as high as 14 percent reflected the fact that demand had still not recovered sufficiently from the depression level of 1933? In the same way, of course, Britain's employment today—Sir Alan Walters' boom notwithstanding—is lower than it was ten years ago. Figure 8.3, showing British employment, makes that point obvious.

An Expansionary Policy

The question today is whether policy can and should be used to bring about a spurt in growth that restores the economy to potential output and wipes out some of the record unemployment. The first issue is whether policy can do anything at all to reduce unemployment. The proposition that policy is basically ineffective is attracting a growing number of adherents, more because it is dramatic and conservative than because of significant evidence in its support. The second issue, assuming policy can be effective, is whether a growth spurt would risk sacrificing the success achieved in disinflation, in reduced inflationary expectations, and in fiscal consolidation. If there were a serious chance or even certainty of increased inflation, then there would be a trade-off in choosing between more growth and more inflation, at best an uneasy choice. But in fact the available evidence offers some confidence—not certainty, by

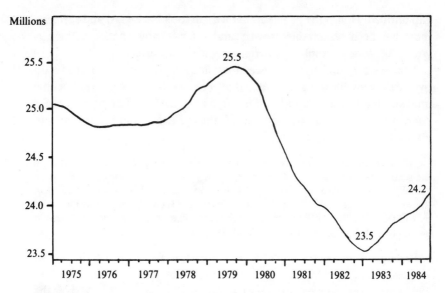

Figure 8.3
The employed labor force. Source: *Dept. of Employment Gazette* and CSA database.

any means—that more rapid growth for a while, and of the right kind, need not put at risk the improved inflation performance. The third question is whether policy-induced extra growth would threaten other important features of the stabilization effort, especially in regard to fiscal policy. We now review the case against policy action.

The Case for Doing Nothing

The case against an expansionary policy has at least six prongs:

- Increased monetary expansion, while perhaps effective in raising demand in the short run, will inevitably spill over into increased inflation, thus compromising the commitment to disinflation.

- Fiscal expansion is undesirable because it *either* leads to crowding out via increased interest rates or real appreciation, thus worsening the medium-term natural balance of the economy, *or* else to monetization, which implies inflation.

- Fiscal expansion is also undesirable because it undermines financial stability via excessive public sector indebtedness, which is unjustified in view of the fact that easy fiscal policy means, more often than not, wasteful public sector activities.

- Any Keynesian-style stimulus to aggregate demand would be unlikely to succeed since firms are employing all the labor they are willing to hire at the going real wage. Unemployment is caused by excessive labor costs, not by a lack of demand. Premature expansion would forestall the necessary cuts in real wages which high unemployment will bring about.

- The unemployment problem is simply misrepresented. Most of the unemployed are "professionally unemployed" in the sense that they are workshy. An increase in aggregate demand would therefore encounter supply limitations and hence be primarily inflationary.

- Policy is both ineffective and undesirable because it destabilizes the private sector's decision making and interferes with optimal resource allocation and the microeconomic quest for increased flexibility and adaptability.

Each of these points contains at least a germ of truth, and it is important to know just how substantive the interlinking objections to expansionary policy in fact are.

Inflation

Consider first the money-inflation issue. The argument that increased money growth always finds its way anywhere and independently of the state of economic activity into inflation is an extreme version of the basic monetarist tenet. It would be supported by evidence such as figure 8.4 (suggested in Sir Alan Walters' article referred to earlier) where current inflation seems in part to be explained by past growth in money. We show the rate of inflation of the retail price index and the growth rate of $M1$ (lagged two years). The linkages between current inflation and previous $M1$ growth are far from tight. In some inflation episodes, for example, 1979–82, the picture looks just right to confirm the tight monetarist link. By contrast, in 1983–84 or in 1973–75 the linkage is simply not there.

It would certainly be a mistake to reject a money-inflation linkage altogether. If money growth were permanently reduced and stubbornly kept low forever, inflation would ultimately abate; *ultimately* the oxygen would run out and inflation must come down. Little is known, however, about the speed with which this consolidation would occur and the price to be paid in the transition. The U.K. experiment (and that in Chile) give, however, some indication. But it is completely clear from all the evidence of industrialized countries that there is no simple, immediate

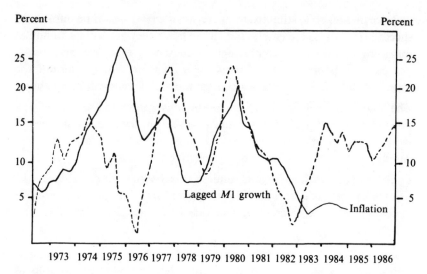

Figure 8.4
Money growth and inflation. (Note: Inflation is the four quarter rate of change of the RPI.
Money growth is the four quarter rate of growth of $M1$, two years lagged.) Source: DRI
database.

link between monetary policy, expectations, and actual inflation. To
understand the medium-term behavior of inflation, it is important to
flesh out the money-inflation relationship and determine the role of
commodity price disturbances (the oil shocks of 1973–74 and 1978–79),
taxes, money demand disturbances, aggregate demand, unemployment,
and the exchange rate in this context.

The fact that inflation is determined not only by money growth but
also by other factors makes the case for expansionary demand policy
more difficult. If inflation were uniquely determined by money growth,
we could simply freeze money growth and that would look after the
objective of price stability. With full success on that front assured, we
could use all other weapons to promote growth, profitability, and
employment. Unfortunately aggregate demand, unemployment, and the
exchange rate do play a role in the inflation process, and very much
complicate the policy problem. The complication comes in two ways:
steady, low money growth is no longer sufficient to bring rapid
disinflation, and the effect of such money growth may, for a while at
least, be primarily felt in reduced activity rather than slower inflation. At
the same time more rapid expansion in demand or a higher level of
demand (relative to potential output), even with a given money growth,
may lead to an upsurge in inflation.

The link between inflation and activity is often presented in terms of a threshold unemployment rate at which inflation remains stable; lower rates of unemployment lead to increasing inflation, and higher unemployment to reduced inflation. Econometric studies suggest that there is, indeed, an unemployment rate consistent with nonaccelerating inflation (NAIRU). Estimates suggest that the level may currently be as high as 10 percent in the United Kingdom (and rising with the actual rate of unemployment). At the present level of unemployment there should, accordingly, be a dampening influence on wage settlements and price inflation at work. In the past two years not much of such a deceleration has been felt, despite high and rising unemployment. One reason has certainly been the ongoing real depreciation of sterling over the last few years.

There is another way of thinking about the inflation-unemployment trade-off. Would those who argue against expansionary policies on the ground of inflation anxieties recommend that the government stand in the way of a boom that springs from a dramatic rise in exports or investment? One is hard-pressed to imagine that the Thatcher government would not stand by cheerfully to harvest all the credit for such "true" growth and not even think about the inflation issue until such time as it might actually emerge. There would surely be no effort to forestall a rise in growth by an immediate tightening of monetary and fiscal policy, lest rapid demand growth reignite inflation. The issue then is a prejudice about the kind of demand growth, spontaneous versus policy induced. There is no evidence that fiscally induced growth (other things equal) is more inflationary than the growth deriving from an autonomous export boom.

If one kind of demand is accepted and another rejected, then the reason is unlikely to be the inflationary impact of strong demand, but must be simply a bias against policy-induced expansion. We return to that question below. But there is a quite different line of argument against expansion, namely that a high level of unemployment, rather than being an unfortunate fact, is in fact a policy instrument deliberately sought and maintained to improve inflation performance. The unemployed are serving in the war on inflation, and they will serve for years to come until the disinflationary stance of financial policy permeates the economy sufficiently to allow lower rates of unemployment, consistent with zero inflation. Moreover, yet higher unemployment is needed to drive down inflation to zero and to maintain it there. This line of thinking brings up very forcefully the issue of trade-offs.

Whatever significance one attaches to the inflation target, there surely must be some level and persistence of unemployment at which unemployment becomes the priority, even if reduction of unemployment means no further cuts in inflation or an actual increase in inflation. The question of trade-offs might be avoided by suggesting that in fact there is no trade-off: only a transition to a noninflationary environment allows a resumption in growth because the very fact of inflation is inimical to enterprise, innovation, progress, prosperity, investment, financial stability, and employment. While that idea is, no doubt, in some people's heads, it is of course sheer nonsense at a rate of inflation of 5 or 6 percent. One would have to believe that any expansion takes the economy straight to double-digit inflation to take this view at all seriously. Yet another way of trying to avoid the dilemma is to believe that, indeed, there are trade-offs, but that the investment in disinflation would be entirely lost and would have to start all over again, unless the course were seen through all the way to zero inflation. But clearly at zero inflation exactly the same arguments would be brought: expansion threatens the great sacrifices made in securing price stability. For some people any year is simply the wrong time to think about unemployment.

Mainstream macroeconomists no longer believe that there are simple, sure ways of controlling inflation, other than to sacrifice all other objectives and singlemindedly use all instruments to counter shocks and disturbances to the inflation rate. The need for attention to monetary growth is widely accepted, though mainly in the way practiced by the Federal Reserve in the United States, with substantial discretion and occasional "money blips." Beyond that it is of course accepted that unemployment and the exchange rate are particularly important influences on inflation. A steep collapse of the exchange rate would unavoidably increase inflation. In the same way a reduction of unemployment would reduce the disinflationary pressure in the economy and, if carried too far, would certainly be inflationary.

The inflation problem, in this perspective, is best dealt with in a twofold way: on one hand, we should avoid overheating; on the other hand, we should use favorable opportunities (oil price declines, appreciation) to achieve some disinflation and hence reduced rates of wage inflation. But within these broad parameters there is a basic acceptance of the idea of trade-offs and the potential for policy to expand demand, in the face of very high unemployment, without the risk of a sharp escalation of inflation. One would certainly add that the policy mix employed to bring about expansion can be designed to minimize the inflation risk. The issue then is the right monetary-fiscal mix and the right kind of fiscal incentive which in conjunction with incomes policy promote growth. Of course incomes policy has a bad reputation, but it is perhaps not quite as bad as that of monetarism.

Difficulties with Fiscal Expansion

Basic objections to deficit finance as a stimulus to aggregate demand center, rightly, on the potentially hazardous effects of deficits. These side effects arise either because deficit finance may carry the seeds of financial instability because of excessive debt accumulation or because of the fact that debt finance distorts the allocation of resources between the present and the future, the government, and the private sector. These issues have drawn a great deal of attention in all industrialized countries and are now at the center of discussion in the United States, where it is strongly felt that the deficit finance strategy, while immensely successful in terms of growth, must be used with care.

The financial instability problem arises in the following manner. The accumulation of debt brings with it the prospect of increased future taxation to service what appears to be an evergrowing debt. As more and more debt accumulates, the high debt service requires levels of taxation that ultimately become intolerable because they affect the efficiency of the economy and private sector enterprise. This burden of taxation cannot be thrown off, assuming no growth miracle or the discovery of natural resources yet untapped, except by repudiation of the debt. As the discussion of the 1920s in Great Britain makes quite clear, repudiation or use of once for all "capital levies" on wealth does not command great popularity, mostly because they might become a habit.

One way out in some countries has been to have bursts of inflation. The process starts with an accommodating monetary policy which pushes down nominal interest rates in the face of inflation. With negative real interest rates the debt falls in real terms even in the face of a continuing deficit. Inflation turns out to be a way of servicing debt, but the economy adjusts. Bond holders realize their fate and debt turns to shorter maturities so that market rates can more readily adapt to the inflation risk. As financial markets adapt to the deficit strategy, more extreme bursts of inflation are required to wipe out public debt, and the very expectation of these policies causes capital markets to turn their attention away from the financing of productive capital to the far more important issue of predicting the course of deficits and inflation. Foreign

exchange crises ensue, and real interest rates soar and collapse alter-
nately; resources are devastatingly misallocated as the capital market
becomes the Casino Royale where the Chancellor of the Exehequer is the
croupier. In the end it is clear that avoiding the destructive taxation
required to service the debt, by recourse to a strategy of inflationary debt
liquidation, carries with it even more staggering costs. Fiscal consolidation, even taking into account the painful costs, becomes a more credible
and, in the long-run, more profitable strategy.

All this is a fair description of Argentina, but it has very little to do
with public finance in Great Britain *today*. This is the case because, in
good part, high inflation in the 1970s has already reduced the debt to
GDP ratio by quite a margin. Today the debt ratio is low by comparison
with earlier years and the real cyclically adjusted budget is in surplus.
Despite a decade of nominal budget deficits the debt to GDP ratio today
is nearly a third lower than it was in 1970.

While the fiscal picture does not justify any great concerns of financial
instability, there is a quite different aspect that does need mentioning.
Mr. J. de Larosiere, the managing director of the IMF, has made himself
a forceful spokesman for the position that a penchant for deficit finance
ultimately distorts the economic landscape and that a return to fiscal
orthodoxy is required on efficiency grounds. Here is what he has to say:[5]

For a variety of reasons the traditional stigma attached to fiscal deficits and
growing public debt gave way to a certain nonchalance on the part of policy
makers. Fiscal deficits no longer required justification, and they did not seem to
have undesirable political repercussions, even when they occurred during non-
recessionary periods . . . Traditional principles that had held that no deficit was
justified if associated with unproductive investment, current expenditure or
revenue, were insidiously abandoned in favour of fiscal activism that made full
employment and the expansion of welfare programs predominant objectives of
economic policy.

An active expression of these concerns is, in the U.K. case, the build-
up of government outlays. Whereas in 1960 they were a bare 32.4 percent
of GDP, by 1984 they had risen to nearly 45 percent. The counterpart of
this level of spending is taxation, present or future, and these high levels
of taxation in turn affect economic efficiency. Supply side economics
represents a revolt against this unstable trend of growing government
and deteriorating economic performance.

Much of this concern is perfectly valid; the problem is what to do
about it. The correct view is to consolidate the public sector over time,
weeding out inefficient programs and using every opportunity that

presents itself to retire debt. But such a course of consolidation cannot be pursued blindly, seeking budget improvement irrespective of the state of the economy. Such blindness might well worsen the fiscal picture even further as deteriorating economic performance, stagnation, lack of investment, and lack of jobs erode the revenue base and sharply increase the need for public programs. Even on a course of fiscal consolidation there must be room for deficits, even large deficits, required to keep the economy on a course of prosperity. As Herbert Giersch, the leading German supply-sider has argued, *increased* cyclical deficits today (of the right kind) are investments in prosperity fully in line with a conservative fiscal policy.[6]

If neither financial instability nor the objectives of fiscal consolidation stand in the way of a cyclically motivated expansion, what other objections might there be? The chief remaining concern is *crowding out*. Here the concern is that public sector deficits require financing. They absorb scarce resources and lead to competition in capital markets where government debt diverts saving from capital formation or net foreign lending. To the extent that deficits are not matched by increased domestic saving, they imply that investment or net exports must be crowded out. The crowding out emerges from competition for scarce saving, which drives up interest rates and draws in foreign capital, thereby appreciating the real exchange rate. A reduction in investment of course is highly undesirable since it reduces growth of activity and jobs. To the extent that net exports are reduced, this implies an immediate fall in activity for at least part of manufacturing.

Whatever the cyclical merits of increased deficits, the crowding out issue is a serious one to contend with. One answer to the crowding out problem is to recognize that with the expansion of output and employment there is a rise in incomes and hence a rise in both tax collection and saving. These will not increase sufficiently to close fully the budget and saving gap, but they will go some way. Furthermore the rise in interest rates induced by fiscal expansion does depend on monetary policy. In the extreme (an unwise choice) the impact on interest rates could be entirely neutralized by accommodating monetary policy. At the other end strict adherence to monetary targets would mean higher interest rates and exchange rate appreciation. There is room between these extremes to look for a policy mix that strikes a balance between the interests of efficiency and price stability. The example of the United States documents in a particularly forceful way that one can have an investment boom in the middle of an extreme fiscal expansion. One reason for this is that the very fact of a sustained expansion is a forceful incentive for investment that may well outweigh some increase in the cost of capital. Another is that, in the United States, investment incentives have helped to offset increased capital costs. The crowding-out argument, on the investment side, therefore is primarily an argument for the right kind of mix. Of course the U.S. example also shows that fiscal expansion draws in foreign saving as the current account deteriorates.

Policy Effectiveness

Whereas the previous objections to policy action focussed on negative side effects, perhaps the most basic challenge comes from an entirely different perspective: monetary and fiscal policy, it is argued, are useless because they will not affect the decisions that private agents make. Either these policies have no effect at all or they are effective because the inefficiency they involve makes everybody worse off. They cannot do anything for the better, and therefore the economy should, for best results, be left to look after itself.

There can be no question that this kind of thinking has significant intellectual support and cannot be dismissed as a crackpot idea. But the appeal to "rational expectations" must also not overshadow the fact that this kind of thinking is quite extreme. It is entirely correct when executed in the framework of highly stylized models, where economic agents are optimally informed and can pursue their optimal decisions without constraints of decentralized decision making, information costs, or lack of access to capital markets. But none of these ineffectiveness results has been demonstrated for anything more closely resembling the world we live in. It may be a puzzle why the unemployed do not succeed, via aggressive wage cuts, in placing themselves in jobs, but it is a fact. Once we accept the fact of wage-price stickiness, the edifice of rational expectations/market equilibrium collapses and the case for policy activism maintains most of its Keynesian vigor. It would be a silly mistake to believe that modern macroeconomics has learned nothing from the rational expectations/market equilibrium school. But it would be equally wrong to suppose that developments of the past ten years have vindicated the main tenets of this movement. If anything the past ten years in the United States confirm, in the most striking way, mainstream macroeconomics:

The main argument of the rational expectations/market equilibrium school of thought is that private agents set wages and prices optimally so as to achieve, at each point in time, the profit and utility maximizing levels of output, employment, consumption, and investment. Their information is as good as that of the government, and hence no role is left for the government except to distort the privately optimal choices by fiscal moves or monetary surprises. On the fiscal side, the predominant idea is that fiscal policy does not have any effect because the public that receives tax relief recognizes that they themselves (or their heirs) will have to pay for the present relief via increased future taxes. Hence they will not respond to reduced taxation by increased spending but rather will increase saving to set aside resources to pay the future taxes. Similarly, increased government spending cannot be expansionary because the implied future taxes tend to reduce private spending. If anything this effect is compounded since government provision of goods and services, in many cases, merely displaces the private provision, though perhaps not with equal efficiency. In this setting the government is viewed with hostility since anything government can do, the private sector can do better. The extremity of the argument reminds one of the great rift at an early postwar meeting of the libertarian Mont Pelerin Society: at issue was whether the British navy should rent or own the battleships.

The impartial observer must feel that all this cannot be very serious and certainly not the best that economics can offer as policy guidance. The sad fact is that it remains the height of academic fashion, even if the lack of empirical support, after 15 years of assertive research and advocacy, has begun to create a problem of credibility. It is worth noting, though, that Thomas Sargent, one of the leaders of the rational expectations/market equilibrium school expressed an early scepticism as to the applicability of these ideas to the case of Great Britain.[7]

... it is difficult to interpret Thatcher's policy action in terms of the kind of once-and-for-all, widely believed, uncontroversial, and irreversible regime change that rational expectations equilibrium theories assert can cure inflation at little or no cost. This not to render a negative judgement on Thatcher's goal or her methods, but only to indicate that the preconditions for the applicability of rational expectations "neutrality" or "policy irrelevance" theorems don't seem to exist in Margaret Thatcher's England. Where these conditions are not met, rational expectations equilibrium models imply that contractionary monetary and fiscal policy actions are likely to be costly in terms of real output and unemployment.

The foregoing discussion has offered some perspective on the difficulties surrounding an expansionary policy stance. Some of these are purely imaginary, others reflect a well-founded concern for inflation risks and the need to watch closely long-term fiscal balance and efficient resource allocation. With these concerns in mind, we now turn to the discussion of a reasonable program for prosperity.

What Kind of Expansion?

Once it is accepted that policy can and should do something about the unemployment problem, matters stop being easy. The choice of policy mix is a political decision involving trade-offs between efficiency and equity. But it also involves an economic problem of determining the relative impacts of the mix upon inflation, short-run employment, and medium-term growth effects. We will deal here primarily with these latter issues.

The choice of policy mix involves decisions on the following points:

- What is the right mix between monetary and fiscal policy? Should money be tight and fiscal policy expansionary, the reverse, or, implausibly, both easy money and an enlarged deficit?

- Should the program focus on stimulating aggregate demand, or should it center on expanding jobs from the supply side?

- If there is policy action on the demand side, should the objective be to maximize the employment impact of a given increase in the budget deficit, or are other criteria (including consumer/taxpayer sovereignty) at least on a par?

- If policies are undertaken on the supply side is the emphasis on inflation, on employment, or on capital formation?

Inflation and the Mix

The key feature of an expansionary policy mix must be to rule out a collapse of the exchange rate. It is well established, in every Banana Republic but now also in industrialized countries, that sharp exchange rate depreciation immediately and sizably adds to the inflation rate. A major depreciation of the exchange rate raises the cost of living because of increased prices of goods that enter foreign trade and because of increased prices of industrial materials that are traded internationally. These price increases directly represent a rise in the inflation rate. But they also spread wider in the economy as they find their way into wage settlements and into the prices of competing products. The exact timing and magnitude of the impact of exchange rate depreciation on inflation may be open to discussion; the fact itself is quite definetely not.[8] The British reduction in inflation owes much to the real appreciation in 1979–81, and the disinflation in the United States similarly would not have been as successful without the strong dollar.

What kind of policy can avoid an exchange rate collapse in the course of expansion? The answer is quite unambiguously a policy of relatively tight money and of sufficiently easy fiscal policy. *Monetary policy should be exchange rate oriented*, ensuring levels of interest rates sufficiently high to attract the capital flows required to finance the inevitable deterioration in the current account. It would definitely be a mistake to use monetary policy to the extent of seeking real appreciation (as the U.S. policies have turned out to do), since the real wage is already too high. The inflation rate is comfortably low, so the emphasis should simply be shifted from inflation to employment, with precaution taken to avoid the most likely risk of exchange rate depreciation.

Of course an easy fiscal policy/tight money mix involves difficulties in the policy framework of monetary targetting. If the fiscal expansion is successful, growth in output and hence money demand may mean increasing the money supply even if the interest rate is allowed to rise to counter exchange market problems. The other difficulty, and this is a more real one, is that increased interest rates would potentially worsen the expenditure mix away from investment toward consumption and government outlays. The details of fiscal policy have to take this risk into account by making provision for compensating investment incentives. Once again, the United States is a case in point: tight money and easy fiscal policy have not stood in the way of an investment boom precisely because the fiscal expansion involved a sizable incentive for investment. This is in sharp contrast to current British policy.

Much less critical to the inflation issue, though perhaps not negligible, is the possibility of using fiscal measures on the supply side chosen because of their favorable inflation effect. Investment incentives might work to expand capacity and thus avoid bottlenecks. A reduction in excise taxes would directly dampen inflation. A reduction in social security taxes on additions to employment would reduce marginal lavor costs and hence might dampen inflation. It must be clear, though, that here fiscal policy cannot do much, or at least not short of vast revenue losses. The inflation impact would therefore not be the primary criterion of choice among different forms of fiscal stimulus.

Employment Priority?

The big question is whether scarce fiscal revenues should be used with the primary objective of creating employment. The question is important because particular fiscal programs, specifically special employment programs, have a much larger employment effect for a given increase in the deficit than, say, personal income tax cuts, investment subsidies, excise tax cuts or subsidies, or public sector investment.

A recent review by Davies and Metcalf reports estimates of the differences in employment impact of various measures which add £1 billion to the PSBR (an increase that represents about one-third of a percent of GDP). Table 8.2 shows a summary of the detailed findings they report.[9]

Table 8.2
Employment effects of £1 billion increase in PSBR (cut in thousands unemployed)

Tax cuts	Public infrastructure investment	Public current expenditure	Employment programs
17–21	38	65	488

Note: The figure for public infrastructure investment is an overall average. Many individual categories of such expenditure have much larger effects on unemployment.

Special employment programs are so much more cost effective *in generating employment* than any other measure because of two features: they involve direct expenditure on labor and the cost is merely the extra cost of employment above unemployment benefits. Any other fiscal measure will involve a significantly larger nonlabor component, will involve higher-paid labor and may imply leakages into saving or import spending. The staggering differences in the employment impact of different programs would appear to make special employment programs the obvious candidate except for this: they are not clearly preferable once longer-term objectives of growth and the valuation of output are taken into consideration. Here is how Davies and Metcalf pose the problem:

It is clear that macroeconomic measures to reduce taxation (income tax, VAT or employers' NICs) are by far the most expensive way of cutting unemployment, at least over over a 2 year period. However, income tax cuts may pay off in the longer term through their supply side benefits. General public spending measures are much cheaper in the shortterm, but it should be noted that infra-structure investment costs more, in terms of jobs created, than current spending. On the other hand, most of the jobs created through public investment are in the private sector, rather than in direct public employment. Special employment measures are *by far* the most cost effective way of cutting unemployment—the next cheapest method is five times as expensive. However, there are serious problems in valuing the output produced under such schemes.

The choices to be made are primarily political, except for the following considerations. Public sector infrastructure investment cannot be neglected merely because there is a budget problem. In fact a recession as deep as the present one is the best time to use the otherwise idle labor to upgrade the national capital stock. Surely the biggest mistake would be to wait for a cyclical recovery of revenue to heap increased public sector spending on top of a strong economy? The other point is that public and private sector investment cannot be neglected because of the risk of bottlenecks. Basing an expansion entirely on investment might generate little employment, at least within reasonable budget costs, but investment should definitely be part of an expansion program. The crowding-out issue raised earlier calls for special attention in this context.

The next observation is that the fiscal expansion program must be forward-looking. We have to ask how, sooner or later, the budget stance can return to consolidation without at that time risking a renewed slide into recession and record unemployment. That perspective suggests that employment programs may be less effective as a measure of sustained expansion unless they represent reasonably permanent job creation in the private sector or investment in skill and mobility that offers the prospect of increased employability.

The most difficult question is what size of fiscal program would offer the prospect of much increased growth without the outright threat of inflation escalation. A short-lived program that is too small is lost like water in the sand, simply because there is no momentum of demand growth and employment expectations. The momentum is essential to lead firms to hire more labor and to invest in expanding capacity, rather than working overtime while charging higher prices. Too large a program might be inflationary, because bottlenecks build up faster than firms can expand jobs and capacity. The spillover into imports might be large, and the inflation and exchange rate consequences would be difficult to contain. Fiscal stimulus of the order of an extra 1.5 percent of GDP for this year and up to a further 1.5 percent the following year, with an eventual phasing out, would be the kind of program that strikes a rough balance between objectives.

International Considerations

All of Europe faces the choices Britain is considering, with as little enthusiasm and confidence, and with much the same urgency. At the same time the United States faces the problem of unwinding the excessively large deficits, and the overvalued dollar, without sacrificing the gains in disinflation and strong growth. The choices abroad will of course influence the opportunities that present themselves to British policymakers. A collapse of world growth would call for a much more expansionary policy as would a collapse of the dollar. But whereas the former is just bad news, the latter at least carries the bonus of making room for noninflationary growth.

The international interdependence emerges especially in two respects. Any country that moves fiscal policy toward expansion in fact subsidizes employment abroad. Import leakages spread the expansionary effects abroad and thus dissipate the domestic cost-effectiveness of a deficit policy. It is clear that joint expansion in Europe would make every country more willing, and more able, to contribute their own fiscal resources to the venture. Exchange markets would be calmer, and growth would be stronger by a very significant margin. Joint expansion has been poh-poohed in the aftermath of the locomotive experience in the late 1970s, but none of the case for it is lost. Just as the world descended into recession jointly in 1980–82, we can get out of the hole by giving each other a hand. There is no need for elaborate targetting or coordination. The point is simply to stop pretending to one another that fiscal consolidation has been a success story and to agree that fiscal expansion should take place now rather than being exactly timed to satisfy election-cycle criteria. In Europe, that means that Germany, the United Kingdom, and France should now take the lead in restoring confidence.

From the U.S. side of the Atlantic it is increasingly obvious that fiscal adjustment must take place on both sides: contraction in the United States and vigorous expansion in Europe. Only in that manner can the recovery be strengthened and given extra gas to run another few years. If fiscal correction does take place here and abroad, extra room exists for a joint effort to talk down real interest rates. The dollar might fall less and growth everywhere would be more balanced, with higher investment, than on the current beggar-thy-neighbor pattern. Clearly lower real interest rates would immensely help the budget problem to the point that extra fiscal programs could be afforded more easily.

Other Possible Changes

The case for fiscal expansion is obvious and uncontroversial. The only problem is to persuade policymakers that there is so big a need, and so little harm, that they can do something now with another helping in time for their reelection. But there are also some more fundamental reforms that are attracting attention. The two most striking ideas are in the area of labor compensation and government employment programs. These ideas are new and immensely controversial. More thought, discussion, and analysis is needed about the details. But these ideas do address in drastic ways the problem of unemployment.

A government employment guarantee for the long-term unemployed has been advocated among others by "Charter for Jobs."[10] The proposal is that the government should undertake to employ at a living wage all such people who cannot find market employment. The saving on benefits now paid to these people might contribute a good part of the extra cost of the public employment program.

Once this major reform has been achieved, another one can follow. There ceases to be a case for giving benefits to the unemployed for an indefinite duration. Where work is guaranteed, we need not offer the alternative of paid leisure. The Swedish government (but not, I see, Charter for Jobs) accepts this logic, and it is a major reason why unemployment there is so low.

Massive public employment programs as a permanent feature are a hard dose to swallow for almost any economist. Even with a hardy disposition for interventionism, few people believe that the government is the best employer of idle labor forever. In fact, what would the government do on a permanent basis with a million people in an employment program? Against this argument we must hold the following reflection: anyone who objects to mass employment programs must, by much the same logic, object to mass *un*employment programs, Without a work test, unemployment benefits may be just that. Moreover from a supply side perspective we can go even further. The fact that some people choose to be on unemployment benefits rather than working (and paying taxes) means that others have to work harder to pay the taxes that finance the unemployment benefits. Clearly a more even-handed approach is worth thinking about before the unemployment culture makes a reversal even more difficult.

The second drastic reform is to change compensation principles in one form or another. A proposal by Martin Weitzman has attracted attention to the idea of profit sharing as a means of shifting the demand for labor and increasing and stabilizing employment.[11] The practice of profit sharing in Japan is worth noting in view of that country's ability to sustain growth and employment so much better than any other industrialized country.

A different idea has already found its way into the labor market, the two-tier system. To the extent that labor market problems involve excessively high real wages and too much rigidity in employment terms, there is a common social interest in relaxing these obstacles to employment. But workers who hold jobs do not have that same interest; they would in fact be paying for other people to get jobs. The obvious answer is to create a system where extra employment attracts lower wages and fewer privileges than are being enjoyed by workers who already hold jobs. The system is unfair, but less so than the present arrangements whereby some people have a job, high real wages, and security and other people don't even have a chance of finding a job. It is interesting to note that in the aftermath of deregulation the two-tier system is already catching on in the United States. When everything is said and done a job is better than rfo job.

Priorities

Whatever the merits of these innovatory ideas—and they offer valuable guides for the future—there are some things that simply must be done now. The top priority is to undo the budget cuts and let prosperity return.

Notes

1. See J. M. Keynes, "Can Lloyd George Do It? (General Election May 1929)," in his *Collected Works, Volume IX, pp. 92, 93–94*, 124.

2. See the study by R. Layard and S. Nickell, "The Causes of British Unemployment," Centre for Labour Economics, London School of Economics, Discussion Paper Nô. 205, February 1985.

3. A detailed account is offered in G. Davies, "The Macroeconomic Record of the Conservatives." Paper presented to a conference on The Thatcher Government and British Political Economy, Harvard University, April 1985.

4. Quoted from his essay "The Right Stuff," in *The Economist*, May 4, 1985, p. 23.

5. Quoted from *IMF Survey*, September 3, 1984.

6. See also the discussion in O. Blanchard, R. Dornbusch, J. Drèze, H. Giersch, R. Layard, and M. Monti, "Employment and Growth in Europe: A Two-Handed Approach," Centre for European Policy Studies, June 1985.

7. Quoted from his essay "Stopping Moderate Inflation: The Methods of Poincaré and Thatcher," in R. Dornbusch and M. Simonsen *Inflation, Debt and Indexation*, MIT Press, 1983, p. 58.

8. For a recent assessment in the British context, see the essay by Wilfred Beckerman, "How the Battle against Inflation Was Really Won," *Lloyds Bank Review*, January 1985. See too the discussion by Jeffrey Sachs in *Brookings Papers on Economic Activity*, 1, 1983.

9. See G. Davies and D. Metcalf, "Generating Jobs," *The Economics Analyst*, Simon & Coates, April 1985.

10. See also Richard Layard, "Cutting Unemployment Using Both Blades of the Scissors," *Catalyst*, Spring 1985.

11. See Martin Weitzman, *The Share Economy*, Harvard University Press, 1984.

Index

DATE DUE

JAN 23 1989		
APR 1 5 1989		
JUN 0 5 1989		
APR 2 8 1993		
DEC 1 4 1996		
GAYLORD		PRINTED IN U.S.A.